# Balancing Work & Family in the Real World

## A Look at Finances, Couple Relationships, and Parenting

Second Edition

**Alena C. Johnson, M.S.**
**Brent C. Miller, Ph.D.**
**Kaelin M. Olsen, M.S.**

Department of Family, Consumer, and
Human Development

Utah State University

HAYDEN
HM
McNEIL

Hayden-McNeil Sustainability

Hayden-McNeil's standard paper stock uses a minimum of 30% post-consumer waste. We offer higher % options by request, including a 100% recycled stock. Additionally, Hayden-McNeil Custom Digital provides authors with the opportunity to convert print products to a digital format. Hayden-McNeil is part of a larger sustainability initiative through Macmillan Higher Ed. Visit http://sustainability.macmillan.com to learn more.

ISBN 978-0-7380-4776-8

Hayden-McNeil Publishing
14903 Pilot Drive
Plymouth, MI 48170
www.hmpublishing.com

Olsen 4776-8 F13

# Table of Contents

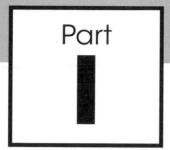

# Part I

# Balancing Work, Family, and Money Management

# Introduction

My name is Alena Johnson and I have written the first part of this book. I will first give an overview of the entire book and then introduce myself and Part I.

Everyone has different areas of their lives they need to balance. For some, it is work and family. For others, it is school, personal life, and community work. Whatever different areas you have in your life, you likely have to work at making sure there is a balance. Sometimes one area tends to dominate the others if we let it. In this book, we mention families frequently, but we understand that single individuals also need help with balance in their lives. This book is titled *Balancing Work and Family in the Real World*, but you can replace "work" or "family" with other areas of your life anywhere in the reading to make it more applicable.

To get the idea of how different parts of our lives interact, let's look at cornstarch and water. Alone, the cornstarch and water have very different qualities than if they are mixed together. You can use cornstarch and water mixed together to thicken sauces and gravies. But as many of you know, you can mix water and cornstarch together to make a very interesting substance. Sometimes this is called "Oobleck." If you mix it together and then put it in a bowl, it will look like a regular liquid, but it will behave very differently. You can actually hit it and it will be hard. You could walk on it if you had enough. But you can poke it slowly and your finger will go right through it. You can roll it quickly in your hands and it will become a ball. But if you leave it alone, it will quickly act like a liquid again, running through your fingers.

When we have work and family separately, they influence our lives differently than when we have both at the same time, just like the water and cornstarch. Quality of life changes as well as resources and demands. Sometimes it even becomes hard to see distinct lines between the two. A mother may get a text from a child while at work and may answer a work email while at the child's baseball game. A father may feel more energized at work because everything is going well at home. Or, he may feel frustrated at home because work is not going well.

Here is an example of how one part of our lives affects another. Brandon has been a very hard worker at his advertising firm. He was very social at work and often did work outside his regular work hours. But lately, he has been getting more involved with his friend Tasha. He has been spending more time with her after work and is also getting involved with her community work with Special Olympics. Can you see several different dynamics here? Brandon may not have outside time to spend on work projects any more. He may not be as social at work. On the other hand, he may feel more fulfilled in his social and personal life, and therefore be more relaxed and confident at work. He may enjoy the time he spends with Tasha and Special Olympics which may help him be a more well-rounded and content employee. We could find many more ways in which his work and personal life interact and will address some of them in the book.

This book has been written by three different authors. Each of us has our own expertise and views on ways to help balance work and family. We have divided the book into three units: Money Management, Marriage Relationships, and Parenting Responsibilities. I will discuss ways that money management interacts with work and family. Brent will teach the unit about how couple relationships are formed, and how marriage and partner dynamics connect with work and family life. Kaelin will introduce ideas that can help parents balance work and family responsibilities. You will find that all three areas have some overlap because these areas of our lives overlap. We have taken the approach that the research in each of our areas can be beneficial in learning ways to create a balance in our lives. Our intent was to use research, personal expertise, and experience from individuals to give you some solid, practical ideas on how to create balance in your life. It is our desire that as you read this book you will find help in creating harmony and peace in your possibly hectic life.

Now, more about myself and this part of the book.

I am a wife, mother of four, and grandmother of three at the time of this writing. I teach Family Finance and Financial Counseling at Utah State University and am an Accredited Financial Counselor. I have spent a lot of time trying to find or create ways to simplify money management and share that information with individuals and families. I really enjoy teaching and sharing ideas about money management, but I don't like paying bills; I suspect you don't either. My hope is that by taking the time to get our finances in order, you and I can have more time and means to spend with our families. My grandchildren are much more fun than my checkbook!

So, to begin Part I, let me ask you an easy question, "Would you rather go on a fun outing with your family or stay home and pay bills?" Most people (I hope!) would rather be doing other things than managing their finances. However, if finances are ignored, problems can arise that take a lot of time to resolve. Gaining a basic knowledge about finances and spending adequate time managing money matters will free up time to be involved in activities you may consider more appealing. Also managing money well will help provide money to fund those activities.

Part I will start out with a chapter about basic money management that can help you balance work and family. Everyone, whether in a relationship or not, can benefit from good money management practices. The next chapter is similar in that it discusses how to deal with debt and not let it affect work and family. Next we will look at good health and how it is intertwined with our finances and the ability to balance work and family well. Then we will look at the important concept of good employment along with layoffs and reduction in income. The last chapter in this section will be a segue into Parts II and III. We will look at families and finances, particularly couples and children. My hope is that you will gain some insights and tools while reading Part I that will help you balance your own work and family more effectively.

*Alena C. Johnson*

# Chapter 1

# Money Management Basics

# Money Management Basics

Everyone can benefit from good money management, no matter what their work or family situation is like. This is the reason we are starting with a chapter on money management basics. Good money management has a lot to do with balancing work and family. For example, employees who are more financially stressed are less productive at work.[1] Also, when people are stressed about finances, they often have trouble with relationships. Finances can affect marital satisfaction[2] and perceived marital instability.[3] Finances are often one of the most frequent topics of arguments[4] and are often associated with more severe marital conflict than most other topics.[5] Learning to manage money well helps people be better employees and helps them strengthen relationships.

Another reason we are starting the book with money management is because, as mentioned, everyone can benefit from good money management. It doesn't matter if you are single, single with children, married without children, or married with children. Your life will go more smoothly if you are practicing good money management. Hopefully you will be able to learn some tools in this chapter that will help you with your own money management. Before we go any further with money management, let me introduce you to the Martin family.

In this book you will read about a fictitious family, the Martins. We use the Martins to help show real-life applications of the topics presented. Our hope is that the Martins' examples will help you see how you can incorporate some, or many, of the tools and techniques discussed in this book.

## The Martin Family

*Rob Martin is an advertising specialist and Maria Martin is a certified nurse assistant. They have been married for nineteen years. Maria has worked off and on during their marriage. She has been a stay-at-home mom since their youngest child was born. Rob and Maria have three children.*

*Their oldest child, Matt, is 16. He started his own lawn mowing business two years ago. He has a head for business and is doing well. He doesn't feel as engaged with school and looks forward to being finished in a couple of years.*

*The next child, Abbie, is 11. Abbie does well in school but prefers to spend time shopping and hanging out with her friends. She and Matt get along most of the time but have occasional arguments.*

*The last child is Luke. He is 5 and just started kindergarten. Luke would rather have a ball in his hands than anything else. He is always playing or watching sporting events. So far he thinks school is okay.*

The fictitious Martin family who has just been introduced consists of a married couple with three children. Our occasional use of the Martin family in this book to illustrate concepts and principles is based on the fact that a married couple with children remains the most common type of family in the United States. But we want to make it clear that the Martin family examples we present are not intended to ignore or devalue other kinds of families. We realize that single parent families, step-families, and many other kinds of families are viable and are usually doing their best to balance work and family issues too. Relatedly, we use the terms "marriage" and "spouse" throughout the book. Again, this is because marriage is still the most common way of forming a family, but the marriage concepts and principles described could also be applied to unmarried couple relationships. Now let's see how money management can help balance work and family.

## Money Management

Good money management starts with well-thought-out goals. Those goals can be incorporated into a budget or spending plan. As part of a budget, a family may need to evaluate income and expenses. Sometimes income will need to be increased and expenses will need to be decreased to make ends meet. Once those aspects are in place, families can also start or add to an emergency fund, a very important part of good money management. Try to find one or two things from this chapter that will help you manage your money more effectively and thus reduce your stress.

### The Martins

*Rob and Maria decided they wanted to gain control over their financial situation. They sat down together and talked about where they were now financially and where they would like to be in the future. They each wanted to save money for emergencies and for future purchases. They wanted to be able to have fun with the family and still be able to pay all their bills and fund their desired savings. After this discussion and some ice cream, the Martins were able to write down some very specific goals. Later, they also included the children in the goal process and as a family decided to write down a goal to take a family vacation to California in two years.*

*After writing their goals as a family, Rob and Maria started to work on a budget. They had kept track of all their expenses for one month so they knew how much they usually spent in each expense category. They found that there were some areas where they could certainly cut back. They spent more money eating out than they wanted. They also had some bounced check fees and a parking ticket that they hoped to not repeat. When they wrote down how much they needed or wanted to spend in each category, the total amount was quite a bit more than their income. Rob and Maria quickly felt discouraged and did not even want to continue working on their plan. Along with their new desire to be in control of their finances, Rob and Maria need some education about money management.*

# Goals

The Martin family started out on the right step. When people start a budget or spending plan, they need to know where they want to go financially. Consider this dialogue between Alice and the Cheshire cat.[6]

> *"Would you tell me, please, which way I ought to go from here?"*
>
> *"That depends a good deal on where you want to get to," said the Cat.*
>
> *"I don't much care where----" said Alice.*
>
> *"Then it doesn't matter which way you go," said the Cat.*

It's the same with budgeting. People need to know where they want to go financially to take full advantage of budgeting. Goals give purpose and direction to budgeting.

Some people have a hard time writing **financial goals.** One way to get started on this step is to use a financial counseling technique called the miracle question.[7] Imagine that during the night a miracle happened. When you woke up in the morning, all your financial problems were gone. Start to think about what your life would be like and how it would be different than it is now. What would you be able to do that you cannot do now? What would you stop doing that you are doing now? How would you feel? Would your family relationships be any different?

The **miracle question** can help a person see what life would be like if their finances were in order. Sometimes it's hard to come up with goals because it's easy to get stuck in the problems of everyday life. Try looking at life as you would like it to be, and then you can determine what goals you need in order to have that desired life.

Once you have an idea of what you would like for goals, it's time to put those goals into writing. Start with a description of each goal, next write a plan to achieve those goals, and finally, write a date by which you would like to have each goal accomplished. If the goals need specific dollar amounts, include that as part of the description, such as, "Save $10,000 for a down payment for a home." The plan should state how the goals will be accomplished. Reducing expenses is one plan for accomplishing goals.

Some goals will be short term and some will be long term. Some goals will be small and others will be bigger and may need to be broken down into smaller tasks. For example, the Martins may have a goal to pay off their credit card debt. Smaller tasks to reach that goal could include using a budget to pay for all expenses so that no new purchases are added to the credit card or adding twenty dollars extra each month on the credit card payment.

It's important to create goals that will be achievable. If the Martins write down that they want to be out of debt in three years but the time frame is too tight, they may not be able to reach that goal, even if they work hard. Be realistic when writing goals. It's also important to write goals over which you have control. Even if the Martins wrote down that they wanted Rob to get a raise at work, they have little control over that goal. It might depend more on the success of the company rather than whether Rob deserves a raise.

Goals should not only be wise and practical, they should also include something fun and exciting. This is a good time to talk to the family and see what they want to work toward. It's hard for children to give up smaller fun things to work toward a lofty goal they cannot see any benefit from, such as a secure retirement for the parents. On the other hand, children may help encourage parents to manage money well if the goal is a family vacation or new electronic equipment. This is more fun for adults as well. Of course, long-term goals need to be addressed as well.

Well-thought-out, written goals are the best place to start a good money management plan. This gives purpose and direction to other financial decisions.

## Tracking

Besides writing goals, it's helpful to **track** all expenses for one month. Write down everything, even down to vending machine purchases. This can be a very eye-opening experience for many people. Everyone has an idea where their money is going each month, but many people do not know *exactly* where. Tracking can provide very accurate information about spending habits. Some families, like the Martins, realize they are spending more in one area than they really want. The Martins were eating out often and spending money there that they really would rather put somewhere else. It was also adding to their credit card debt. Without tracking and then making a plan for spending, it's easy for money to slip through anyone's fingers.

I have my students track their expenses for one month as part of a larger assignment. I get interesting comments from the students. One day I received an e-mail from a student that said, "I just wanted to say that it is not even halfway through February and I am dying at how much we are spending when we don't need to be! This tracking assignment is awesome, and I feel like it is really going to help me." You may have the same experience if you track your expenses.

One easy way to track is to carry a small notebook and write down each purchase when it's made. Some people keep receipts and then wait until the end of the day and write down everything from the receipts. This is fine as long as purchases without receipts, such as small cash purchases, are also recorded. People who use a check-book for most purchases can keep track in their check register. They will also need to be careful with cash purchases and make sure they are recorded.

After tracking for one month, expenses can be grouped into categories. For example, there may be a category for food purchased at grocery stores and another category for eating out. Add up all the purchases in each category for one month. This will give a good picture of overall spending and provide a great start for budgeting.

# Budgeting

Some people do not like the word "budget." It comes with negative feelings. If you feel this way, just change that word to "spending plan." A budget is a great way to *plan* where your money is going. You decide ahead of time how much you want to spend in each category. This is also the time to look back at the goals written and include them in the budget. Goals give purpose to the budget. The Martins want to eliminate their credit card debt. They also want to save and feel that they are in control. A budget is a great way for them to accomplish those goals.

One good reason to budget is to make ends meet, or live within your means. Spending less than you make is a good habit to get into. If everyone always spent less than they made, there would be no need for bankruptcy or home foreclosures. Using credit is an easy way to spend more of one's income each month. Budgeting can help control spending and reduce purchases using credit.

After tracking for one month, start with a budget worksheet. This can be a purchased or an already created form, a computer program, a new form created by you, or even a blank piece of paper. Write down all income and each expense category you need. Tracking can help with the categories. Even if using a pre-made or purchased form, it's good to customize the form to suit your needs. You may need to add a category for pet supplies, gym membership, or dry cleaning. Then decide how much you are going to put into each category. Again, the tracking is very helpful for this. Look at how much you spent for food purchases while tracking. Decide if that was a reasonable amount for the next month. If you think it was, you can put that same amount for food on the budget you are creating. Or, you may decide that you want to eat out less and will need to spend a little more at the grocery store.

## Budgeting Methods

During the month you will need to keep track of how much you spend in each category. This can be done by tracking again. Some people prefer to track all the time. This helps them keep a close eye on expenses and reminds them to stay within their budget. There are other ways to determine how much is spent each month which I'll call budgeting methods. No one method is a perfect way for everyone to budget. Some people do really well with one method while others do well with another. It depends on skills, time, and personalities.

### Envelope System

To use the **envelope system**, a family places cash for certain categories in an envelope marked for each category. If a family allocates $350 for food for a month, they would put the $350 in an envelope marked "food." And so on. The envelope system works well for categories over which a person has control during the month. For example, it works especially well for entertainment. The family uses money from the envelope for entertainment during the month, and when the money is gone, it's time to find free entertainment.

This is a simple yet effective method for budgeting. There are a few cautionary measures that need to be taken. First, make sure the money is in a safe place. Also, when shopping, it might be better to just take out what is needed for a specific purchase instead of taking the entire envelope. Finally, it's best to use the envelope system for categories with smaller amounts of money. It's better to pay bills such as rent or mortgage and utilities with a check instead of cash.

When my husband was in graduate school, we were always short on money. He was very busy with teaching and school, and I did most of the money management. Even though he made more of our income than I did, when he needed to buy something, he would have to come to me. That was stressful for him. He had to ask for the money he made. It was also stressful for me. I was trying to do the best I could with the little income we had. If he said he needed new running shoes I would say something like, "Now? We just don't have the money." He always put off asking as long as he could, but would get to the point where he really needed some things.

Then we decided to use the envelope system for clothes. We each got a little money every month for clothes. He usually saved for months and then bought several things at once. I didn't mind because that was no problem to our budget. I tended to spend mine every month but felt great freedom in being able to do that. Even though we didn't get a lot for our clothes money, I knew that I could really spend it on clothes. I didn't have to feel guilty that I wasn't using it for groceries. This system helped lessen our stress and strengthened our relationship.

The envelope method worked so well for us with clothes that we decided to use it in other areas such as personal allowance and entertainment. We use other methods for other expenses but find that the envelope method works well for these categories for us. You may find you like to use this method for a lot of categories, a few categories, or not at all.

### Checkbook Method

For people who use their checkbook register regularly, the **checkbook method** works well. This involves not only writing down checks and subtracting them as usual, but also keeping a running balance of a few categories right in the checkbook register.

Vertical lines can be drawn on the checkbook register to indicate various budgeting categories. When a check is subtracted from the running total of the entire balance, it's also subtracted from the category to which it belongs (Figure 1.1). Expenses that have a category written in the checkbook are subtracted from that category, and others are just subtracted from the running total.

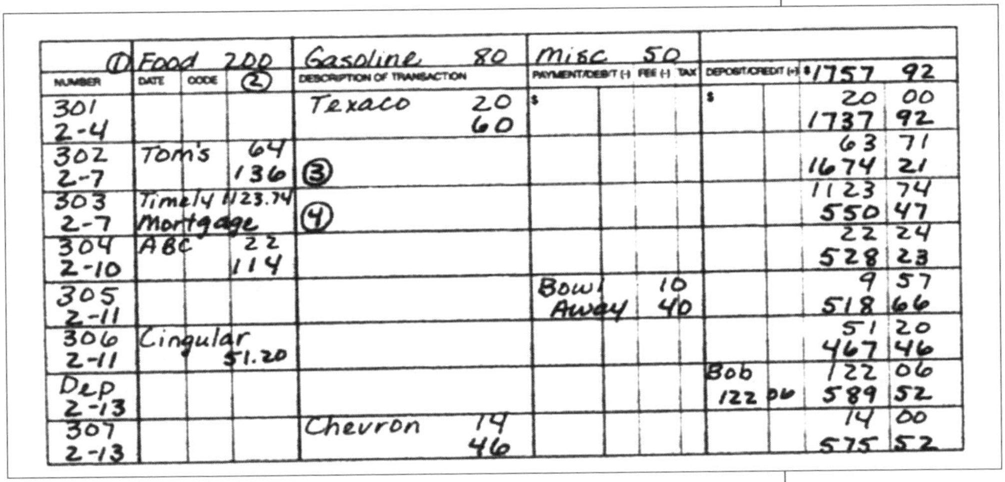

**FIGURE 1.1.**

To use the checkbook method, label each column (1), enter how much is allotted for that category (2), and subtract purchases from the category as soon as they are made (3). Purchases that are not included in one of the listed categories should be written down, but not subtracted from that category (4).

Most people have just a few categories that they really need to keep track of during the month such as food, gas, entertainment, and miscellaneous spending. These categories can be the ones that are written in the checkbook and monitored during the month. People who use a checkbook register regularly may find this method of budgeting to be simple and easy to use.

### Computer Programs

For anyone who has a computer and basic skills, computer programs can work well. Some programs are available online for free and others can be purchased. Some people really enjoy using this type of budgeting system, especially if they are on a computer frequently. However, it's not a requirement to good money management. These systems work well for some people, but not everyone.

### Worksheet

As mentioned earlier, budgeting works well if you have a worksheet to lay out the entire budget. You may want to find a copy of a budget sheet or create one on a spreadsheet. A simple worksheet can be found at http://usu.edu/fchd/housing/fchd3550Worksheets.cfm. You can either have a worksheet that shows only the budget or you can have one that also keeps track of spending, more like a ledger.

### Combination

Many people like to use a combination of two or more methods. People can use the envelope system for clothes, food, and entertainment. They may use a purchased system for tracking all other purchases, and their own worksheet to create and evaluate their budget. As stated earlier, different methods work well for different people. It's good to try different methods and different combinations to find what works best for you.

## Evaluation

Along with choosing and implementing a budgeting method, it's good to evaluate a budget frequently. Lives change and budgets need to change with them to be effective. Think of a budget as a ball of clay to be sculpted. A person starts with this ball and works with it, molding and shaping as they go. Then they may say, "Here is my budget. I think it will work." But after a few months they may have a change in income or an extra bill to pay. The budget needs to be changed. So the clay is again molded and worked until it becomes the new budget. This process needs to be done often to keep the budget working for the family.

## Stumbling Blocks

There are a few situations that can make budgeting very difficult. Some people decide budgeting does not work because of these stumbling blocks. However, the following three stumbling blocks can be planned for, making budgeting a much smoother process.

1. **Irregular expenses.** These expenses are the ones that you know about, but they don't come every month. They are expenses such as birthdays, getting children into school, athletic group fees, car registration, car insurance (if not

paid monthly), and property taxes (if not paid with a mortgage payment). Each of these expenses can be a problem for budgeting if not planned for. An easy way to make sure there is money for these purchases is to have a **revolving savings account.**

Start by writing down when each of these unexpected expenses is due and how much they will be. Then total all the expenses for the year. Divide that amount by 12. The amount that is left is how much needs to be set aside from the monthly budget to cover these expenses. A revolving savings worksheet can be found at http://usu.edu/fchd/housing/fchd3550Worksheets. cfm.

An easy way to handle this savings is to set up an automatic withdrawal from checking into savings each month. This way the money is always taken out and set aside for these expenses. Then when these expenses come, instead of playing havoc on the budget, the money is already set aside. This is a great way to overcome the first stumbling block.

2. **Large unexpected expenses.** These expenses can be medical bills, appliances breaking, car repairs, etc. When any of these comes along, it's very hard on a budget. The solution to this stumbling block is to have an **emergency fund.** Setting a little aside each month to cover these unexpected expenses can greatly increase the likelihood of successful budgeting.

3. **Small unexpected expenses.** These expenses come along in the form of donating to a wedding gift at work, children's school fees, speeding tickets, flowers for a funeral, supporting a local fundraiser, etc. An easy way to make room for these in a budget is to have a miscellaneous category in a budget. It's impossible to plan for these expenses because they are not known about beforehand. But having a **miscellaneous category** in the monthly budget gives a person a place from which to take the money.

## Living within Means

As stated earlier, it's important when budgeting to keep spending below income. However, as the Martins found out, this is not always an easy task. The Martins found out they did not have enough money to cover all their spending. When this happens, there are three options: 1) increase income, 2) decrease expenses, or 3) combine the two.

## Increase Income

There are several ways to increase income. Some ways involve employment and others do not.

### Added Employment

This first option to help live within means needs careful consideration. Extra work can have a large impact on the family and should be thought about and discussed. If only one spouse is working and decides to pick up more work, that can be a burden not only on the working spouse, but also on the spouse at home, especially if there are small children at home. If a stay-at-home spouse decides to start working, remember to look at costs involved with the work as well as other considerations such as who will drive children to their activities and be home to monitor household activities. Deciding how much family members should work is a complex decision that needs a close look.

### Improved Work

Besides increasing hours worked, a family can also seek improved work. A working person could look for a better paying job or ask for a raise at their current job. Sometimes this can be a long-term goal when education is involved. Sacrificing to gain a better education can be of great benefit for a family.

### Others

There are other ways to increase income that do not involve regular employment. Here are some ideas:

- Sell unused assets and property
- Use a hobby or skill
- Adjust tax withholdings (if you get a large refund each year)
- Rent a room if zoning or landlords allow
- Clean houses, remove snow, mow lawns, help people move, etc.

Be creative and see if you can come up with a way to make more income. Here is a story to illustrate how we handled it one time.

When our children were involved with extracurricular activities at school, we required they pay half the fees. We were willing to pay half because we valued those experiences. But we required them to pay half to remind them that "money doesn't grow on trees" and so they would appreciate the experience more.

When our daughter started marching band, she engaged in the fundraising activities through the school to earn her half of the fees. However, she didn't make enough to pay for her entire portion. I thought about it and told her one day that I would be willing to give up some of our strawberries if she wanted to pick them on a Saturday morning and take them to the farmer's market. To my amusement, her first question was, "How early would I have to get up?" Sleep is a precious commodity in her life.

We ended up deciding that my husband and I would get up with her, help her pick the strawberries, I would go with her to the market, and then we would split the proceeds. In only two Saturdays she was able to earn the rest of her fees.

The next year we were talking about what she would do to earn money and she said she actually kind of liked going to the market. It was just the picking she didn't really like.

We hope that she learned that when you need money, there are a lot of different ways to get it. Sometimes you just need to be a little creative.

## Reducing Expenses

The best plan of action for many families is to reduce expenses. If increasing income is not a good option but expenses are greater than income, it's time to reduce expenses. The tracking experience is a great place to start. After tracking, a family can look at expenditures and evaluate each one. It's common for many families to spend more on eating out than they want to. At the time of each purchase it seems like a good idea, often because of lack of time or energy. But in the long run, these purchases can add up and there is really nothing to show for them.

There are many ways a family can reduce expenses. One is to create and keep a good budget. Deciding ahead of time how much will be spent on each expense category can help eliminate the extra spending. Another way is to evaluate each expenditure from the tracking and decide if they are even used or needed. Some things such as a magazine subscription or an expensive cable package can be eliminated or at least reduced. Sometimes money goes out to pay for items that are not even being used or could be changed and put to better use.

### Unnecessary Expenses

A good way to reduce expenses is to take out unnecessary expenses that can sneak in when we aren't paying attention. These would include speeding or parking tickets, late fees from video stores, bank fees, and even letting food spoil. A family may be amazed at how much money goes toward such items. Making a good food plan, watching what is in the fridge and pantry, and noting what needs to be used before it spoils can help reduce wasted food. Carefully monitoring checking accounts can be especially effective in reducing banking fees. Other cautions such as driving the speed limit and turning in books and videos on time will reduce those added expenses. A little planning and control can help the family reduce expenses.

### Reducing Debt

One of the most effective ways to help spend less than we make is to pay off debt. If the Martin family gets rid of their credit card debt, they will have more money to live on each month. If a car is paid off, the amount of the car payment can be added to other debt or toward savings. Eliminating or reducing debt is even better than extra income. Extra income must be taxed before it can be used. Taking away a payment from a budget is money that can be used without additional taxes. For example, if a family has a $400 car payment and then they pay off that loan, they now have the entire $400 to save or pay off debt.

### The Step-Down Principle

I want to introduce the **Step-Down Principle**.[8] This principle is a way to incrementally improve a situation. In this chapter, we will see how the Step-Down Principle is used for expenses. Later we will use it for time and nutrition. The idea is that every step down improves the situation.

Here's how it applies to food purchases. The top step could be to go to a restaurant and pay for the food and a tip. This can be very expensive for a family. The next step down could be buying fast food. The next step down might be buying prepared food or a mix at the grocery store. The last step could be cooking from scratch at home, which would be a lot less expensive. Figure 1.2 shows how this looks on a staircase.

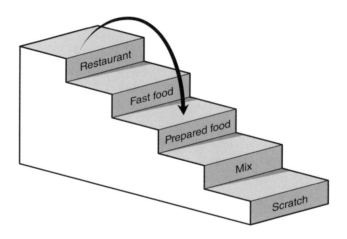

**FIGURE 1.2.**

The Step-Down Principle can be used in other ways for food purchases. In addition to considering *where* the food is purchased, people can consider how many times they eat out. Most people I know really enjoy eating out. But perhaps eating out could become more of an occasional activity instead of a regular one. If people normally eat out 12 times a month, they could change that to 8, 6, 4, or 2. They just step down the number of times they eat out instead of not eating out at all. Or perhaps they could step down how much food they purchase when they eat out. Instead of eating a full meal, they could leave out the appetizer. Maybe they could leave out the appetizer and drink. Water is healthier than soda anyway. What about not ordering dessert, or at least sharing it with someone?

Does stepping down make much difference? Yes! I priced out the cost of four pancakes on each of the steps on Figure 1.2. Just stepping down two steps, from the restaurant to prepared food, was a 78% savings! The great part of the Step-Down Principle is that people don't need to step down all the way; just one or two steps can make a big difference.

One reason I like to share the Step-Down Principle with people, especially when it comes to food, is because I have found that a lot of families spend a lot of money on food. When the economy is down or a family is having their own tough time, they often do not take big vacations, buy new cars, or upgrade homes. But they still spend a lot of money on food, especially eating out. This seems to be especially true with the young adults I teach at the university. Anyone who is busy finds themselves stopping for fast food unless they make plans to avoid that. How are you doing in this area? Is this a place you could improve a little? Besides helping your finances, there is a good chance stepping down with money will also improve your nutrition.

The Step-Down Principle also works well with clothes and entertainment. For clothing, the lower steps can include sales and clearance shopping. Entertainment can include matinees instead of evening shows and going to the library for videos instead of renting them. Stepping down can work for categories such as communications, transportation, gifts, vacations, and even housing. If a family finds they just cannot meet their obligations, moving to a smaller, less expensive home can ease their burdens.

> *The Martin family made a goal to go to California for a vacation in two years. They discussed how they could step down to achieve this goal. The children were willing to give up some of their usual spending in order to reach this goal. It helped that they did not need to give up each purchase altogether, they just needed to find a less expensive way to make those purchases.*

The entire family can be involved with the Step-Down Principle. The next time you are going to make a purchase, ask yourself, "Can I step down?"

## Savings

The last concept in good money management that we will cover is savings. I can't stress enough the importance of savings. Savings is one of *the* most important parts of good money management. When I was a financial counselor I would sometimes have people in my office in tears because their lives were so messed up. I often thought if they would have had just one thing, an emergency fund, they would not be in the situation they were in.

Having savings can bring harmony into your life. However, many people in the United States do not have much savings. The National Income and Product Accounts organization calculates a national personal savings rate each year. In 2005 the national personal savings rate went into the negative side, meaning there was more spending than income.[9] According to their calculations, it hasn't been negative since the Great Depression.

Many people, like the Martins, spend their lives living paycheck to paycheck. They spend everything or more than they make, leaving them very vulnerable to financial disaster. Having savings gives people options that they wouldn't have otherwise. These options can include starting a business, returning to school, buying rental property, surviving a layoff, etc.

There are many reasons to save. Maybe you want to focus on an emergency fund, or maybe you are in the position to want an increase in wealth. While you are thinking about savings, here are four important types of savings to consider.

1.  **Emergency Fund.** As mentioned, one of the most important types of savings is an emergency fund. An emergency fund is for larger, unexpected expenses or loss of income. Anyone without an emergency fund is teetering on the edge of financial devastation. Some people, with amazing luck, never end up tumbling over the edge, but many do make that dreaded fall. When something like large medical expenses occur without an emergency fund, a family can be faced with severe financial stress. On the other hand, when there is an emergency fund available to use when financial hardships arise, life can continue without the added stress.

    Many experts recommend having three to six months worth of expenses in an emergency fund. This can be a great deal of money for anyone struggling with life's basic money issues. One way to get started is to set a monthly goal. This can take the large, possibly overwhelming goal of an emergency fund and break it up into small, easier to accomplish goals such as a monthly amount to save.

    Creating an emergency fund is one of the best financial moves a family can make. This one savings account can be the means of keeping a family from financial difficulties and even financial ruin. If everyone had a good emergency fund, there would be much less cause for home foreclosures, debt defaults, and even bankruptcy.

2. **Revolving Savings.** As discussed earlier, a revolving savings account can help smooth out a budget by planning for the irregular expenses that come up throughout the year.

3. **Future Purchases.** When major purchases are always bought on credit, a family ends up spending a lot more than the original purchase price. On the other hand, when a family saves for future purchases, they can be on the receiving end of interest instead of the paying end. Most families may have no alternative to debt for homes and even cars. With careful financial management, most other purchases can be saved for and not put on credit. This practice can save thousands of dollars over a lifetime.

   There is a way that you might be able to eventually pay cash for vehicles. If you purchased a car with a loan and kept the car after it was paid off, you would have a period of time without a car payment. If, however, you continued to make a payment, only this time to yourself into a savings account, you could have a large amount saved by the time you needed a new car. Plus you might have the first car to trade in. You might not have enough to pay cash for the second car, but the second car would then be paid off faster than the first car—allowing more time to save before the third car. If this is continued over time, eventually you would be able to pay cash for a vehicle. Would you rather earn interest over your lifetime or pay it to someone else?

4. **Retirement.** Some people have described retirement like a three-legged stool. The three legs are social security, a work retirement plan, and personal savings. If each leg is sufficient in strength, the stool, or retirement, is sturdy and secure. If any are lacking, other sources, such as employment, must make up the difference.

   Having a work retirement plan is a great employee benefit. Be sure to find out if there is a plan you can contribute to and if the employer will match funds.

   Even with social security and a work retirement plan, most people also need their own savings to have the type of retirement they desire. The government has given tax breaks to individuals desiring to save for retirement. These tax breaks can be very helpful for retirement savings. One of these breaks comes in the form of an Individual Retirement Account (IRA).

Retirement savings is a place where compound interest can work its best magic. If people start to save for retirement early, they can do amazing things with small amounts of money because of compound interest.

Other good means to save for retirement can include owning rental property and selling a business or a larger home. The important aspect is to make goals and plans to save early for retirement.

## How to Save

Finding a way to save can be the hardest part of saving. As with the Martins, often every cent is used for expenses each month. First, try treating savings like a bill that must be paid. Include the allotted savings amount in a budget and put the money in savings as soon as income is received. Some people try to wait until the end of the month, or pay period, before they put anything into savings. Often, there isn't anything to put into savings at that point. Pay yourself right along with the other bills, or even better, first! Also, don't forget to use the ideas from this chapter to increase income and decrease expenses to find money to put toward savings.

# Summary

What are you going to do to help reduce the financial stress in your life? Are you going to write goals, start a budget, increase income, try the Step-Down Principle, or treat savings like a bill? Choose something right now that you plan to work on, and then get started! Hopefully you will be able to have more control over your finances and bring more harmony into your work and family life.

### The Martins

The Martin family had a lot of work to do. They wrote goals, made a budget, and came up with ways to decrease their expenses. They also considered having Maria start working again to help pay off their credit card debt. Making these adjustments was not easy for the Martin family. They were used to eating out, going to movies, and making other purchases as they wanted. But this spending behavior was causing them stress. They had a greater desire to get control over their finances than they had desire to spend, at least most of the time.

The Martins found they needed to make a few adjustments to their original budget like spending a little more at the grocery store in order to spend a lot less eating out. The revolving savings account helped with the irregular expenses. By using the Step-Down Principle, they have been able to add an extra $20 each month towards paying off their credit card debt. They have also started saving $50 each month toward their emergency fund. The children have started finding ways to reduce expenses also and the entire family is working toward their goal of a family vacation to California in two years. Rob and Maria are planning to start an IRA as soon as they pay off their furniture loan.

*The Martin family is now committed to their goals, but it's not always easy to do what they need to do to accomplish them. They are getting better at sticking to a budget, even when the children ask for things they used to buy frequently but are cutting back on now. They have made a lot of progress but still have a long way to go. At this point they will need to find ways to stay motivated and keep working toward becoming more in control of their finances.*

## References

[1] Financial Distress Among American Workers Final Report. Available at http://www.pfeef.org/press/press-releases/Financial-Distress-Among-American-Workers.html

[2] Dew, J. (2008). Debt Change and Marital Satisfaction Change in Recently Married Couples. *Family Relations*, 57: 60–71. doi: 10.1111/j.1741-3729.2007.00483.x

[3] Gudmunson, C. G., Beutler, I. F., Israelsen, C. L., McCoy, J. K., & Hill, E. J. (2007). Linking financial strain to marital instability: Examining the roles of emotional stress and marital interaction. *Journal of Family and Economic Issues*, 28: 357–376. doi: 10.1007/s10834-007-9074-7

[4] Stanley, S. M., Markman, H. J., and Whitton, S. W. (2002). Communication, Conflict, and Commitment: Insights on the Foundations of Relationship Success from a National Survey. *Family Process*, 41: 659–675. doi: 10.1111/j.1545-5300.2002.00659.x

[5] Papp, L. M., Cummings, E. M., and Goeke-Morey, M. C. (2009). For Richer, for Poorer: Money as a Topic of Marital Conflict in the Home. *Family Relations*, 58: 91–103. doi: 10.1111/j.1741-3729.2008.00537.x

[6] Carroll, L. (1960). *Alice's Adventures in Wonderland and Through the Looking-Glass*, 1960 edition, New York, New American Library. p. 62

[7] Waddell, F. (2007). *Solution Focused Financial Counseling*, 2007 edition, Virginia, Genesis Press. p. 116

[8] Johnson, A. (1999). *Changing Financial Behavior: The Step-Down Principle*, Proceedings of the Association for Financial Counseling and Planning Education, November 1999, 157.

[9] Reinsdorf, M. B. (2007). Alternative Measures of Personal Saving. Available on the internet at: http://www.bea.gov/scb/pdf/2007/02%20February/0207_saving.pdf

# Chapter 2

# Dealing with Debt

# Dealing with Debt

One of the best ways to help balance work and family is to reduce debt. For most people, it looks like this:

**LESS DEBT = LESS STRESS**

A key component to good money management is knowing how to manage debt. Many families have found that debt is their main financial concern. Credit and debt are often easy to get, but not easy to pay back. This chapter will examine various forms of debt and how to reduce debt, as well as consider credit histories and credit scores.

### The Martins

*The Martins have had some problems with debt. They are especially struggling with their credit card payments. They also have a mortgage, two car payments, a furniture loan, and they owe the dentist for a dental crown. Their credit card payment is their biggest concern because of the high interest rate. They would also like to pay off the furniture loan quickly which is a six-months-same-as-cash loan. The dentist has worked out a payment plan for them and is not charging interest. Eventually, they would like their only debt to be their mortgage. For now, they are going to focus on getting the credit card balance paid off and not adding to it.*

## Debt

What impact do you think debt has on balancing work and family? When you get to Chapter 5, you will read about a study that surveyed newlywed couples and asked what was problematic in their marriage.[1] The most problematic area for wives and second most problematic area for husbands was "debt brought into marriage." There are some legitimate reasons to incur debt:

- to fund education
- to fund a new business
- to fund major purchases that might not otherwise be available such as a home or car

For many people, being able to borrow money is very helpful in being able to fund these things that might not be available otherwise. If used wisely, debt can be part of good money management. For example, if students get student loans to pay for their education, their income may improve enough after graduation to make the loan well worthwhile.

Of course there are disadvantages also. Some of the negative aspects of debt are:

- ties up future income
- borrower pays interest to the lender
- borrower pays more for purchases because of the interest
- borrower has an obligation to someone else

Once people have incurred debt, they are committed to paying off that debt, which ties up future income. That debt takes away options when people get paid. Part of that income is already committed to debt. Instead of earning interest for themselves, they are paying interest to someone else. This interest adds a lot to the cost of an item. For example, if people buy a bedroom set for $3,000 on credit at 18% interest for 5 years, they will end up paying $4,571 for that furniture. It's even more incredible for homes. A 30 year mortgage of $210,000 at 5% interest would raise the total cost of the home to $405,837—almost twice the original amount! Unfortunately, most people do not have enough money to pay cash for homes or even cars. It then becomes a matter of using debt wisely.

It's easy to get into too much debt quickly. Lenders may tell individuals that they qualify for the debt and the borrower may think, "They are the experts. If they say I can afford this loan I must be able to afford it." It's important to figure a budget with debt payments and see if the new debt is easily incorporated into a budget. Sometimes other purchases may need to be sacrificed to accommodate the new debt. Even when it appears the debt will be fine, it may become burdensome later. Some people acquire debt and then have a job layoff, a reduction in hours, or added expenses such as medical debt. Suddenly, that easy-to-pay debt is a problem.

> *Rob and Maria Martin felt that their debt was going to be fine when they first got loans. Then they had added expenses such as braces for Matt and a dental crown for Rob. They also got other debt with small payments, thinking the new debt would be easy to pay, only to find those payments made it impossible to live without using their credit card for basic expenses.*

It's best to keep debt below levels that are often considered reasonable. There are many different forms of debt that can be acquired and each one has special considerations.

## Payday Loans

One of the biggest debt traps consumers can fall into is using **payday loans.** These loans seem innocent at first, but can lure unsuspecting borrowers into a painful commitment. Payday loans, also called check cashing loans, cash advance loans, or postdated check loans, charge fees for loans for short periods of time. A typical loan may charge ten dollars for a one hundred dollar loan for one week. Borrowers write a check for $110, which will not be cashed for one week, and they walk out with $100 in cash. At the end of the week, they can go back and pay the $110 in cash and get their check back, allow the business to cash the check, or "rollover" the loan for another week with another $10 fee.

Although $10 may not seem like a huge fee for a loan, on an annual basis, that is 520% interest! No one would get a car loan at 520% interest. If borrowers keep the loan for only one week, they will pay only the $10 (in this example), but many borrowers use the rollover option and pay yet another $10 fee. This often happens because borrowers were short on money to begin with. When they get paid, they still owe the $110 to the lender, which leaves them short again. Some people continue to roll the loan over week after week. Each week the fee is added on to the original loan. This is a terrible trap for people with money management problems. Some states have even banned payday loans completely.

## Six-Months-Same-as-Cash

The Martins purchased some furniture on a **six-months-same-as-cash** loan. These loans can be fine if the loan is really paid in full before the six months are up. The problem many people run into is that often the lender has worked out a small payment for them that will not pay off the loan in the allotted six months. If the borrower does not pay off the loan within six months, interest is charged from the beginning of the loan, not on the balance at six months. Many people start out with good intentions to pay off the loan in time in order to pay no interest, but they find money to be tight and make only the minimum payments. Then they do not get the benefit of the interest-free loan and owe interest from the beginning of the loan. Again, these loans can be fine if they are really paid off within the six months.

## Credit Cards

If used wisely, credit cards have great benefits. Some of the benefits include:

- protection against fraud
- use of the float period
- added insurance
- rewards
- for emergencies
- for reservations and rentals
- convenience
- building credit without paying interest

When making purchases online, it's better to use a credit card than a debit card or check. There is more protection from fraud with a credit card. If credit cards are lost or stolen and used by a thief, cardholders will only be liable for up to $50 of the purchases if reported within 60 days to the credit card company. If cash is lost or stolen, the owner has no protection.

It's also nice to have a **float period** with credit cards. People can make a purchase using their credit card in the middle of the month and not need to pay for it until they get the statement the next month. This float period works along with the grace period, which is the time between when a person makes a purchase and when the credit card payment is due. If people always pay off their credit card balance each month, they will not need to pay interest on the purchases made with the card.

Insurance can be a great benefit to using a credit card. When people rent a car using a credit card, that card may provide auto insurance on the rented car—saving renters the added insurance costs. Some cards provide life insurance while flying for people who purchased their airline tickets with the credit card. Before depending on this insurance, such as when renting a car, be sure to find out if the credit card actually provides the insurance.

Credit card companies often offer **rewards programs.** These can include air miles, cash back, or gift cards to various businesses. These rewards can be fun and beneficial if people using the card do not pay more in fees and interest than they are receiving in benefits. Also, some people end up spending more on purchases trying to "earn" rewards. Beware of this trap.

In case of an emergency, credit cards can be very helpful. If you are driving out of town and have a problem with your car, a credit card can pay for the needed repair. Credit cards allow people to pay for emergencies without carrying a lot of cash or worrying about a business not taking personal checks.

Credit cards are needed to make hotel reservations and to rent automobiles. Credit cards are convenient to carry and use. Also, people can use credit cards, pay the balance off each month, and build credit without ever paying interest. Because of these benefits, using a credit card can be part of a good money management plan. However, credit cards are also one of the easiest misused forms of debt. It's easy to get and use credit cards and they can quickly become a financial problem.

Some of the negative aspects of credit cards include:

- Interest
- Fees
- Overspending
- Minimum payment option

Credit cards usually have higher interest rates than other types of debt. Sometimes people use credit cards for purchases because, though they don't have the money right then, items are on sale. If they pay only the minimum payment each month, the good deal will be lost because of the added interest. For example, let's say that you find a riding lawn mower that is regularly $3,500, but it's on sale for $2,575. You might think, "I don't have the money right now, but that's such a good sale, I will get the mower now and put it on my credit card." However, if you use a card that has 18% interest and the minimum payment is 4% of the balance or $10 (whichever is higher), the payments would last 10 years and 4 months, and you would pay a total of $4,035.73 for the mower. What happened to the good deal? You would have been better off to wait to buy the mower until you had the money saved, even if you had to pay full price.

Some credit card users pay as much in fees as they do in interest. Some of the fees are:

- late
- over-the-limit
- annual
- transfer
- cash advance

First, try to find a card without an annual fee. There are enough credit cards without annual fees that people should be able to find one without that fee. Second, never make purchases that will put the balance over the limit of that card. You actually have to "opt in" to go over the limit now. Third, always make payments on time. Be aware that transferring a balance from one card to another will often result in a fee charge. Making a cash advance from a credit card will usually include a fee also.

The biggest credit card trap for some people is the ability to **over-spend.** It's easy to use "plastic" and not think about the total balance on the credit card or about paying back the debt. For some people, a credit card does not seem like real money. These people would not spend as much if they were using cash and actually seeing the money go away. Yet with a card, it's easy to continue spending until a financial burden has been created. Keep in mind that using more than 50% of your credit limit can hurt your credit score.

Even when the credit card bill comes, low **minimum payments** may seem manageable. Some people may think, "The minimum payment is only $25. I can pay that." Paying the minimum payment will keep people current on their payments, and no negative marks will go on their credit report. However, making only the minimum payment will stretch the debt out for extreme amounts of time and increase the amount of interest paid. If the minimum payment on a statement is $25, the interest portion of that payment may be $15. That means that only $10 is actually going toward paying off the balance. Also, if cardholders keep adding purchases to the debt on top of the current balance, the card may never be paid off.

If used wisely, credit cards can be part of a good money management plan. Using credit cards wisely includes finding a card that has no annual fee, paying the balance off each month, and avoiding anything that will cause a fee to be charged, such as going over the limit, transferring balances, and taking cash advances. The best practice is to *pay off your balance each month*. Wait—did you catch that? **The best practice is to pay off your balance in *full* each month.**

## Mortgages

Buying a home is a dream for most families and one that can be part of good financial management. Most people need to borrow to get into a home. Since people need to pay for housing anyway, buying a home can be a good idea. Buying a home gives individuals an opportunity to build equity while paying for housing. Buying is not right for everyone, however, especially anyone who moves frequently. As far as investments go, because of paying interest, investing elsewhere might be more profitable.

If people do decide to borrow to buy a home, they need to be very careful about the mortgage. The first place to start is to make sure the loan is affordable. When you sit down with a mortgage loan officer to see how much you can qualify for, the loan officer will plug information into a computer program. The information usually includes debt payments and income. The program will then calculate how much people qualify to borrow. However, there are many things the program does not take into consideration. The program does not ask how many members are in the family, how much is spent each month on medical expenses, or how much the family gives for charitable contributions. Even though people may qualify at that time, the program does not take into consideration that they may need a new car within a year or are expecting a baby. All these situations need to be taken into consideration by the people buying the home. They need to create their own budget and decide how much they can afford.

While doing a projected budget, people should find out what expenses will increase or be created because of the home. Utilities may increase, purchases may need to be made such as a lawn mower, and repairs will certainly need to be paid for at some point. All these added expenses need to be included in the budget. It's wise to budget 1–3% of the value of the home for maintenance each year.

The mortgage itself needs to be evaluated carefully. One question to ask is if the rate is a variable or fixed interest rate. **Adjustable Rate Mortgages** (ARMs) can be good if a person plans to stay in their home for a short period of time such as two to three years and if the loan has good caps that will not allow the interest rate to suddenly increase dramatically. The reason they can be good is because ARMs usually start out with a lower interest rate than a fixed mortgage. If you aren't planning to stay a short period of time, a fixed interest rate is better. That way, you know what you are going to have to pay for the entire loan.

Two other questions to ask are, does the mortgage have a balloon payment or a prepayment penalty? **Balloon payments** are a clause in a mortgage that states that a large lump sum of money is due on a specific date. This is done to help the individual qualify for a loan they might not otherwise be able to qualify for. Given that they could not qualify for the loan without the balloon payment, they most likely will not be able to make the balloon payment when it becomes due.

A **prepayment penalty** is a fee that is charged if the loan is paid off early. Any loan with a prepayment penalty should be avoided. Personally, I am a fan of paying extra on a mortgage to pay it off early and reduce the amount of interest paid. However, a prepayment penalty makes that savings less beneficial. If you pay the mortgage off early, either because you pay extra along the way or you decide to sell the home, you would have to pay the prepayment penalty.

Another aspect of a mortgage that needs to be taken into consideration is **mortgage insurance.** Mortgage insurance is an insurance that protects the lender in case borrowers default on the loan. This is not the same as homeowner's hazard insurance, which protects the homeowners from hazards such as fire. Mortgage insurance protects only the lender, and the costs are added to the monthly mortgage payment. Because this insurance does not benefit homeowners, it's good to avoid the insurance or work toward getting it taken off if possible. Some loans will remove mortgage insurance once the borrower has paid down the balance to reflect 20% equity, others will not.

Buying a home can be a good financial move for many people if it's done wisely. Start by getting a mortgage that is easily affordable. Next, make sure the mortgage does not have added features that will make the loan hard to pay such as exploding interest rates, balloon payments, or prepayment penalties. Try to avoid or work toward eliminating mortgage insurance. Finally, make the mortgage payment a top priority. It's good to pay the mortgage payment first, before other bills. Protect that investment and that shelter.

## Home Equity Loans

At first glance, a **home equity loan** seems like a good way to borrow money. The loan is usually tax deductible and may have a low interest rate, though that may be temporary. Home equity loans come with one big catch, however. The home is the collateral for the loan. Collateral is something that can be taken away if a loan is not paid. Therefore, if you miss payments on a home equity loan, you could lose your home. Some people getting a home equity loan think they will be able to make the payments, only to realize later they are having a hard time doing so. Problems can arise in each family, and those problems can make debt payments hard to pay. Be very careful when considering a home equity loan, and also make it a priority when paying bills.

# Debt Reduction

Do you ever worry about debt? Does it cause any stress in your life? Reducing debt can be an important part of a good money management plan for many people. Following are a few things that can help people reduce their debt.

1. **Stop Adding to Debt.** When trying to reduce debt levels, the first step needs to be to create a budget that will incorporate all necessary expenses so that no new debt is acquired. Some people will need to reduce discretionary expenses, such as eating out and going to movies, in order to include all necessary expenditures in their budget.

2. **Pay Extra Toward Debt Payments.** Adding even a little extra to each debt payment can greatly reduce debt levels and interest payments. On a $3,000 loan at 15% interest with $50 payments, it will take 112 payments to pay off the loan and the total paid will be $5,600. If borrowers paid just $20 a month more on this loan, or $70 each month, it would only take 62 months to pay off the loan and the total amount paid would be $4,340—a $1,260 savings!

3. **Make Power Payments.** A good method for reducing debt more quickly is to use **power payments**. Once a debt is paid in full, the money that was going to that debt can be added to another debt until it's paid off (Figure 2.1). Then both payment amounts can be added to another debt, and so on until all debt is paid off. Making power payments will greatly reduce the amount of time and money it takes to get out of debt. A computer program developed by Utah State University Extension called PowerPay is available at https://powerpay. org. This program is easy to run and can show people how much they can save and how long it will take them to pay off debt using power payments. This information can be helpful in creating a debt reduction program.

Power Payment Calendar

| Month | Credit Card | Dept. Store | Furniture | Car |
|---|---|---|---|---|
| Jan | 80 | 50 | 100 | 250 |
| Feb | 80 | 50 | 100 | 250 |
| Mar | | 130 | 100 | 250 |
| Apr | | 130 | 100 | 250 |
| May | | 130 | 100 | 250 |
| Jun | | | 230 | 250 |
| Jul | | | 230 | 250 |
| Aug | | | | 480 |
| Sep | | | | 480 |
| Oct | | | | 480 |
| Nov | | | | 480 |
| Dec | | | | 480 |

**FIGURE 2.1.**

# Credit Reports

Credit reports (also called credit records or credit histories) are a very important part of good money management today. They are a record of how a person manages debt. When you get a loan from a company, that company reports to a credit bureau how well you are making your payments. Then if you apply for new credit, the new lender may request a credit report from the credit bureau to help them make the decision of whether or not they want to lend to you. If you have been doing well making payments to the first company, the second company may feel you are a good risk and approve the loan.

Besides new lenders, there are others who look at credit histories. Some of them are:

• **Employers.** Some employers will request a credit record of a potential employee to see how they manage their own finances. They may do this for a variety of reasons. One is that the position applied for may include working with the company's finances and the employer wants to know that the potential employee can do well with their own finances. Another reason is that research has shown that a financially stressed employee is more likely to be less productive than one who is not having financial problems.[2]

- **Landlords.** Some landlords, especially those who own larger complexes, may request the credit history of a potential renter. These landlords assume that a person who makes debt payments well will also be likely to pay their rent payments.

- **Insurance companies.** Some insurance companies, especially auto insurances, will request a credit history of current or potential clients. These companies have conducted studies that indicate that people who are more risky with their finances tend to be more risky drivers and get in more accidents. Therefore, insurance companies will likely charge higher premiums for those that have poor credit reports.

People should request a copy of their own credit report periodically. This can be done by going to www.annualcreditreport.com or by calling 1-877-322-8228. Everyone is entitled to one free credit report from each of the three major credit bureaus each year. The major three credit bureaus are:

1.  Equifax (equifax.com)

2.  Experian (experian.com)

3.  Transunion (transunion.com)

A good way to monitor credit reports is to order one every four months, spreading the reports throughout the year. Be sure to go to www.annualcreditreport.com to get your report. Other sites will charge you for credit reports or automatically sign you up for a service where you pay a monthly fee. After receiving a credit report, look for potentially negative items, mistakes, and fraud.

## Potentially Negative Items

Usually towards the beginning of the report there will be a line with the words "potentially negative items." Next to those words should be a zero. If there is anything other than zero it means that person has some problems with his or her report. Common problems include late or missed payments or going over the credit limit on a credit card. More severe items would be defaulting on a loan or even bankruptcy. It's very important to always make full, on-time payments on all loans.

## Mistakes

Sometimes there are mistakes on an individual's credit report, items that do not belong to that person. These can be resolved by contacting the credit bureau and explaining the problem. Usually the credit report will come with instructions on how to dispute an item.

## Fraud

A very important reason to request a credit report frequently is to look for fraud. This is often one of the first places individuals may find out they are victims of identity theft. If a thief has opened new accounts in a person's name, or if a person suspects they are a victim of fraud, they should quickly contact each credit bureau and have a fraud alert put on their account. A fraud alert will notify new lenders that no new credit should be extended because this person has been a victim of fraud.

## Credit Scores

Along with credit histories, individuals have **credit scores**. A credit score could be considered a summary of a credit history shown by a number. There are various companies that produce credit scores. One of the most common is the FICO score (Fair Isaac and Company). Scores range from 300 to 850 and the average is around 675. A score of around 720 or above is considered a good score.

There are many factors that contribute to a credit score. Of course, having negative items on a credit report will lower the score. These kinds of items might include bankruptcies, loan defaults, late payments, etc. Other less obvious reasons can also lower the score such as using too much of the available credit. If a credit card has an available limit of $6,000, using over $2,000 of that balance could hurt the credit score.

Credit scores can also be lowered when people apply for many sources of debt and each of those lenders pull a credit report. A credit score is not lowered if an individual requests their own credit report, however. Also, the score is not really hurt if a person is shopping for a car or a home and comparison shops at different businesses within a one-month period. For example, if a person is looking for a car, and they go to four different dealers and those dealers all request a credit report for the individual, there is little harm to the score. On the other hand, if that individual applies for a car loan, a furniture loan, a mortgage, and a credit card within a short time period, there is more impact on their score. Requests that are not initiated by the individual do not hurt a credit report. This would include pre-approved credit card offers.

As mentioned earlier, credit reports are used in a variety of ways, and it's very important to have a good one. This can be done by making full, on-time payments with all debt. If negative items do appear on a credit report, credit scores will be lowered. The way to fix a credit report is to make those full, on-time payments over a period of time.

## Summary

Are you wondering what debt, debt reduction, and credit reports have to do with balancing work and family? Remember, less debt equals less stress. Less stress provides a more peaceful environment for strengthening family relations. Also, less debt gives people more options when it comes to employment. What if you had a job you didn't like, but it paid well? If you had little debt you would have the option of looking for a job you liked more, even if the new job paid less. When you have higher debt levels or poor credit scores, you have fewer options.

### The Martins

*Rob and Maria realize they have had some debt problems which have shown up on their credit report. They have been late on a few payments and even stopped making payments on one bill for a while. As part of their new money management plan, they have gotten control of their spending and have been making all their debt payments on time. They are close to paying off the dentist and plan to make power payments by using that payment to put toward the debt with the highest interest rate, the credit card. By making good, on-time payments the Martins will be able to improve their credit report and credit score.*

References

[1] Johnson. A., Schramm, D. G., Marshall, J., Skogrand, L., & Lee, T. R. Newlyweds' Financial Issues and Educational Solutions for Strengthening Marriages, Association of Financial Counseling and Planning Education Conference, November 2004.

[2] Garman, E. T., Leech, I. E., & Grable, J. E. (1996). The Negative Impact of Employee Poor Personal Financial Behaviors on Employers, *Financial Counseling and Planning,* Vol. 7, 157–168.

# Chapter
# 3

# Good Health

# Good Health

You may be wondering why there is a chapter about health in the money management section. You may also wonder what health has to do with balancing work and family. First of all, health care can be a large expense for some people. The more you can take care of your health the less you will need to spend on health care. As far as balancing work and family, think about the last time you were sick. Did you have a hard time being productive at work? Did you have a hard time being patient with your spouse or children? Good health is actually a huge part of balancing work and family. This chapter will look at nutrition, exercise, and revitalization.

### The Martins

*Maria was feeling rundown and tired all the time. She felt little enthusiasm for life and just focused on getting through each day. It seemed as though she caught colds easily. When the family wanted to do activities, she reluctantly went with them or made an excuse to stay home. A friend asked her to start walking with her for exercise. Maria told her friend that she could not fit walking into her busy day. The truth was, she had no desire to exercise. Maria realized she was not enjoying life and something needed to change. She decided to start with a visit to her doctor and have a physical.*

Have you ever had a time in your life when you felt like Maria? Many people have. There are a lot of things that could be contributing to her current feelings about life. There may be lack of good nutrition, lack of exercise, and increased stress. How are you doing in those areas?

## Nutrition

When it comes to good nutrition, there is a fine balancing act between good nutrition, reducing spending, and time management. When I was a little girl my grandma had a game called "Tip-it." There was a little plastic man suspended on top of a balance with three prongs sticking outward. On each prong, a row of colored discs were lined up. With each turn, depending on what color the spinner landed on, the player had to rearrange the discs. It didn't take me long to realize, even at my young age, that when a player took a disc off of one prong and put it on another prong, the man on top became less stable, and could eventually fall off.

Balancing time, money, and nutrition when it comes to food is like that game. When people are short on time, they may buy more fast food. That purchase causes them to spend more money and most likely reduces their nutrition intake. When people decide to increase their nutrition, they may decide to cook at home more often. This may have a good effect on finances, but will likely require more time. The trick is how to best achieve a balance so the man doesn't fall off.

You already learned about the Step-Down Principle for reducing expenses. Now we will apply it toward nutrition.

## Nutrition

Remember, with the Step-Down Principle, the more you step down the more improvement you see. Here's an example with pizza. The top step could be a pepperoni pizza with extra cheese. The next step down could be a pepperoni pizza without extra cheese. Then we could step down to a cheese-only pizza. Another step down could be to add a lot of fresh vegetables. The last step down could be to include a whole wheat crust with the vegetable pizza. The next time you want pizza, see how many steps you can step down.

You can step down with milk going from whole milk, to 2%, to 1%, to nonfat. What about condiments? Starting with mayonnaise you could step down to light mayonnaise, nonfat mayonnaise, or even mustard. Instead of white rice or white bread could you step down to brown rice or whole wheat bread? For beverages you could start with a sugary soft drink and go on down to water. Even looking at how processed the food is can be stepping down to good health. Are you getting the idea? There is an endless list of ways to use the Step-Down Principle to improve nutrition.

Here are a few easy-to-implement but very good ways to improve your health:

- Eat more vegetables
- Eat more fruit
- Eat more whole grains
- Drink more water
- Eat less sugar
- Eat less fat

Start with two or three of these suggestions. Which ones do you want to work on? It is not too hard or overwhelming if you start with just a couple of these suggestions.

## Time

Obviously, if people always cooked from scratch, they could save a lot of money and have better nutrition. But people don't always have time to cook from scratch when they are balancing work and family. Here's how the Step-Down Principle relates to time. Each step represents less time. So the first step would be to cook from scratch. The next step down could be to prepare some ingredients ahead. The next step down might be to make and freeze meals ahead of time. The last step might be to buy prepared food or just eat out. However, eating at a restaurant can actually be more time consuming by the time you order and wait for your meal to come. But it does take less energy.

Notice what happens to money and nutrition when you step down with time. They tend to get worse. That is why I talked about the balancing act at the beginning of this section. There are ways to reduce time spent when cooking at home compared to buying food away from home *and* still achieve lower expenses and better nutrition.

I mentioned freezing meals. If you have some freezer space to do this, you can save a lot of time. This can be done on a large or small basis. First of all, if you have limited freezer space you might freeze only ingredients. For example, I like to buy, wash, and cut up green peppers and onions. This does take time, but it takes less time to cut a large amount all at once than cutting them each time I need them. I also like to buy meat in bulk when it is on sale, cook it, and freeze it. Then I can quickly add the precooked meat to recipes. With meats and vegetables, you can either freeze by portion or freeze with an ice coating. This can be done by putting the prepared item on a cookie sheet in the freezer (if you have room), leaving it for a few hours while an ice coating forms, then putting the frozen item in a freezer safe container. The benefit of the ice coating is that you can take out just the amount you want at any time.

If you have more room, you can freeze entire meals. This can be done by doubling a recipe every time you cook and putting half in the freezer. Another way is to spend time making several recipes at once and freezing several meals. I have a few neighbors who do this on a regular basis and love it. They often buy all the ingredients on Friday, being sure to watch the advertisements for sales, then spend Saturday making many meals to put in the freezer. If you want to try this, there are several websites that have recipes and more freezing tips.

Besides freezing, you can try using a slow cooker. You can assemble the ingredients the night before and put them in the slow cooker in the morning. Your dinner can be cooking all day and be ready to go when you get home. There are also a lot of recipes on the internet for slow-cooking.

Another great way to save time is to use the delayed time bake feature on an oven. This option does not work for meats, however. But there are other things you can put on time bake besides meat. I can put potatoes or rice in the oven and set the oven so they are done when I get home from work. I have also had meat in the refrigerator ready to put in the oven, set the oven, and asked one of my children to put the pan of meat in the oven when they get home from school.

There are many ways you can save time when cooking at home besides what has already been mentioned. When I was first married, my older sister showed me how to set up my kitchen to be more conducive to cooking. She suggested I put anything I need for cooking in a corner area. That way I can stand in that corner and reach many of the ingredients I need and also the bowls, measuring cups, and utensils. Another thing that helps me is to print off some of the recipes that I use frequently and put them on the inside of one of the cupboard doors of the corner I cook from. I have those on the back of the cupboard that has my measuring cups in it.

Planning a menu is a very helpful way to cook from scratch more. Sometimes just deciding what to make is half the battle. If you know what you are going to cook, have all the ingredients, and maybe prepared part of it beforehand, cooking is not so time consuming. I have seen some systems that list all the ingredients needed for about 20 main courses. The same 20 recipes are used every month, with leftovers and occasional eating out filling out the remaining days in a month. If you can come up with 20 healthy meals your family likes and you plan ahead in order to have all the ingredients, it isn't so hard to cook.

Alright, think back to the "Tip-it" game. I have tried to share some ideas about how you can balance time, money, and nutrition when it comes to food. But this can be a little tricky. There is one way to step down in each of these areas and still keep the man balanced on top. That way is with *family meals*.

## Family Meals

Cooking and eating meals together as a family can help you reduce costs, reduce time, and improve nutrition. When I realized I wanted to write about **family meals** in this chapter I started looking for articles about the benefits of family meals. The amount of research on this subject is huge! I found out there is a lot more than just balancing time, money, and nutrition. According to one article, "Teens who take part in regular family meals are less likely to smoke, drink alcohol, use marijuana and other drugs and are more likely to have healthier diets as adults."[1]

Besides all those good results, family meals can be less expensive; they can be more nutritious; and everyone can help, making the preparation and cleanup less time consuming. This can be a great bonding time for the family. Sometimes people have to work around obstacles that come along, such as schedules. But with some persistence, many people can have at least several family meals a week. The benefits are well worth the effort.

Let me share a meal that our family likes to have that incorporates several of the techniques I have discussed in this section. They are called Taco Toppers. First cook rice according to directions, with taco seasoning added to taste. Each person puts the rice on their plate and tops with any of the following: grated cheese, black beans, black olives, corn (or corn salsa), tomatoes, romaine lettuce, salsa, lime juice, guacamole, crushed tortilla chips, etc.

This is how I use some of the techniques for this meal. I use brown rice to improve the nutrition. I put the rice in the oven in the morning on time bake to save time. Cook white rice for 1 hour at 350°. Brown rice takes 1 ½ hours at 350°. There is no meat in the recipe so the cost is low. I can wash and cut the romaine lettuce the night before or buy pre-cut lettuce to also save time. I can also ask family members to open the can of beans, cut the tomatoes, or cut up olives. The meal is ready in a matter of minutes after we get home. What family recipes do you have that you could plan for balancing time, money, and nutrition?

## Exercise

Just as nutrition is a big part of good health, exercise is vital, too. How are you doing with exercise? People may think they are too busy balancing work and family to exercise. But exercising can actually help people have more energy to do the tasks they need to do every day. What people need to do is figure out how to fit it into their schedules. People don't have to take a full hour every day to exercise; they can actually break it up into 10-minute segments. Six 10-minute segments will give them much needed exercise. Can you think of ways to include several 10-minute blocks of exercise each day?

Maybe you prefer to get up a little earlier and get the full time in before going to work. Maybe you prefer to exercise right after work to help reduce stress. One idea for balancing work and family is to include children in your exercise. Play basketball, tennis, or racquetball. Swim, or go on a bike ride with your children. Involving children sends two messages to them. The first is that physical activity is important to you, and the second is that you want to spend time with them.

It also helps to make some type of commitment. Sign up for a class, or exercise with a friend or family member. People are more likely to keep up on regular exercise if they have committed to it.

When I first moved to the town where I now live, I called the pool at the local high school and signed up for water aerobic classes. I have had four knee surgeries and prefer exercising in the water. After a while, I asked a neighbor if she wanted to go with me. She started going and we took turns driving. Then, after a couple of years of classes, the instructor told me she was quitting and asked if I wanted to take her place teaching. My first thought was, "Are you kidding? I take this class to reduce stress, not create it!" But after thinking about it for a while, I decided it might be nice to get paid for exercising. I had taken water aerobic classes for years and from several different instructors. I was able to build on what I already knew from them, and I became certified. I have been teaching now for many years.

This story shows different levels of commitment for me. I began by taking a class. Then I shared a ride with a friend. Then, I had a much larger commitment when I started to teach. Besides getting paid, there are several benefits to teaching. On cold, winter mornings, I can't decide it is too cold to go outside to make my way to the pool to exercise. Also, I find that I work harder when I teach. What can you do to create a commitment to exercise?

If you are wondering how much you should exercise, here are some guidelines for adults from the website of the Center for Disease Control.[2]

Choose one of the following:

1.　150 minutes per week of moderate to intense aerobic activity AND 2 days of muscle-strengthening activities.

2.　75 minutes per week of vigorous to intense aerobic activity AND 2 days of muscle-strengthening activities.

3.　An equivalent mix of the above-listed times of moderate to vigorous aerobic activity AND 2 days of muscle-strengthening activities.

The moderate to intense aerobic activity can be something like brisk walking and the vigorous to intense aerobic activity can include jogging or running. The muscle-strengthening activities should work all major muscle groups such as legs, hips, back, abdomen, chest, shoulders, and arms.

If you haven't been exercising at all, first check with your doctor, then start with small amounts and build up. As you start exercising you will most likely notice that you have more energy. Then when you add more exercise you might get even more energy. You will start to look better and feel better. Hopefully exercise will become a part of your life and something you don't want to do without.

# Revitalization

Revitalizing yourself and reducing stress can significantly improve health. Life can become almost unbearable when people have lots of stress and no time to renew. Hopefully you will find some ideas from this section of the chapter to keep your life in balance.

## Choose an Activity

First, try to find something that rejuvenates you and relieves stress. Here are some ideas:

- Listen to soothing music
- Exercise
- Read
- Take a hot bath
- Talk with a good friend
- Play with your children
- Meditate
- Garden
- Walk through a park
- Watch a favorite movie

Second, try to figure out a way to regularly incorporate this activity into your life. A regular schedule can help. For example, every day when you get home from work, you can play with your children for 30 minutes before you get into the craziness of the evening.

Third, make a conscious decision to let the activity really revitalize you. Let me make a comparison. I really like dark chocolate. I have made a deal with myself. If I have done well with my eating for the day, I allow myself to have a small piece of dark chocolate (only 35 calories) that evening. If I eat the chocolate quickly while I am doing something else, I won't really enjoy it. Or, I can put the chocolate in my mouth, slowly let the smooth chocolate melt in my mouth, and consciously realize that I am enjoying the taste immensely. I'm enjoying just writing about it! There is a big difference for me in those two methods of eating dark chocolate. The same can be true about the activity you have chosen to reduce stress and revitalize yourself. Sometimes we need to actually say, "This is nice. It is just what I needed."

## Sleep

Getting enough sleep helps revitalize our bodies. Lack of sleep has been associated with physical and mental impairments, irritability, anxiety, weight gain, depression, etc.[3] I learned years ago that I am not a happy person if I don't get enough sleep. I have learned that I have to make sleep a priority in my life. My family also likes it when I get enough sleep!

Besides making sleep a priority, you may find that exercise helps you sleep better. A lady at my water aerobics class told me that when she had stopped coming to class for a while, she had a hard time sleeping. This is true for many people. You may need to find out the best time for you to exercise. When I first started teaching water aerobics, I taught in the evening. I didn't have a hard time going home and going to sleep. However, there were others that said they had a hard time slowing down enough to go to sleep after they exercised. Find out the time that works best for you.

At the beginning of this new year I decided to make a new year's resolution in connection with my schedule. I made a plan to quit my evening activities at 9:00 p.m. Then I would read a book between 9:00 and 9:30 for enjoyment, not work. At 9:30 I would start getting ready for bed and try to be in bed by 10:00. At 5:30 a.m., I would get up and exercise before I started my day. How have I done with my goal? Well, I have been really good about getting up to exercise (mostly because it was already a habit) and pretty good about getting to bed on time. But I have been pretty lousy at doing the reading between 9:00 and 9:30. I need to make a renewed effort to add this back into my schedule.

## Pay Off Debt

Does this seem like a funny thing to add into a section of revitalization? Have you ever paid off debt? How did it feel? I personally think it is a very revitalizing experience! High levels of debt can cause stress. That stress seems to be adding to health problems. According to one study, those with high debt stress also had more ulcers, depression, heart attacks, migraines, anxiety, etc.[4] Although no one can be certain that the debt is the cause of the health issues, the correlation seems relevant. So, do yourself a favor and pay off some debt!

## Simplify Your Life

The more simple your life is, the less stress you are likely to have. Here are several ideas about simplifying your life.

1.  **Pay Off Debt.** Wait. Did I already say that? Besides reducing stress, paying off debt can also simplify your life. It is worth mentioning again.

2.  **Reduce Activities.** Many people have too much "going on." They may be involved in many good activities, but even the good ones can cause stress. Take a close look at your schedule and see if there is something that can be dropped. Sometimes even children are so involved with different activities that they have little free time to just be kids.

3.  **Say No.** Part of simplifying life is to learn to say "no" nicely. This can be really hard to do. Choose which activities you really want to be involved in and say no to the rest. These activities will hopefully be ones that add something good to your life.

4. **Delegate.** When possible, give tasks to others. Children and spouses can help around the house with cleaning, cooking, yard care, etc. At work, are there things you can ask others to do? Sometimes people feel that it might be less stressful to do work themselves instead of showing someone else how to do the work. This may be true for one-time activities. Anything that is done regularly, however, is worth passing on.

5. **Reduce Possessions.** Sometimes we have to spend time, money, and energy taking care of our possessions. Reducing those possessions can simplify our lives and maybe save money too!

## Summary

At the university where I teach, we have a "Wellness Director." I asked her if she knew anyone I could interview for this chapter of the book. She gave me the name of a lady with a great story. Here it is:

*I have struggled a lot with weight all my life but it seemed to get worse after I had children. I stayed at home all the time in my sweat pants. I had a low self-esteem and no excitement for life. Then a friend asked me to go with her to a nutrition class. It changed my life. I decided to try the simple nutrition facts I had learned at the class. I started with small changes, but they produced results, and then I made more changes.*

*This same friend also asked me to start walking with her. It was hard for me to leave my children at home to exercise, but I found other ways to exercise without leaving my house, such as videos and a treadmill. When I could walk with my friend, we started saying things like, "Let's run to the stop sign." Then we ran a little further and a little further. Eventually, I became a "runner."*

*My life is very different now. I am excited about life. I have self confidence and know that I can get through hard times (which I have had to do). I make sleep, exercise, and good nutrition a priority in my life. I found out there was an athlete inside me. I eventually started running marathons. Some people ask me how I have the energy to get up early to exercise and to run marathons. I tell them that exercising gives me more energy! Even though I have small setbacks sometimes, I gave away all my larger clothes or had them altered. Now I look good and feel good, and I don't plan on ever going back to how I was before.*

What lessons does this inspiring story teach? This lady had a friend that helped her get started. She learned some good nutritional facts and started implementing them slowly. After incorporating good nutrition in her life she added exercise. She now makes sleep, exercise, and good nutrition a priority in her life. By doing this, she has the self-confidence and energy to face challenges head-on.

What can you do to be a healthier person? I highly encourage you to choose a few things to start with now. Will you get more sleep? Eat more vegetables? Start adding more physical activity to your life? Drink more water? Plan a time to revitalize yourself? Pay off debt (one of my favorite things)? Just a few simple activities can make a big difference in your health.

### The Martins

*Maria went to see her doctor. He did a blood test and gave her a general physical. He also talked to her about her lifestyle. He found out that she didn't get enough sleep, frequently ate junk food, and didn't exercise. He talked to her about the importance of adequate sleep, nutrition, and exercise. The blood test did show that Maria had a low vitamin D level. Her doctor suggested she take a regular daily vitamin as well as a vitamin D supplement. Maria also started making other changes in her life.*

*Rob and Maria try to eat at home more and involve the family in those meals. They asked the children to try to be home at their set dinner time on most days. Each one has an assignment as part of dinner. They find that they enjoy sharing how their day was with each other, have more nutritious meals, and even save a lot of money by not eating out as much.*

*Maria took her friend up on her offer to walk. They decided to start with three days a week. Maria also tries to get to bed earlier each night. She doesn't always make her goal with this but her added effort does make a difference. After a few weeks of these improvements, Maria started to have more energy. She found she wanted to do more activities with the family. She simply enjoys life more. An added bonus is that she has lost a few pounds. She finds this to be encouraging and decided she wants to keep her new lifestyle.*

### References

[1] KidsHealth. *Family Meals.* http://kidshealth.org/parent/food/general/family_meals.html

[2] Center for Disease Control. *How much Physical Activity Do Adults Need?* http://www.cdc.gov/physicalactivity/everyone/guidelines/adults.html

[3] http://www.sleep-deprivation.com

[4] Jeannine Aversa. *Stress Over Debt Taking Toll on Health.* http://www.usatoday.com/news/health/2008-06-09-debt-stress_N.htm

# Chapter
# 4

# Employment

# Employment

Some of the other chapters in Part I don't talk a lot about work. This chapter, on the other hand, is all about work, a very important part of the balancing act. To start this chapter, ask yourself, "What does good employment mean to me?" Maybe a good income is your top priority. Or maybe you are just as concerned, or more concerned, with having a job that you like, that brings you satisfaction. Having good benefits can be important as well as having a work environment that is friendly and where you are appreciated. This chapter addresses these different aspects of good employment, and other various topics related to employment, such as deciding on a second income, negotiating with employers, what to do when there is a reduction in income, and how to respond to unemployment.

### The Martins

*Luke asked if he could join a beginning soccer club. Rob and Maria decided he could join, but when they went to sign him up at the community recreation center, they found out there wasn't a coach for the team. The person at the registration desk asked if either of them could coach the team. Rob said he would like to but didn't know if he could manage it with his work schedule. He said he would check into it and get back to them.*

*The only time the team could get the practice field was at 4:00 p.m. on Thursdays. Rob works until 5:30 every day. He really wanted to take this opportunity to be involved with Luke and with the community, so he decided to talk to his boss and see if anything could be arranged.*

*Rob was a little nervous to approach his boss so he decided he would be most effective if he had a plan before going in. Rob waited until his boss was alone in her office and everything seemed calm. He explained the situation and asked if it would be possible for him to leave two hours early on Thursdays and work an extra half hour on the other days of the week.*

*At first Rob's boss seemed unwilling to work with him. She explained that if Rob didn't finish his work on Thursdays, others may be held up from doing their work on Fridays. She said Rob had always been a good employee and wished they could work it out. After thinking for a minute she asked Rob if he would be willing to finish up his work Thursday nights at home.*

*Rob thought this was a reasonable compromise and agreed to the situation. He thanked his boss for working with him. When Rob got back to his office he called the city recreation department to tell them he could coach the soccer team. Then he called a very happy Luke to tell him the same news.*

## Harmony

My husband sang in a Barbershop Quartet for a few years. They were an amateur quartet that performed for enjoyment only. When the quartet first started singing together, it took some time for them to learn to blend and build off of one another. Sometimes when they performed, they sang out a chord that just didn't sit right with me, even though I am by no means an expert. Other times they would hold a chord, and it just felt good. It felt sweet to my ears and was not only a pleasant sound; it was almost a pleasant *feeling*. My husband said this was when it was really fun to him. This is the beauty of **harmony**. Our lives can be like chords from a quartet. Sometimes, different parts of our lives don't seem to work together, and we have that uncomfortable feeling that something is not "right." As you read through this chapter, think about striving for harmony in your life. That means you have the sweet feeling that everything is working together.

## Finding Good Employment

Good employment can mean different things to different people. Let me tell you a story about my oldest son. He graduated with a dual major in finance and economics. He wanted to work for a small-town bank. He was fortunate to find such a bank and get a job as a loan officer with them. After a training period, they transferred him to his permanent branch in a small community. My son and daughter-in-law bought a home and settled in. After a while, my son called me and asked, "Mom, what would you think of me being an elementary school teacher?" My response was something like, "Where is this coming from?" He then explained to me that the bank was changing his job responsibilities. What started out as a more service-oriented job was turning into a sales-oriented job, probably because of the economic downturn at the time. This was not what my son wanted to be doing for the rest of his life, so he asked himself what he would rather do. What he came up with was teaching elementary school.

He is now a certified elementary school teacher teaching third grade. He told me a while ago, "I'm doing what I should be doing." I don't think my son and his wife will have as much money as they would have had if he had continued on as a banker, but he is a lot happier. Another perk for him is having summers off. He, his wife, and children enjoy camping, hiking, biking, and other outdoor activities. Now they will have more time to enjoy those activities as a family. You may be surprised to hear me say this in a section about finances, but there is more to life than just money.

### Find Work You Enjoy

People can be happier in all aspects of their lives if they *enjoy their work*. It's hard to be pleasant with spouses and children after working all day if that work has been tedious. Sometimes people don't have choices and need to just find any job to pay for the basic necessities. This is often the case in a down economy. Unfortunately, many people get stuck in those jobs and never find a job they like. But often, people do have choices.

My husband and I took a short trip to Yellowstone National Park the first week of January one year. You may think that is a crazy thing to do in the winter. The temperature did get down to –30 degrees the last day we were there, but it was beautiful, and we had a wonderful time. While we were there, we found it interesting to talk to the various employees about working there. To get into the park, we rode in a "snowcoach." The driver stopped to let us take a picture of the beautiful Firehole River Falls and said, "This is *my* office." That got us talking, and he said that he had "quit working competitively" several years ago and was much happier. I thought that was an interesting way to put it. Also, our cross-country ski instructor said in order to live that lifestyle you have to give up some of the "creature comforts" of life, but it was worth it to him.

That may sound a little extreme to you, or you may wish you could have such a job. Whichever way you feel, I hope you are not one of those people that works at a job you hate to pay for things you don't even really want or need. Sometimes people get jobs and start buying more things when their income increases. Often this includes taking on more debt. Then they have to keep working and working to pay for those things. It can be a vicious trap. My point is that keeping debt low and spending in check may make it possible to take an enjoyable job, even if it pays less, like my son and the people we met in Yellowstone.

## Family Friendly

As you look for work that will help you achieve your goals in life, you might also want to look for a company that is friendly and supports employees and their families. Some companies are much better at this than others.

I have a friend who was having very serious medical problems. Her husband needed to stay home with her for some time. He talked to his employer, and his employer said he would be able to use the **Family and Medical Leave Act (FMLA)** to be able to help out at home. This sounded like a family-friendly company to me, but it gets even better. This company has a policy that for every year you have worked for the company, you get a set number of days of *paid* leave with the FMLA. This pay made a big difference to my friend and her family.

The FMLA provides up to 12 weeks of unpaid, job-protected leave per year. It also requires that an employee's group health benefits be maintained during the leave. "FMLA is designed to help employees balance their work and family responsibilities by allowing them to take reasonable unpaid leave for certain family and medical reasons."[1]

Policies, such as the FMLA, can be resources parents can use to help balance their work and family responsibilities. However, even though policies such as this are available, employees need to feel that they can use these policies without being penalized. A study about workplace policy found that the workplace attitude may be just as important as policy.[2]

## Good for the Family

Another important component is to decide what will work best for your family. There are many configurations that work for different families. Sometimes part-time work can be an excellent option for working parents. My own position is a three-quarter time position. This works out well for our family because it gives me the freedom to do more work at home than my husband who works full-time. This arrangement works for our family, though it might not work for yours.

One time, while talking with my daughter and her friend, the friend mentioned that her dad always did her hair before school when she was growing up. I asked her if this was because he liked to or was good at it (thinking of my husband's lack of skill in doing little girls' hair). She said it was because her mom worked and her dad stayed home. I was in the process of writing this book at that time and asked if I could interview her dad. This is the story her dad told to me.

*My wife and I met when we were both in college majoring in pre-med business. I eventually figured out that I didn't belong in pre-med and started in Engineering. Our plan was for me to get my degree and then put her through medical school and residency. After that we would both work part-time. The first part of our plan went as scheduled as I worked to put her through medical school and was on track for management. Then when my wife started residency, we had to move. At this time we had two children. I was working and she was putting in about 80 hours a week. We tried a nanny but didn't like the influence she had on the children. We took turns being home with the children but this meant I was getting about four hours of sleep a night. Not only was the lack of sleep very hard, I also felt like I was losing my family.*

*For a while I cut back to twenty hours a week but even that was difficult. I felt like things were slipping out from under me. We finally decided I would be a full-time dad. It was a tough decision. I enjoy working. Staying home has been challenging. But the rewards have been worth it. I have been able to be a part of my children's lives in ways that most fathers can't experience. I have been very involved. This has allowed us to raise our own children. There have been many sacrifices along the way, but it has been worth it.*

Notes

The dad in this story is not alone. According to one article, 176,000 men have left the workforce to raise children.[3] Many more than that are still the primary caretaker of children and are supporting wives in their jobs. There are many reasons for this new trend. Sometimes it is an economic choice, especially if the father lost his job during the recession. Sometimes it is a lifestyle choice based on the desire to have a parent in the home. Some fathers realize they can have deeper rewards bonding with their children than bringing home income. There may be a situation where the husband has more time to take care of children and still pursue a career than the wife does. Whatever the reason, as I mentioned before, it is good to find the best way to balance work and family in your own family.

Dr. E. Jeffrey Hill has done extensive research on the interactions of work and family. He shares a story of how a flexible work schedule helped him harmonize work and family.

> *For thirteen years I struggled to juggle a demanding IBM career with the needs of my family. In 1990 I started working from my home office, instead of an IBM facility. The difference in my life was immediate. Instantly, I gained an hour a day because I did not have to drive to and from work. Instead of dragging into work and needing to unwind after a "fast-lane" commute, I could roll out of bed early with an exciting idea and immediately key it into the laptop. Later, I could get the kids up for family devotional and breakfast. Because I was working from home, I could listen for baby Amanda while my wife Juanita went to aerobics, shopping, or ran errands. When Abigail had the lead in the fourth-grade play, I could be there on the front row at 11:00 a.m. When work got frustrating, I could put Emily in the jogging stroller and go for an invigorating run. The dissonance would dissipate, and I could return to work refreshed. I usually took about 30 minutes off work mid-afternoon to visit with the kids when they came home from school. Jeffrey and I would often play a 10-minute game of one-on-one basketball.*
>
> *On the work side I found myself more focused, energized, and productive. Without the interruptions of co-workers, I was able to deliver higher quality products in less time. The arrangement worked so well that soon four of my colleagues were working from home with similar results. Within four years more than 25,000 IBM employees were working in what became known as the "virtual office."[4]*

As you can see from Dr. Hill's story, it can be beneficial to ask about **flexible work schedules.** At one point in our married life, my husband worked in a large city about 30 miles from our home. Without traffic, he could make this commute in about 30 minutes. With rush hour traffic the commute could take 30 to 60 minutes longer. His employer offered flexible work hours at that time, and my husband was able to go into work before rush hour and get home before rush hour. This gave him more time to spend with our family.

Although families don't always have a lot of options in employment, families should explore any available options that will provide more harmony within the family unit. This may include working part-time, one spouse staying home with children, working different shifts, flexible work hours, working from home, etc. This topic will be addressed more in the next section.

### Good Benefits

The last part of good employment that I would like to mention is having good **benefits.** If you ever have the option of deciding between two jobs, I hope you won't overlook the important aspect of employee benefits. These can include various insurances, retirement plans, paid leave, flexible spending accounts, merchandise discounts, etc. Sometimes people look only at salaries and forget the important role that benefits play in family financial management. Health insurance alone is an important benefit that can help balance work and family. Although I am not going to spend any more time on this topic, I do want to stress the importance of looking at a benefit package when looking at employment.

## Deciding on a Second Income

When looking for good employment, couples also have to decide if they will both work or if there will be only one main breadwinner. There are many aspects to this decision. Sometimes both individuals want to work. This may be for fulfillment, to keep up-to-speed and qualified, for self-esteem, or even for social reasons. Another reason, of course, is for more income.

Sometimes couples decide they need to both work in order to make ends meet. When looking at the income a second job will bring, they forget to include the costs as well. One of the biggest expenses when working is **taxes.** Couples may not realize that a second income is taxed at a higher rate. The reason is that when a couple files jointly, they get the same deductions, exemptions, tax credits, etc., whether just one or both of them are working. Therefore, a second income would be taxed more because the couple doesn't get another set of deductions, exemptions, and tax credits along with the additional income. There are many other expenses to consider such as daycare, transportation, and work clothes. Also, when both people work, more money is usually spent on fast food. The list can go on and on.

Here is an example of a nonworking spouse considering accepting a job offer for $40,000 annually. The employer provides some life insurance worth $10 per month. The employer also includes a health care plan, but the new worker is already covered under the plan of the first employer. The family is currently in the 25% federal income tax bracket and in the 5% state income tax bracket. The total net amount of the extra $40,000 income is a mere $14,260, thus adding only $1,188 a month to total earnings. This is only about 35 percent of the gross additional income.

## How to Assess the Bottom Line Benefit of a Second Income

### 1. Additional Income

| | |
|---|---|
| Annual earnings | $40,000.00 |
| Value of employee benefits | |
|    Life insurance ($10/month) | $120.00 |
|    Health care plan (include only if enrolled) | |
| **Total Additional Income** | $40,120.00 |

### 2. Additional Expenses

| | |
|---|---|
| Federal income taxes (25% rate × $40,000) | $10,000.00 |
| State/local income taxes (5% rate × $40,000) | $2,000.00 |
| Social Security taxes (7.65% × $40,000) | $3,060.00 |
| Transportation and commuting (50 weeks @ $50 per week) | $2,500.00 |
| Childcare (9 months after-school only) | $3,600.00 |
| Additional lunch expenses (50 weeks at $20 per week) | $1,000.00 |
| Work wardrobe (including dry cleaning) | $1,800.00 |
| Other work-related expenses | $200.00 |
| Additional evening meal expenses due to additional reliance on take-out and restaurant dining ($100/month) | $1,200.00 |
| Additional home-care expenses due to work time commitments | $500.00 |
| **Total Additional Expenses** | $25,860.00 |

### 3. Net Value of Second Income

| | |
|---|---|
| Total Additional Income | $40,120.00 |
| Minus Total Additional Expenses | $25,860.00 |
| **Net Benefit of Second Income** | $14,260.00 |

A couple may decide it's worth a second person going to work for $40,000 a year, but what about $14,000 a year? The lower income paints a much different picture. When making the decision to increase employment, ask these four questions:

- What costs will come with the employment? (i.e., taxes, gas, extra food, clothes, day care, etc.)
- What will be gained after those expenses?
- What will be lost with the employment? (i.e., time, household chores, yard work, time with family, cooking healthy food, exercise, etc.)
- Will the amount gained be worth what will be lost?

Discussions about these matters are very important. Remember that there may be other reasons to work as mentioned earlier, but if the main reason is income, it's good to look into the costs also.

Another interesting point is brought out in the book *The Two Income Trap: Why Middle-Class Mothers and Fathers are Going Broke.*[5] When there is a second income, most families use that second income, not to save, but to pay for living expenses. When this happens, couples give up a **safety net.** The safety net is having a non-working individual who can go into the workforce if the working individual loses his or her job. During 2008 and 2009 when there were massive layoffs and soaring unemployment among men, more women returned to the workforce.[6] Some families had the option of sending the wife to work if the husband got laid off. If both were already working to make ends meet, that option is gone.

When trying to decide what is best for your family, you may think, "If we have only one working adult then we might not be able to make ends meet. If we have two working adults we lose our safety net. What is best?" Here is a suggestion for each way. If you decide to have only one working parent, try to find ways to decrease expenses. There are many things the nonworking individual can do to cut costs. You will find suggestions in Chapter 1. If you decide to have both individuals work, set aside some of each paycheck for an emergency fund. You will also find information about an emergency fund in Chapter 1.

## Negotiating with Employers

In order to obtain good employment that works well with your family, you may find you need to negotiate with an employer. This may include **negotiations** about work schedules, as in Rob's situation, or about pay, benefits, or responsibilities. If you remember back at the beginning of the chapter, Rob had several things going for him when he wanted to negotiate with his employer. He had been a good employee, he went in with a plan, and was willing to be flexible. The attitude of the company has a large part to do with negotiations, but is not impossible even in unfriendly environments.

Having good work schedules may be an important part in work/family harmony. One aspect of flexible schedules is being able to have dinner together as a family. As mentioned in Chapter 3, there have been many studies looking at the importance of a **family dinnertime.** One study found that employees working long hours had more negative effects of the long work hours if they had to miss dinner because of work.[7] The authors of the study suggest that employers find ways to provide flexibility to employees allowing them to have a family dinnertime. This may include some negotiation but the benefits can be tremendous.

Here are some key points to keep in mind when negotiating with employers.

- Build a good relationship before negotiating. Try to always be a team player and be willing to step up to the plate. You may even want to take on jobs that others are not willing to do. Rob's boss said that Rob was a good employee, and she wanted to work with him. This relationship was built slowly over time, and when Rob needed to work out a solution with his boss, his hard work paid off.

- Look at your employer's point of view. Before starting negotiations, consider what the employer's needs are. Think about how your request will impact the company or other employees. Be tactful. Search for an outcome that will be beneficial to both of you. You may even want to point out to your employer why this desired solution will be a good situation for him or her.

- Be willing to compromise when possible. Before talking to your employer, decide what you would be willing to give up in the negotiation process if necessary. Good negotiations usually involve compromise on both sides. Try to be sensitive to when it's best to give in and when it's best to stand up for yourself.

Remember, you are asking for a change because you want to be a good, productive employee which is a benefit to your employer as well. This will, of course, require a positive approach to negotiations.

## Reduction in Income

Sometimes, despite good negotiations, families still find themselves with a reduction in income. This situation can be extremely difficult, especially if money was tight before the reduction in income. This reduction may come with a little warning or it may come suddenly. Let's look at each situation.

### Time to Prepare

During the down economy of 2008 and 2009, our university, like most others, was dealing with major budget cuts. My husband and I both work at the university and we wondered if both of our jobs would survive those cuts. I started looking at our spending and thinking about ways we could cut back if we had to. Then it dawned on me, "We don't have to wait until one of us loses our job to cut back, we can start now and be more prepared if we do." This might be a good attitude for all of us to have in general, but especially when the economy is down. My husband and I are still both employed, but we did go through a round of furloughs, which reduced both of our incomes for several months.

If you have any warning that a reduction in income is going to take place, there are several steps you can take to help brace yourself for the blow. Here are some ideas to survive a reduction in income.

1. **Reduce Spending Right Away.** Sometimes if people hear that they are going to have a reduction in income, they tend to wait until the reduction comes to make changes. Maybe this is a

form of denial, but it wastes precious time that could be used to prepare for the cutback. In Chapter 1, you learned about the Step-Down Principle, which can help you figure out how to cut back spending.

2. **Pay Off Debt.** I am a big fan of paying off debt at anytime. But paying it off before a reduction in income is very helpful. Think about how much money you would need to meet all your expenses for three months right now. Now think about how much you would need if you had no debt. There is possibly a big difference! Chapter 2 gave you ideas on how to pay off debt more quickly.

3. **Save.** Imagine how good you would feel if you have little or no debt and a nice amount of savings. Seriously, stop a minute and think about that. What a good feeling! If you start with reducing your expenses, then you will be able to put more money toward your debt payments and also start or add to an emergency savings account. These are three simple but important steps to becoming financially stable.

## No Time to Prepare

Sometimes you don't have time to prepare for that unexpected reduction in income. There are still ways that you can survive. The first thing to do is to switch to a **crisis budget.** This is a budget that only includes necessities. If people have time to prepare for a reduction in income, they can cut back on *some* wants. When they don't have that time to prepare, they need to cut back on *all* wants. This is difficult. It takes determination. Sometimes in people's lives there are expenses that seem like needs. But faced with the possibility of not having enough money for food, people realize some of those needs are really wants. Keep in mind that this crisis budget is most likely temporary. That thought can help you and other family members get through a tough time.

Another way to keep spending down is to think about **resources** that you can use that don't cost money. I have a personal story about this topic. This didn't happen after a reduction of income, but it will still convey the point I am trying to make. The point is, sometimes resources, which haven't been considered, are available.

We moved into a new house several years ago. There was no yard, just dirt and lots of rocks. We decided we wanted to put in a sprinkling system before we planted grass. We had a LOT of rocks in our yard so we rented a large trencher to dig the trenches for the sprinkling system. It worked very well. Unfortunately, right after we dug the trenches it rained hard for three full days. This caved back in all our trenches. It took us a long time to get the trenches cleaned out, the sprinkling system in place, and the trenches filled back in. After all that, it was getting close to the end of summer. We really wanted to get the grass in and growing before cold weather hit, but we needed to spend a fair amount of time raking up rocks. At that point we were running out of time, we were out of money, and we had pretty much used up the resource of our children's help. We didn't know what to do.

Then one day I thought of an idea. Our children were pretty tired of the yard project, but our children had friends! I talked to the family and proposed the idea of having a rock raking party. They could all invite as many friends as they could, I would feed them all pizza, and then we could all rake rocks. At first our children thought that was a poor excuse of a party and not necessarily a nice thing to do to their friends. But I could see their minds working as they realized that having their friends help would eliminate a lot of work on their part. They were in!

I was actually feeling a little funny about the idea myself, especially when one of the friend's mother called. To my surprise she said, "You are brilliant. My son is excited to come to your rock raking party." The friends all came. I made pizza. They all jumped in and got the entire yard raked in less than two hours. We even had ice cream after. Everyone went home happy, and we had our project done.

There may also be **community resources** that can help during a down time. For example, the school district may have a free or reduced lunch program for school children, or you may find heat assistance through a local program. You may be able to qualify for food stamps, which can be a great help in providing food for the family, especially with a reduction in income.

What resources could you come up with to save money? You may have more than you think. I hope my rock raking story helps you start thinking of resources you have that could save you money. This way of thinking may help you survive a cutback in income.

# Unemployment

Even worse than a reduction in income can be losing a job altogether. If you are experiencing this situation, you may be going through a lot of emotions. You will likely have a hard time paying bills, and you may feel personally attacked. Job loss can, however, be a time to take a good look at your life and make changes to improve it.

## Stages of Grief

Some people experiencing a job loss may go through what have been called the stages of grief. These stages have been in and out of favor in the scientific field, but may still help some people understand what they are experiencing. Here are Dr. Elisabeth Kübler-Ross' original stages, and how job loss applies.[8]

**Denial.** In this stage people can't really believe they are going to be without an income. Sometimes they continue to spend as if the job loss was not really going to happen.

**Anger.** Some people get very angry with a boss or even the economy. Life is certainly not fair at this point and individuals may try to blame someone else for their own situation.

**Bargaining.** Sometimes individuals losing jobs will try to negotiate with a boss or even a higher being. They try to change the path or make some type of arrangement.

**Depression.** Once depression sets in, people are often not motivated to look for other work or figure out how to reduce spending. Some people stay in this stage longer than others and find they have a hard time moving on.

**Acceptance.** During this stage individuals can usually look at life with a clearer picture and decide what needs to be done. They are more likely to apply for work and get their life "in order."

## Paying Bills

If you have lost your job, you may find that there is just not enough money to pay all the bills. Sometimes bills must be prioritized: high, medium, or low priority. The question to ask is, "What may happen if I don't pay this bill?" This question can help you determine which bills are **high-priority debt.** Of course, not paying any bill will result in a negative mark on your credit history. However, if there is no way to pay all the bills, consider the consequences of not paying.

Usually high-priority debt includes debt that has collateral such as mortgages and auto loans. This is called **secured debt.** If you do not make the payments on secured debt, the collateral can be repossessed or foreclosed. There are programs available to help individuals work through some mortgage problems.[9] Other important bills may include utility payments and health and auto insurance. Of course, you need to make sure there is money for food, also.

Debts and bills that are lower-priority may include credit cards, store cards, and medical bills. These are **unsecured debt.** There is no collateral to take away if the debt is not paid. That does not mean the debt will go away. There will still be consequences, but the consequences are less severe. Again, not paying these debts will show as a negative mark on a credit history.

Another alternative is to try a **work-out plan** with a lender. If you explain your situation to lenders, they may work out a plan with you that will allow you to continue making payments, but on a modified plan. This may include a lower interest rate or reduced payments.

One more important point along these lines is to try not to take on any more debt. Often when people have financial problems, they think the solution is to get a loan. This may help for a short period of time but usually causes more trouble in the long run. Use this route as a last resort.

## Choose a New Path

Finding out you are losing your job can be devastating. On a more positive note, it can also be an opportunity to make major changes in your life. My brother has been through a few layoffs, and I asked him to share some insights he has. His thoughts came down to two ideas that he wanted to share. They fit in well with this section. Here are his comments:

1.  **A layoff can be just what you need to get a better job.** *Most people dream about finding a better job than the one they currently have. But if you are getting by okay with your current job, you are less likely to do a lot towards finding a better job. You are mainly just glad you have a job, especially in times of economic downturn, and you are not likely to invest large amounts of time into looking for something else. But getting laid off gives you large amounts of time, and though your main worry is just finding something, you also have a much greater chance of finding something better than you did while you were employed. If you do find something better, you can look back and say, "I never would have gotten this job if I hadn't been laid off."*

    *That is very true for my current job, which I like far better than my previous one. I didn't even have to invest any time to get it—I only needed to get laid off! My current office had considered offering me work for two or three months, but had never called me because they felt sure I wouldn't leave my job. Then they happened to hear from somebody else that I was out of work, and called me almost immediately.*

    *I have been laid off three times in the past eight years. All three times, it led me to a higher-paying job that I liked better.*

2.  **Getting laid off does not make you less of a person or less of a professional.** *Even if your layoff is entirely due to company financial problems or corporate changes—that is, it's not at all related to your performance—it's very easy to let the layoff affect your feelings of self-worth. You may find that it becomes even harder to avoid these feelings if you go a long time unemployed. It's important to remember that even very highly paid people with great resumes and lucrative degrees get laid off. It's not like you have suddenly become less qualified! You are as qualified and valuable as ever. You may even use some of your unemployed time to make yourself more qualified and valuable.*

*In my previous job, I was on a team of four, and two of us got laid off because of shrinking company budgets. Several people (including me and my co-worker who also got laid off) made the comment that the two who got laid off were the two who really "got it": we designed and wrote the best new teaching materials, and were the reviewers/editors who anticipated problems and fixed errors before a product went online. Our two team members who did not get laid off had a reputation in our office for always doing everything the same way, even when that way didn't make sense, and for not noticing weaknesses or problems with the products before users noticed them. The layoffs were handled by an office in a completely different part of the country, which never explained what the basis was for their choices of who was let go. (I suspect they simply looked at the salaries, and kept the two highest-paid team members.) Being a veteran of two previous layoffs, I had gotten good at not taking it personally, but my laid-off co-worker was devastated and seemed to feel almost like she had been wrongly found guilty of some crime. When my new employer called to offer me my present job, he also asked me if I knew of anyone else who would be good for their new project. And so now, my formerly devastated co-worker and I are working together on a project that is much more fulfilling and creative, in an office where our talents and abilities are far more appreciated and utilized.*

Although it's very difficult, try to avoid feeling personally attacked if you get laid off. Also, take the time to evaluate your current situation and think about the possibility of taking a new and better path.

## Summary

Because good employment is such a large part of being able to balance work and family, look for work that you enjoy, is family friendly, is best for the family situation, and has good benefits. You may want to consider having one family member work part-time or stay home with children. Consider working from home or negotiating for flexible work hours. There is not a "one-size-fits-all" when it comes to good employment for each family.

Try to reduce spending, pay off debt, and increase savings when there is sufficient employment. These measures will certainly reduce the stress associated with a reduction in income or unemployment. If unemployment does occur, take the time to evaluate your situation and determine if you should stay on the same path or make some changes. Mostly, think about what you need to create harmony in your life.

### The Martins
*In this chapter, you can see that Rob was able to negotiate with his employer and find a way that he could coach Luke's soccer team. Rob was able to work this out because he had been a good employee for the company and was willing to compromise to create a good situation for both him and his employer.*

References

[1] United States Department of Labor website: http://www.dol.gov/dol/topic/benefits-leave/fmla.htm

[2] Pedersen, Minnote, Kiger, Mannon. 2009. Workplace Policy and Environment, Family Role Quality, and Positive Family-to-Work Spillover. *Journal of Family Economic Issues.* 2009, 30:80–89.

[3] Alex Williams, "Just Wait Until Your Mother Gets Home. *The New York Times* 2012 (online). Available at: http://www.nytimes.com/2012/08/12/fashion/dads-are-taking-over-as-full-time-parents.html?pagewanted=all&_r=0

[4] E. Jeffrey Hill, "Harmonizing Work and Family Life: One Man's Perspective." *Marriage and Family*, 2–6, 2001, April Available at: http://www.byucemedia.org/cw/family/pdf/Hill_JeffreySYLLABUS1.pdf

[5] Elizabeth Warren and Amelia Warren Tyagi, *The Two Income Trap: Why Middle-class Mothers and Fathers are Going Broke.* Basic Books, Cambridge, MA.

[6] Kelly Evans, "In Downturn's Wake, Women Hold Half of U.S. Jobs." *The Wall Street Journal* 2009 (online). Available at: http://online.wsj.com/article/SB125797318108844061.html

[7] Jenet I. Jacob, Sarah Allen, E. Jeffrey Hill, Nicole L. Mean and Maria Ferris, "Work Interference with Dinnertime as a Mediator and Moderator Between Work Hours and Work and Family Outcomes." *Family and Consumer Sciences Research Journal.* Available online at: http://fcs.sagepub.com/cgi/content/abstract/36/4/310

[8] Dr. Elisabeth Kübler-Ross. http://en.wikipedia.org/wiki/K%C3%BCbler-Ross_model

[9] www.hud.gov

# Chapter 5

## Family and Money Management

# Family and Money Management

Anyone working with couples and families finds that money issues are often at the forefront of problematic areas. This chapter focuses on financial issues within the family. Finances can be the source of family stress and are often stated as one of the top reasons for divorce or other marital problems. Evidence of financial problems within families comes in the form of high bankruptcy rates, sky-rocketing home foreclosure rates, large amounts of consumer debt, and low savings rates.

First we will look at couple relationships and the way those relationships interact with finances. Then we will do the same with children and finances. This chapter will lead into the next two sections of the book.

Key factors for couples include learning to communicate about money matters and working together to create financial goals and plans to reach those goals. Also, good money management can be taught to children in the home when the stakes are small and the consequences are not as devastating as they can be in adulthood. When money is managed well, those family members that are employed are even less stressed at work and don't feel the constant need to increase their income. Having good, working, financial management within the family will help eliminate stress and increase balance.

### The Martins

*As you have read about the Martins in the past few chapters, you have seen the financial problems they have had. Maria and Rob got thinking about how those problems began.*

*Maria and Rob Martin started out their marriage not worrying too much about money matters. They didn't have a lot of money, but they didn't need to spend a lot either. Soon they found they wanted to buy new furniture, electronic equipment, a new car, and take a nice vacation. Maria and Rob did not agree on which of those purchases was most important. They began to argue about expenses and did not agree on what was considered a need and what was a want. Maria felt that a cell phone was a need and Rob felt a new car was a need. They bought some items on credit, only to realize that the next time they got paid they did not have enough money to pay all their living expenses and all their bills.*

*These financial problems became more intense as their lives progressed,
adding into the picture other issues such as children, concerns about insurance, trying to fund retirement, and still being able to spend money on things
they each enjoyed. These issues led to the debt problems they had later in
their marriage. As money got tighter, Maria and Rob seemed to argue about
other problems that, before they had money problems, seemed small and
insignificant.*

*Early in their marriage, Maria and Rob did not have financial goals or any
type of money management plans. They did not use a budgeting system,
and they did not have a savings program. Their financial situation needed
some direction, and instead of feeling hopeless and frustrated, they wanted
to feel in control. When they experienced these frustrations, they often wondered if they each needed to take on additional employment even though
they were already stressed with the work they had.*

## Money Management

As shown in the above example, the Martins' money management practices, or the
lack thereof, can cause relationship problems. Even if other areas in a marriage are
not problematic, financial problems can magnify them into problems. As discussed
in Chapters 1 and 2, money problems, such as too much debt, can carry a high cost
to society as a whole in the form of higher interest rates and fees due to bankruptcies
and loan defaults. On an individual level, when people have financial problems,
they often pay higher interest rates and fees due to a poor credit record. Bad credit
in turn can make getting a new loan harder or more costly, not to mention other
problems like higher car insurance, difficulty renting, and even not being able to
gain employment. Employers are finding that individuals with money problems
make less productive employees.[1] You can learn how to address these issues through
incorporating good money management into different stages of life like engagement,
marriage, and with children.

### Engagement and Money

I have watched engaged couples spend hour upon hour planning every detail of
their special day, even down to what napkins they will use. They also talk exten-
sively about their future, including such topics as how many children they want,
what their dream house would be like, and the fun vacations they want to take
together. But too often, financial management is not discussed. Engagement is a
perfect time to start discussing money matters. If every couple spent as much time
planning their financial future as they did their wedding day, there might not be
such a high rate of bankruptcy!

### Look at the Past

A good place to start is to get to know each other financially. People might know
their fiancé's favorite color, their favorite ice cream flavor, and what their favorite
movie is, but may not know anything about that person's financial upbringing and
history with money. Couples can start out by asking each other questions about
what they remember about money while growing up such as:

- Did you get an allowance?
- What was spending like in your family?
- Was money tight in your home?
- Did you work outside the home when you were a teenager?
- Did your parents talk about money issues in front of you or with you?
- How did your parents handle money?

Sometimes knowing about people's past can help others understand why they feel a certain way in the present. For example, if you lived in a home where the breadwinner was frequently laid off from employment, you may feel concerned about having adequate savings at all times. These concerns will likely affect how you manage money as an adult. Besides looking at memories about money, it's good to discuss any past financial behaviors that might have an effect on the financial situation in marriage. Bringing out into the open any problems with bounced checks, late payments, or overspending can help reduce stress later when married. It's good to discuss all financial issues before marriage.

## Look at the Present

Although it doesn't sound very romantic, it's good for each person to order a credit report and look at them together. Discuss any amounts of debt for each person. Imagine coming home from a wonderful honeymoon and finding a bill for a high credit card debt in the mail. A very difficult situation in a marriage can occur when one spouse finds out the other has brought debt into the marriage. Disclosing that debt before marriage is better. I have had students come to my office many times and tell me that they have been married for a few months and just found out that their spouse has debt they did not know about. This is hard on a marriage. Besides talking about debt, talk about other money matters, such as how much each person makes and what bills they have. Ideally, an engaged couple could even work out a marriage budget based on what they know their income and expenses will be. Going into a marriage with specific plans is a great way to start.

Another area to discuss is what is often called **money personalities**. Several different authors, such as Mellan[2] and Solomon,[3] have created names for specific money personalities. Some people tend to save money; some tend to spend. Some people don't like risk at all and others love it. There are people who enjoy using money for status and someone else who uses it for security. Often one person does not understand why the other has certain money behaviors and vice versa. Exploring each other's money histories and money personalities can help increase communication and understanding.

Along with exploring money personalities, a couple can learn about the **money attitudes** of each other. A starting place is to find out what each person likes about money. Ask questions such as:

- Does money bring you pleasure, security, or power?
- Do you prefer to spend or save money?
- Do you tend to be frugal, or do you like to spend spontaneously?
- What would you do if you were given one thousand dollars today?

Discussing money personalities or attitudes along with money memories can bring a unique understanding to the relationship that will help improve future financial communication.

## Plan for the Future

Engagement is a great time to write down specific financial goals. Starting a marriage with financial goals increases the likelihood that good financial practices will be incorporated into that marriage. After goals are written, the next step is to figure out how to accomplish those goals. Creating specific plans for accomplishing goals is a key step. Again, it's good to ask some questions:

- Who will pay the monthly bills?
- What budgeting or money management systems will we use?
- How much will we save each pay period, and where will we save it?
- How will we decide upon and fund our fun purchases?

Engaged couples can begin to learn how to build upon each other's strengths and to help each other in weak areas. For example, if Maria Martin loves to buy shoes and has a hard time walking away from a much desired pair, even if unneeded, she can work with Rob to create a balance between feeling the freedom to buy an occasional pair of shoes and staying within a budget. Maria may also be a very organized person. Rob can appreciate and build upon that strength as they begin to organize their financial situation. Maria may be especially good at creating and maintaining a budget.

## Communication

Engagement is a great time to start good communication patterns about finances. Money matters have an emotional impact, and a couple can easily get into heated arguments about money if they have not established good, open communication about finances. It's easy to blame someone else for problems, even financial problems.

Although engaged couples may not yet have as many financial problems as a married couple, it's important to start off with good communication patterns. People can learn to state how they feel when talking about money and avoid blaming others. For example, Rob Martin might say to Maria that her shoe buying is causing a financial problem. In reality, although her shoe buying could be adding to the problem, it's likely not "causing" the problem. Instead of placing blame, Rob could say to Maria, "I feel concerned about our financial situation. I would really like to get out of debt and start saving. Can you think of any way we can work together to accomplish this?"

In the second example, Rob is not blaming Maria for their problems, but he is stating how he feels about the situation and asking for her suggestions. He could even offer a suggestion about how he could cut back on spending. Stating his concerns this way will help Maria feel like she can talk about the situation openly without immediately becoming defensive. When people feel defensive, they tend either to fight back or become silent to end the discussion.

Communication is very important for goals, for purchases, and for money management in general. Couples should spend time dreaming a little about what they would like their future financial life to be like. Throughout our married life, my husband and I have enjoyed talking or "dreaming" about what we want our financial life to become. We share our feelings about what we think it will feel like when we are totally out of debt. We talk about vacations we would like to take as a couple and as a family. We imagine what retirement will be like if we have enough money to have our dreams come true. Dreaming is a good place to start, but we can't stop with the dreams. We need to turn those dreams into goals.

When setting goals, some couples find that they have different ideas. There could even be conflict because of different values and hopes for the future. It's important that couples talk about their values and what is important to each of them. For example, an accomplished pianist may have the *need* to own a piano and should share that need with her spouse. For someone else, owning a piano might only be a *want*. This type of information should be shared, discussed, worked through (which may include compromise), and then become part of goal setting.

One last aspect of communication is talking about major purchases. Even if just one person handles the monthly bill paying and money management, it's important for each person to talk about major purchases. Other larger financial decisions should also be discussed so that each person, not just the one handling the money, is aware of and part of the process. Couples can start this good communication when engaged and set a pattern for future money management.

The ideas and suggestions in the "Engagement" section are not only for those who are engaged. Although that is an ideal time to go through those steps, a married couple will also benefit from them, especially good communication.

## Marriage and Money

How important is good money management in marriage? Financial issues are often stated as one of the top reasons for divorce. One study collected data from newlywed couples about a wide variety of marital issues such as communication, in-laws, finances, intimacy, and conflict.[4] When asked to indicate which areas of their marriage were problematic, 20% of the wives and 18% of the husbands listed debt brought into marriage. This was the highest score for wives and the second highest for husbands, followed by balancing job and marriage. Couples who did not bring any debt into marriage had the highest marital satisfaction scores. Even those who brought small amounts of debt into the marriage ($1,000–5,000) had significantly lower marital satisfaction scores. Husbands with the highest amounts of debt ($20,000–50,000) had the lowest marital satisfaction scores. In this study, debt was certainly at the top of the list of problematic areas for these newlyweds.

Another study looked at the strengths, instead of weaknesses, in marriages.[5] Couples who felt they had great marriages were asked to be part of this study. Among other things, these couples were asked about their financial management practices. The major results from this study were that these happy couples communicated about finances (especially major purchases), had plans about how their finances would be handled (including who would handle the day-to-day money management), and tended to be debt-free or were working on becoming debt-free. Some stated that having little or no debt kept some of the stress out of their marriage. They also tended to be frugal and live within their means. These couples did not report any incidents of over-spending. They did talk about fun vacations and little splurges they gave to themselves, but they were usually well within their budget limits. It becomes very clear very quickly what helps strengthen marriages.

Having good couple communication and wise financial practices in a marriage is a great first step to having a solid financial base in a family. The next step is to include children in the picture and make sure they are learning good money management skills.

## Children and Money

Imagine that you are a parent of a thirty-seven-year-old man. He knocks on your door one day and asks if he can borrow enough money to make his house pay-ment. He apologizes for asking but says he spent his paycheck on new electronic equipment. How would you feel about this situation? Most people would cringe at the thought of having adult children come ask for money because they were not managing their own money well.

Teaching children and teenagers wise money management is not an easy thing. Sometimes it requires parents to say "no" to things they would really like to give their children. Parents love their children and want them to have a good life. Some parents want their children to "have everything I never had." The over-indulgence of children can give them an unrealistic view of life. These children may feel that they deserve the good life and that they should not have to work to obtain that life.

A great time to teach children good money management practices is during childhood and the teen years. The stakes are much smaller at these ages than when they are adults. But it takes the self-control of parents to be able to teach these principles.

My husband and I have tried to teach good money management practices to our children. We have given them a monthly allowance, and they are expected to budget for all their activities. One of our sons has an insatiable sweet tooth. When he was younger he often spent his allowance on candy and soda pop early in the month. I wasn't happy about this, not only for financial reasons, but also for health reasons. But we decided to wait it out a little and see what happened. One time my son's friend called to see if my son could go to a movie. My son asked me if he could go, and I asked, "Do you have the money?" He replied "no" with a very disappointed look. As hard as it was, I decided to say, "Then you can't go." I thought all was going well until his friend said, "That's OK, my mom will pay." Now the situation was even harder. I could have also paid his way, but I wanted him to learn good money management practices. I decided to stick to the plan and told him he couldn't go unless he could pay his own way.

Even though this was hard on both of us, he did finally learn that if he spent all his allowance on treats he couldn't afford any activities for the rest of the month. Maybe he won't come back to ask for money when he is thirty-seven. The consequence at his age was a missed movie. As an adult, it could be a missed mortgage payment. The interesting part of this story was that I told it in a college class one time and a student raised her hand and told me I was "awful!" She said, "It was just a movie. Let the kid go to the movie!" What do you think?

## A Good Example

One of the best things a parent can do is be a good example when it comes to money management. Parents who try to teach one behavior and yet demonstrate another behavior will not have much success with teaching. Children may or may not listen to what parents say, but they usually watch what their parents do. For example, parents may tell a child they cannot afford to buy a video game the child would like to buy. However, if the parent then turns around and purchases a new CD for themselves, the child does not know what to believe. Most likely the child will continue to ask for the video game because they see that there really is money for extra purchases.

Parents can come up with guidelines and rules for spending as well as goals within the family. It's good to include children, especially older children, in this process. For example, a family could have a discussion about a vacation. Everyone could give their input about the destination, and everyone could also give ideas on how to reduce spending to be able to afford the vacation. This involvement will help children be more committed to the goals. If parents say, "We are not going to go to any movies for eight months so we can save for a vacation," the children will likely be frustrated with that rule. But if the children help plan the vacation, are excited about it, and help decide on the means for getting enough money to pay for it, they will be more willing to go along with the rules. Parents then need to set a good example and stick to those rules.

## Communication

Just as it's important for spouses to communicate openly about money, it's equally as important for parents to communicate with children about money. In some homes, it's not only hard for spouses to talk about money matters; it's even more difficult for them to talk with their children about money matters. One of the best times to talk about finances is when children ask questions. A child may ask, "Dad, why do people put money in a bank?" At this point the child will be more willing to be engaged in a discussion on compound interest than at any other time.

When talking with children about money, just as in talking with a spouse, it's important to not attach any blame to problems. Parents can talk about concerns they have, and all family members can suggest ways to solve the problems.

## Teaching

Some children will get formal financial education in a school setting. Others will only get what they learn at home. Even when children learn about money management in school, the home is an ideal place to put this information into practice. Parents can teach their children many things about money. Four areas that should certainly be covered are: budgeting or spending, saving, borrowing or credit, and security.

1. **Budgeting.** As soon as children learn about money, they can start learning to budget. At the age of about five or six, children learn that a dime is worth more than a nickel even though the nickel is larger in size. At this point, a child can also learn to budget. One of the easiest ways to help children learn to budget is to get small jars or boxes and label them with different spending categories.

There can be jars for such categories as spending, long-term savings, short-term savings, and donations. Parents can help set guidelines for how much is put in each jar every time the child receives money.

One good way to start this process is to give children an **allowance.** This allows children the opportunity to learn budgeting principles. A child must have money in order to learn to manage it. Some parents say they do not want to just "give" their children money. These same parents often pay for children's activities such as going to a movie. If children are given an allowance and expected to budget for activities and other purchases, parents can teach hard-to-learn principles at an early age.

Some parents tie allowances to chores.[6] This works well for some families, as long as there is a good level of organization. Parents must decide how much making a bed is worth, along with all other chores, and keep good records of each chore. Other parents, who do not wish to keep such detailed records, have a set of chores each child is expected to do before getting his or her allowance. With this method, instead of taking away money if the chores are not done, privileges can be taken away. For example, a family may have a rule that children cannot play until their work is done. This works well for children who are not money motivated. Some children would say it's not worth the money to have to clean the bathroom. Parents can attach the chores to something that does motivate each child.

Some parents have specific chores that each child is expected to do, and they also have a list of extra chores the children can do for extra pay. This gives children an opportunity to earn extra money when needed, but also teaches them that they need to work to get that money. This is actually what I did when my son wanted to go to the movie but did not have the money. I allowed him to do an extra job and earn some extra money. It was my compromise.

There is not one money management method that works best for every family, or even for every child within one family. Parents need to look at available resources, including time and money and also personalities of their children. Parents can try different methods to find one that works. Here is an idea of how I tried something new.

I had three sons in a row and then had a daughter. I didn't have many clothes issues with my sons. One son I couldn't even get to go shopping. When my daughter became a teenager, it was a different story. When we would go shopping, it seemed like she wanted every item of clothing that she saw. I got tired of making decisions every time we went shopping. So I decided to use the example of my sister, who uses an extensive budgeting system with her children, and started a clothes budget with my daughter. We sat down together and wrote down what I would probably spend on clothes for her for an entire year. Then we divided that by twelve and that was her monthly budget. At first she thought it was kind of fun. But when it came time to start a new school year, she realized she hadn't saved any money to buy new school clothes and suddenly it wasn't as fun. Again, I had a hard time, but stuck with the plan.

This daughter soon realized she could buy a lot more clothing items if they were on sale. She learned to shop at stores that were less expensive and loved looking at clearance racks. The decision-making process was taken off my shoulders and given to her. She not only learned to make wise spending decisions but she also learned good budgeting techniques. She learned to save for a few months before school started so she could get new school clothes.

2.  **Saving.** When budgeting, children can start a good practice of saving. Parents can start teaching about savings with the small jars or boxes. Parents can consider at least two types of savings: long term and short term. It's good to teach children about long-term savings. They can save for college or their first car. Parents may want to require that children save a set percentage for long-term savings. Be careful not to discourage children from saving by requiring a large percent in long-term savings.

    A way to encourage children to save is to focus on short-term savings for something they want to buy. Maybe a child wants to save for a skateboard. Saving for something they want to buy will help children feel more motivated to save, and they can also learn to see the benefits of savings when they get to purchase the desired item. Hopefully, this will carry into their adult life. Again, parents can be good examples of this behavior.

    Once children save enough to put into a savings account in a financial institution, they can learn about **compound interest.** Parents can teach children that compound interest works like rolling a snowball down a snow-covered hill, which gathers snow and becomes larger as it rolls toward the bottom. When money is put into a savings account it will gain interest. The longer it's left there, the more interest it will gain. Interest will even be earned on interest. Children often get excited about this concept. Teenagers can even be taught about investing and the importance of time when reaping the benefits of compound interest.

3. **Borrowing.** At some point, everyone has to make the decision about going into debt. For children, it may start with borrowing from parents. Eventually they will receive credit card offers, possibly well before they are ready for such commitments. Parents can teach important concepts to children about debt and credit.

   After sitting through a lecture on credit cards, one of my college students asked, "You mean if I have a two thousand dollar balance on my credit card, I will have to pay back more than the two thousand dollars?" I was very surprised that she had made it to college without figuring that out. Parents can teach children very valuable lessons about credit before they ever get that first credit card offer in the mail.

4. **Security.** Just as each adult needs to be careful about identity theft and other fraudulent practices, children, especially teenagers, need to be taught how to prevent such problems. Parents must teach children how to protect their social security numbers and any account numbers they may have.

## Summary

This last chapter in this section has dealt more with relationships than work. Keep in mind however, that work tends to go more smoothly when relationships at home are good. Also, when finances are in disarray, individuals feel stress, which can cause problems at work. If families are overspending because they are filling too many of the "wants," there may be even more stress if couples take on more work or have a hard time making payments.

*The Martins*

*Rob and Maria can continue on their road to good financial management by communicating effectively. This includes open communication about feelings without blaming the other person. Rob and Maria can each talk about what memories they have about money as children and teenagers and even as young adults. Next, if Rob and Maria can continue to implement the new plans they have been making, they will be able to reduce the arguments they have over money and will very likely reduce the arguments they have in other areas of their marriage. They will start to feel a sense of control and the peace of mind this control will bring.*

*Rob and Maria will also need to work with their children and teach them good money management skills. They can start with a family discussion about goals. Rob and Maria can start an allowance with each child and work with the child to establish their own goals for spending and saving. They will need to decide what purchases their children will need to make with their allowances. The older children, Matt and Abbie, may benefit from a clothing allowance also. This will take some work and diligence on the part of Rob and Maria, especially if the children are used to just asking for anything they want. But the hard work will pay off as the decision-making turns to the children and is taken off the shoulders of Rob and Maria.*

## Ending Thoughts

The Martin family has been through a lot in Part I of this book. They have made some great changes in their lives. They are eating healthier and are including more physical activity in their lives. Maria especially has made healthy lifestyle changes. She is feeling better than she has in years.

Rob and Maria are also improving financially. They have created goals, have a great budget, and are starting to save for a family trip. They are already reducing their expenses by not eating out as much. They also realize the need to have an emergency fund and have started saving. One of their goals is to get out of debt. They have started by addressing their credit card debt. First they are trying to not use their credit card anymore and are using the money they save from reducing their expenses to pay more on their credit card bill each month. As the Martin family begins to gain control of their financial situation, they will find they have less stress which can help them be more productive at work and have more time to develop more positive family relationships.

I hope that these five chapters have been helpful for you in your pursuit to balance work and family. I also hope you will be able to manage your money well so that you can be a more productive employee and strengthen your family relationships in order to create harmony in your life.

References

[1] Armour, S. Personal Finance Employee Education Foundation. *Worker's Financial Stress May Hurt Productivity.* http://www.personalfinancefoundation.org/features/Workers-financial-stress-may-hurt-productivity.html

[2] Mellan, O. (1994). *Money harmony.* New York: Walker & Company, 1994.

[3] Solomon, S. (n.d.). *Money habitudes.* Retrieved May 15, 2009, from http://money-habitudes.com/Tips4Talk2YourHoney.pdf

[4] Johnson, A., Schramm, J., Marshall, J., Skogrand, L., & Lee, R. (2004). *Newlyweds financial issues and educational solutions for strengthening marriages*, Proceedings of the Association for Financial Counseling and Planning Education, November 2004.

[5] Johnson., A., Skogrand, L., DeFrain, J., & Horrocks, A. (2007). *Financial management practices of couples with a great marriage*, Proceedings of the Association for Financial Counseling and Planning Education, November 2007.

[6] Eyre, L., & Eyre, R. (1994). *3 steps to a strong family*. New York, New York: Simon & Schuster.

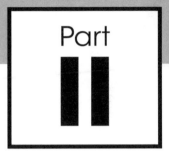

# Part II

# Balancing Work, Family, and Marriage Relationships

# Introduction

Welcome to Part II of this book, the part most focused on marriages and families. The preceding section emphasizes financial and work-related issues, and the section at the end of the book emphasizes parenting and childcare. So in between—in these next five chapters—information is presented about how couple relationships are formed, and how marriage and partner dynamics connect with work and family life.

My name is Brent Miller, and I completed degrees in psychology, family studies, and sociology at three different universities. Both my wife and I grew up in Utah, and we moved to Minnesota for graduate school and to Tennessee for my first faculty position. We returned to Utah State University where we had been students, and where I have been a faculty member now for over 30 years. I also have been Head of the Department of Family and Human Development, and Vice President for Research, here at USU.

My wife and I have three children and six grandchildren—and the latter really are more fun that the former (sorry kids, but you understand!). I am the oldest of the three coauthors, nearing the end of my career.

During my faculty career at USU I did a lot of research, using social science methods to study marriage and family issues. Much of my research focused on correlates and consequences of adolescent sexual behavior and pregnancy; in later years, I also studied and wrote about the adjustment of adopted children. Our family took sabbatical leaves to the state of Washington and to Washington D.C., where I worked for research companies and the federal government in marriage and family-related research capacities.

Marriages and families are vitally important. All of us have (or had) parents and grandparents, and other extended relatives, and nearly all of us will form couple relationships—usually marriages. Most of us also will have and/or raise children. Marriage and family issues usually are fundamental to people's values and priorities in life, so it is fitting to address these topics.

Part II begins with Chapter 6, which describes how biological sex and gender roles form basic templates for the marriage, family, and work-related activities of our adult lives. Chapter 7 is about how individuals come together as partners, couples, and spouses. Chapter 8 describes the norms, processes, and dynamics of marriage relationships. Chapter 9 presents a background about becoming parents, and how we confront the many issues that arise when we are expected to simultaneously parent children, enrich marriages, and be productive employees. Chapter 10 is the most specifically focused on work and family conflicts—when conflicts are most likely to arise and what can be done to reduce and resolve them.

I hope that you learn a lot from this section of the book. Even more, I hope that you enjoy and benefit from what you learn.

*Brent C. Miller*

# Chapter 6

## Gender, Gender Roles, Families, and Work

# Gender, Gender Roles, Families, and Work

"It's a boy," or "it's a girl"—these are the first words spoken about most newborn babies around the world. One of those phrases probably was the first thing ever said about you, and it almost certainly was the first thing said about your parents. The announcement of a baby's gender is based on his or her biological sex, usually first observed during delivery. But now, in advanced societies, a developing baby's gender can be learned prior to birth by genetic testing or by ultrasound during pregnancy. Each of us is biologically male or female, based on our genetics, hormones, external anatomy, and internal sex organs. Regardless of how a child's sex becomes known and is announced, the world is strongly differentiated—dichotomized actually—by our biological sex, also sometimes called "gender."

It is not quite so simple, however. Biological sex is ambiguous at birth for a small percentage of infants, because their genitalia are not fully formed, or because they have characteristics of both sexes.[1] People with this condition are called **hermaphrodites**, and I introduce this concept here because it vividly conveys how biological sex, and our related gender identity, is so dramatically important, but is also usually taken for granted. Can you imagine what it would be like as a parent, or grandparent, not to be able to say whether your newborn child is a boy or a girl? What would you tell people when they asked about your baby? What would you say? "I don't know", or "I am not sure"? How would you choose a name? What about clothes, toys, colors? What about the child's future? Biological sex is at the absolute core of who we are, how we regard ourselves, how we are treated by others, how we relate to one another, and how we imagine and create our futures.

I stated that **biological sex** is determined by the combination of anatomy, internal sex organs, and genetics. Actually, biological sex is driven by genetics—females have double XX chromosomes, and males have XY chromosomes—in every body cell. This basic genetic endowment drives the sexual differentiation of male and female hormones, gonads, and brains during embryonic and fetal development.[2] Most obviously, the "private parts" of our sexual anatomy differentiate and our genitals become externally visible; a male has a penis and a female has a vagina. But unseen internally, males also have testes, a prostate, seminal vesicles, vas deferens, and so on, whereas females have ovaries, fallopian tubes, a uterus, etc.

In contrast to biological sex, but related to it, **gender identity** is one's own perception and belief about him or herself as a male or female.[3] Masculine and feminine gender identities usually develop gradually throughout childhood and adolescence, consistent with biological sex, and with others' beliefs and actions toward us. Here too there can be complications or confusion. Sometimes a person feels like they are, or should be, the other biological sex. Sometimes such **transgendered** persons act on their beliefs by obtaining sex change operations and hormonal treatments to make their biological sexual characteristics more congruent with their psychological gender identities.[4]

The general public tends not to be very aware of hermaphrodites and transgendered people; this is because they are relatively rare in the population and because sexual identity issues are highly personal. Atypical gender identities tend to be kept secret or private, because they are strongly stigmatized. I remember a neighbor girl a few years younger than me who was quiet and reserved when we were growing up; it wasn't until more than a decade after we finished high school and I had moved away that I learned "she" now had a male name and was living life as a man. Occasionally such cases make national news, like when a person who has undergone a sex change operation seeks to participate in a sports competition under their new gender identity, but where their original biological sex might have given them a competitive physical advantage. In some cases of higher-level athletic competition, genetic testing is done to allow (or prohibit) certain individuals from participating in one gender category or the other.[5]

More commonly, some children become sensitive to gender identity issues from having been given a gender neutral name (like "Chris") that could belong to either a boy or girl; in school, they might get placed on the gym class roster for the other (wrong) sex. It could be more seriously irritating to some people if their parents gave them a name usually associated with the other gender, like when a boy is named "Sydney" or a girl is named "Michael" or "Charlie." In his later years of life, my own father preferred (and went by) his initials because he disliked the feminine sounding names he was given at birth. The late singer Johnny Cash sang a famous and colorful song about this gendered naming situation:

> "My daddy left home when I was three
> And he didn't leave much to ma and me
> Just this old guitar and an empty bottle of booze.
> Now, I don't blame him cause he run and hid
> But the meanest thing that he ever did
> Was before he left, he went and named me "Sue.""

Well, he must o' thought that is quite a joke
And it got a lot of laughs from a' lot of folk,
It seems I had to fight my whole life through.
Some gal would giggle and I'd get red
And some guy'd laugh and I'd bust his head,
I tell ya, life ain't easy for a boy named "Sue."[6]

(2 of 10 verses)

Fortunately, the vast majority of infants are either clearly male or female at birth and, unlike "Sue" in the Johnny Cash song, they usually are given typically male or female names. Being recognized as a girl or boy, and being given a gender appropriate name, sets in motion a lifelong core for each person's gradually evolving gender identity. The social and cultural worlds around young girls and boys are structured differently, reinforcing their masculine or feminine self-perceptions. This is most evident in traditional developing societies, where tribal boys and girls might be segregated, and where only boys are allowed to do some things, and only girls are allowed to do other things. But even in the United States, traditional practices persist in intentional and sometimes haphazard ways. It is still quite common to dress little boys in blue and provide them with "masculine" toys, like trucks and tools. Many little girls still are dressed in frilly pink clothes and they are given feminine toys, especially dolls, as practice for taking care of young children.

Although biological sex and gender identity are crucial to the roles that we play throughout life, some activities are not gender segregated. To equalize life opportunities for males and females, many advanced societies deliberately require that both sexes be treated the same. There are laws in the United States, for example, against sexual discrimination in education, sports, and employment. But biological sex and gender roles are still influential, because some kinds of work and sports remain dominated by one gender. Both boys and girls play soccer—sometimes on the same teams—but wrestling and football remain very strongly segregated, especially at older ages. Most importantly for the focus of this book, gender issues are deeply involved in marriage and family life, and in the world of work.

To conclude this introduction, it is important to recognize how biological sex and gender issues permeate our lives, so that we can better understand ourselves and others, and more readily find or achieve success and fulfillment. Even more fundamentally, gender can be crucial in defining what we seek in life, and how we go about pursuing and attaining our goals. Most of us also seek to blend our own gender role expectations with a marriage partner, who has a gender identity and gender role expectations of his or her own.

*The Martins*

*Rob and Maria's children each developed typical male and female gender identities, so they have not had unusual gender issues in their family. But, like every couple, Rob and Maria have had to figure out who does what around the house, and how they will manage childcare when the children are young. Their decisions for Maria to be a stay-at-home mom for most of this time, and for Rob to be the main income earner, reflect their somewhat traditional gender roles.*

## Who Does What in Marriages and Families?

Gender roles in marriages and families were traditionally viewed as the wife/mother providing warmth and nurturance, and the husband/father acting as the protector and provider.[7] These traditional gender roles in marriages and families were supported by religious teachings, and institutionalized in a variety of ways. In early childhood socialization, boys were more likely than girls to have played with tools and trucks, and girls were more likely to have played with dolls. Going further, certain kinds of work around the house and different educational subjects were seen as more appropriate for boys, and other activities and subjects as more appropriate for girls.

Marriage and family roles in your grandparents' generation expected men to maintain the car and other mechanical things, fix gadgets, do outside house and yard work, and handle the family finances. Traditional mothers spent much more time than fathers parenting children—especially infants and young children—and they also were more likely to be in charge of food and clothing—shopping for groceries and clothes, and preparing and serving meals. These patterns have not totally disappeared, and might still describe your parents, or even you to some degree. But at the present, a small minority of households in the United States consist of a breadwinner husband and stay-at-home wife.

Most of us share some gender role expectations about who will do what in our families. Certain household tasks might be relatively gender neutral (like caring for a pet) but others still carry gender role expectations (like feeding the baby, or fixing the car). It is interesting to think about these issues for yourself, but it can be more important and useful for you—and for your partner—to understand what you think and how you both feel about these things.

You might want some things to be done by one or the other of you (servicing or fixing the car, doing the laundry, changing the baby's diapers). If your partner agrees, the two of you can specialize in doing certain things rather than trying to do them together, and you could get more stuff done that way. But you might also want certain things to be done by both of you working together—for example, making major purchases and parenting. Then, too, there are many things that either of you could do equally well. If either of you could do something equally well, and you don't have gender role expectations or preferences about it, then who does what might just depend on who is willing, or who has more available time and energy.

The exercise in Table 6.1 could be especially useful when completed by couples who are approaching a long-term relationship, like getting married. It could be even more interesting for females (wives) and males (husbands) to complete this separately, and then to compare and discuss their answers together.

**TABLE 6.1**  Gender Role Expectations in Marriage, Family, and Work

| Who do you think should do the following things? | | | | | | |
|---|---|---|---|---|---|---|
| Activities | 1<br>WIFE<br>all or<br>mostly | 2<br>WIFE<br>more than<br>HUSBAND | 3<br>EQUAL<br>WIFE or<br>HUSBAND | 4<br>HUSBAND<br>more than<br>WIFE | 5<br>HUSBAND<br>all or<br>mostly | 6<br>BOTH<br>together |
| Shop for groceries | | | | | | |
| Cook meals | | | | | | |
| Clean up after eating | | | | | | |
| Wash dishes | | | | | | |
| Shop for clothes | | | | | | |
| Do laundry | | | | | | |
| Iron clothes | | | | | | |
| Make bed(s) | | | | | | |
| Collect/empty trash | | | | | | |
| Clean toilet(s) | | | | | | |
| Sweep floors | | | | | | |
| Pay monthly bills | | | | | | |
| Arrange health care | | | | | | |
| Buy major appliance/car | | | | | | |
| Change the baby | | | | | | |
| Feed the children | | | | | | |
| Clothe the baby/children | | | | | | |
| Make plans for children | | | | | | |
| Talk with teachers | | | | | | |
| Help with homework | | | | | | |
| Go to back-to-school | | | | | | |
| Attend children's sports | | | | | | |
| Attend children's music | | | | | | |
| Work full time | | | | | | |
| Maximize career | | | | | | |
| Leave work if kids sick | | | | | | |

## Gender Differences in Work

As previously noted, men were traditionally "breadwinners" as their major family role, being employed for pay outside the home. The major roles for most women traditionally were focused in the home, especially being a wife and mother. Among middle- and upper-class women historically, working at a job outside the home was viewed negatively and discouraged.[8] For many women, however, employment was part of their life experience, even though it might have been considered optional, secondary, part time, and in many cases was postponed until the children started school, or even until they were older. In contrast to these employment patterns for middle- and upper-class women, combining work for pay with family roles always has been necessary for most single-parent mothers[9], and for women in lower[10] socio-economic level two-parent families.

Consistent with childhood gender socialization, gender differences are reflected in the kinds of work later done by adult women and men. The fact that men and women tend to work in different kinds of jobs and industries is referred to as gendered work segregation.[11] Men are much more likely than women to have blue collar jobs in production, machine operation, and repair than women.[12] Conversely, women are much more likely than men to have secretarial jobs in administrative support.

Some jobs are even more extremely gender segregated, reflecting the differential childhood socialization of girls and boys. For example, the female dominance of jobs such as childcare workers (95% of the workforce), nurses (over 90% of the workforce) and elementary school teachers (85–90% of elementary teachers) is familiar to everyone.[13] But, equally striking is the extent to which men dominate careers in engineering, constituting about 98% of all engineering industry workers in 1978, and still nearly 90% of engineers today.[14]

## Education, Training, and Preparation for Employment

Some of the large and persistent gender differences in men and women's employment patterns must be related to their preparation for work. To the extent that some careers, especially better paying careers, require a college degree, men seeking these jobs used to have a distinct advantage over women. Males in the United States were historically much more likely than females to attend—and especially to graduate—from college. In 1960, males were almost twice as likely as females to graduate from college (65% vs. 35%), but this gender difference declined gradually until parity in college completion was achieved in the 1980s.[15]

In recent decades, trend data in educational attainment shows that women have become significantly more likely to graduate from college than men. Currently, over 60% of both bachelor's and master's degrees are awarded to women in the United States, suggesting that females are increasingly better prepared to hold higher paying jobs.[16]

## Changes in Women's and Men's Work Roles

Consistent with these trends of increasing education for women in the United States, their employment has increased dramatically over the past half century. About 75% of all women ages 25–44 now participate in the labor force of the United States, compared to 82% of same aged men.[17]

Even more striking in recent decades is the rapid increase in *mothers'* labor force participation. Between 1950 and 1960, only about 30% of mothers with children under 18 were working for pay.[18] By 1975, 47% of mothers with children under 18 were employed, and by 2007, that percentage had risen to 71%.[19]

Employment rates are lower among mothers than among women of the same age without children; during the prime childbearing years (ages 25–45), women with children are about 9% less likely to be employed.[20] Lower employment among mothers is strongly affected by educational attainment, however, such that the employment gap between women with and without children is largest among women who have the least education, and smallest among mothers with advanced degrees. Even if they have children under 18, about 75% of mothers who have advanced degrees are in the labor force.[21]

Attitudes have been changing along with behavior. In 1977, among dual-earner couples, seven out of ten (70%) men thought it was better for men to earn the money and for women to care for the home and children (in spite of the fact that their wives were working).[22] By 2008, less than four in ten (only 37%) of men in dual-earner couples felt that way, perhaps reflecting the fact that family income has become increasingly dependent on women's earnings.

Men's work at home also has been changing. One major study found that married men's overall housework has increased by more than a factor of 2 (from 4.4 to 9.7 hours per week) in the past four decades and their "core" housework (e.g., cooking, cleaning, etc.) has increased by over a factor of 3 (1.4 to 4.6 hours per week) during this time. Through the same decades, married women's time spent on housework has remained relatively stable.[23]

Because the historically observed college graduation advantage of men over women has been reversed, it should not be surprising that, among young couples today, both partners expect to be employed. Relatedly, marital and family roles today are more likely to be played based on personal preference, training, and expertise, rather than on traditional gender role expectations.

## Work, Pay, and Gender

Adults generally have to be concerned about earning enough money for the family's food, clothing, and shelter. But beyond these mere survival needs, virtually all parents want more money to buy better conditions and advantages for themselves and their children. What amount of income is "enough" depends on many things (expectations, number of family members, etc.). Having two incomes will bring in more money than having one income, but dual employment also might entail additional expenses, especially expenses associated with the ages and needs of children and childcare (see Chapter 3). How money is budgeted and managed also can be as important as the amount of income per se (see Chapter 1).

People have different attitudes about money, how it should be spent, saved, and managed. In 2012 comedian Jimmy Fallon had a popular commercial with a baby who grabs attention because she vigorously rejects getting any more money; the ad is entertaining because everyone knows that turning down money is nuts. Universally, people would rather have more money than less, or staying at the same low level of income. Everybody would like a raise in pay.

Consequently, there is great interest in how much people are paid, and in pay equity for people doing the same jobs. A widely shared norm is that everyone doing a job should be paid the same amount (other things being equal), but it is a well-known fact that women are paid less than men, on average.[24] There is a saying: "Another day, another dollar." I remember years ago seeing a sign with the slogan "Another day, another 69 cents," intended to communicate that when men earned a dollar, working women at that time only got 69 cents, on average. While the discrepancy in pay for men and women has narrowed over the years, it is still significant; overall, women earn about 80% of what men are paid.[25]

Regardless of gender, employees want higher wages or salaries so that they can pay the bills, have money to meet other needs, and satisfy some wants. So it doesn't seem fair that men, on average, are paid more than women, even when doing the same jobs. Why are women paid less than men? The presumption is that there is pay discrimination based only on gender. Are women paid less than men just because of their gender, or are there other factors that help explain the gender-based salary differential?

Pay tends to increase with work experience, so years of employment need to be controlled to make valid comparisons. Do men and women have the same years of experience on the job? Are they the same about taking time off from work? Then, too, it was noted above that some industries and kinds of jobs are extremely gender segregated, so that whole groups of male and female employees receive quite different levels of pay based on their job category (e.g., mostly female childcare workers vs. mostly male engineers).

A recent study that focused on explaining why women are paid less than men found that it is not necessarily because employers discriminated against female employees.[26] This study found that women and men view the employment landscape quite differently, and much of the segregation in applying for jobs and hiring into certain kinds of occupations occurs because women place a higher value on work/life balance—women do not identify themselves with some higher paying job categories where work/life balance is most negatively affected.[27] In other words, women tend not to identify with some aggressive and demanding high paying jobs that are stereotypically masculine, so they do not apply for those jobs; instead, women systematically choose lower paying occupations than men, but the jobs chosen by women tend to have better work/life balance.

In spite of the average lower wages of women than men, it is still the case that many wives earn as much or more than their husbands.[28] The Bureau of Labor Statistics estimates that about 40 percent of working wives earn more than their husbands. Given the change to women now completing a larger proportion of college degrees than men, this could signal a major future shift in marital power.[29]

### The Martins

> Working at a lower paying job, and being off-and-on in the labor market, reflected Maria's priority on the children and maintaining work/life balance. But now that five-year-old Luke is beginning school he will require less childcare, so Maria and Rob are facing a turning point. This could be a time for Maria to reconsider her options and start a different career. In any case, she will probably have new full-time work expectations that will require Rob's work commitments to be readjusted for them to achieve satisfactory work/life balance. Maria and Rob can see that their children probably will enter their own future relationships expecting to divide work and family roles more equally, especially when providing childcare and earning income.

## Summary and Conclusion

Everyone starts out life being either male or female, based on biological sex. Gender identity develops gradually, usually congruent with biological sex, and gender role training and expectations prepare young people for future marital, family, and work roles.

There are still strong expectations for men to provide financially for their families, and social norms still seem to hold mothers more responsible than fathers for parenting and childcare. But these gender role expectations are less strongly held than in the past, when two-parent traditional families with a male breadwinner and female homemaker were the norm. Today, when there are two parents in the home, the typical pattern is for both partners to be employed, and both to be actively involved as parents. But, there also are many more single-parent families now than in the past.

In recent generations—and especially in recent decades—there has been a marked shift toward less gender role differentiation in marriages and families. Some gender differences remain in the activities of husbands and wives, and many household tasks shared by young couples become more gender role segregated after children arrive. But, in general, there is a clear trend toward increasing gender role convergence in marriage, family, and work lives.

### References

[1] Money, J., & Ehrhardt, A. A. (1996). *Man & Women, Boy & Girl*. Lanham, MD: Jason Aronson, Inc.

[2] Planned Parenthood. (n.d.). What is Biological Sex? In *Female, Male & Intersex*. Retrieved from http://www.plannedparenthood.org/health-topics/sexual-orientation-gender/female-male-intersex-26531.htm

[3] Egan, S. K., Perry, D. G. (2001). Gender Identity: A Multidimensional Analysis with Implications for Psychosocial Adjustment. *Developmental Psychology*, 37(4), 451–463.

[4] Namaste, V. (2000). *Invisible Lives: The Erasure of Transsexual and Transgendered People*. Chicago, IL: The University of Chicago Press. Retrieved from http://books.google.com/books?hl=en&lr=&id=kBiImQOBgzEC&oi=fnd&pg=PR11&dq=transgendered&ots=6b3u8QNbKU&sig=GMSQt_0OAVjQj_tXkE40EC3nCUQ#v=twopage&q&f=false

[5] Torre, P. S., & Epstein, D. (2012). The Transgender Athlete. *Sports Illustrated*, 116(22), 66–73.

[6] Silverstein, S. (1969). A Boy Named Sue [J. Cash]. At San Quentin [record]. New York: Columbia Records.

[7] Vella, F. (1994). Gender Roles and Human Capital Investment. *London School of Economics and Political Science*, 61(242), 191–211.

[8] Reid, L. (2005). Employment Exits and the Race Gap in Young Women's Employment. *Social Science Quarterly* (Blackwell Publishing Limited), 861242–1260.

[9] Misra, J., Moller, S., Budig, M. J. (2007). Work-Family Policies and Poverty for Partnered and Single Women in Europe and North America. *Gender & Society*, 21(6), 804–827.

[10] Damaske, S. (2011). *How Class and Gender Shape Women's Work.* Huntington Beach, CA: Oxford University Press. Retrieved from http://www.oup.com/us/catalog/general/subject/Sociology/Women/?view=usa&ci=9780199791491

[11] Reskin, B. F., & Hartmann, H. I. (1986). *Women's Work, Men's Work: Sex Segregation on the Job.* Washington DC: National Academy Press.

[12] Bond, J. T., Thompson, C., Galinsky, E., Prottas, D., (2002). *Executive summary: Highlights of the National Study of the Changing Workforce.* New York: Families and Work Institute.

[13] Cartwright, B., Edwards, P., & Wang, Q. (2011). Job and industry gender segregation: NAICS categories and EEO-1 job groups. *Monthly Labor Review,* 134(11), 37–50.

[14] Marsh, B. (2012). Jobs Where Gender Segregation Persists. *The New York Times.* Retrieved from http://www.nytimes.com/image pages/2012/09/30/opinion/30coontz-gr1.html?ref=sunday

[15] Buchmann, C., & DiPrete, T. A. (2006). The Growing Female Advantage in College Completion: The Role of Family Background and Academic Achievement. *American Sociological Review,* 71(4), 515–541.

[16] Adebayo, B. (2008). Gender Gaps in College Enrollment and Degree Attainment: An Exploratory Analysis. *College Student Journal,* 42(1), 232–237.

[17] Hoffman, S. D. (2009). The changing impact of marriage and children on women's labor force participation. *Monthly Labor Review,* 132(6), 3–14.

[18] Pew Research Center. (2009). *The Harried Life of the Working Mother.* Retrieved from http://www.pewsocialtrends.org/2009/10/01/the-harried-life-of-the-working-mother/#prc-jump

[19] Galinksy, E., Aumann, K., & Bond, J. T. (2008). *2008 National study of the changing workforce: Times are changing—Gender and generation at work and at home.* New York: Families and Work Institute. Retrieved October 13, from http://familiesandwork.org/site/research/reports/Times_Are_Changing.pdf

**Notes**

[20] Boushey, H. (2005). *Are Women Opting Out? Debunking the Myth\**. Center for Economic and Policy Research. Retrieved from http://cahiers.cerium.ca/sites/politiquessociales.net/IMG/pdf/opt_out_2005_11.pdf

[21] Boushey, H. (2005). *Are Women Opting Out? Debunking the Myth\**. Center for Economic and Policy Research. Retrieved from http://cahiers.cerium.ca/sites/politiquessociales.net/IMG/pdf/opt_out_2005_11.pdf

[22] Galinksy, E., Aumann, K., & Bond, J. T. (2008). *2008 National study of the changing workforce: Times are changing—Gender and generation at work and at home.* New York: Families and Work Institute. Retrieved October 13, from http://familiesandwork.org/site/research/reports/Times_Are_Changing.pdf

[23] Bianchi, S. M., Robinson, J. P., Milkie, M. A. (2006). *Changing Rhythms of American Family Life.* New York: Russell Sage Foundation.

[24] Sloan Work and Family Research Network. (2008). Questions and Answers about Women in the Workforce: A Sloan Work and Family Research Network Fact Sheet. Retrieved from https://workfamily.sas.upenn.edu/sites/workfamily.sas.upenn.edu/files/imported/pdfs/womenwork.pdf

[25] Longley. R. (n.d.). *Why Women Still Make Less than Men.* Retrieved from http://usgovinfo.about.com/cs/censusstatistic/a/womenspay.htm

[26] Knowledge at Wharton. (2012).*Why Do Women Still Earn Less Than Men? Analyzing the Search for High-paying Jobs.* Retrieved from knowledge.wharton.upenn.edu/printer_friendly.cfm?articleid=3058

[27] Knowledge at Wharton. (2012).*Why Do Women Still Earn Less Than Men? Analyzing the Search for High-paying Jobs.* Retrieved from knowledge.wharton.upenn.edu/printer_friendly.cfm?articleid=3058

[28] Bureau of Labor Statistics. (2011). *Women in the Labor Force: A Databook.* Retrieved from http://www.bls.gov/cps/wlf-databook-2011.pdf

[29] Mundy, L. (2012). *The richer sex: How the new majority of female breadwinners is transforming sex, love and family.* New York, NY US: Simon & Schuster.

# Chapter 7

# Forming Couple Relationships

# Forming Couple Relationships

What are your hopes and dreams for a close relationship? Do you want a traditional marriage or nontraditional relationship? Maybe you will have one or more casual partners looking for the right person, gradually becoming more committed? Do you have feelings or beliefs about the timing of sex, or cohabitation before marriage? Would you prefer a long and careful courtship and engagement, or could you decide and become partners quickly? Do you think you will get married? If so, when…how old will you be when you get married?

Most of you reading this book are in your late teens or early twenties. You are in the prime years for forming couple relationships. The majority of older adolescents and young adults in the United States are all about hanging out, dating, hooking up, cohabitating, becoming engaged, or otherwise trying to figure out if (or when) they should form a more committed relationship. Many of you have been through such experiences with one or more partners, and some of you have already married.

At the same time, most late adolescents and many young adults also are still in school, college, or training to prepare for future careers. Many of you are working part or full time to support yourself, and maybe to cover some or all of the costs of your education beyond high school. Before discussing couple and family issues in relation to work, however, it will be useful to establish a broader context for understanding the formation of couple relationships.

### The Martins

*Rob and Maria began their couple relationship more than 20 years ago, when they first met and were initially attracted to each other. Their becoming a couple proceeded through a series of filters that they didn't consciously plan or think about at the time, but it resulted in their being alike in many ways (about the same age, same race, compatible religions, with similar values and outlook on life). Their similarities help them understand each other, and having similar perspectives facilitates their communications and adds to their emotional and physical intimacy.*

## Starting Out

Humans are social beings. We begin life completely helpless—kept alive and nurtured by others through our most dependent years. In advanced western societies, like the United States, infants are typically cared for in small family groups, helped out by extended family members and organized group care. Parents usually form a unique emotional and physical closeness, referred to as **bonding**, with their infants and young children.[1] Some of you also know more about childcare from having been an older sister or older brother, or you might know about infant and childcare most vividly from being a parent yourself. In any case, the point is that we begin life being cared for, and as we mature we learn to care for others. Our lives initially depend on, and come to revolve around, close social relationships.

Throughout infancy and childhood most young people form their closest relationships with parents and siblings. In the first year of life, infants usually form an especially close and important **attachment** to their primary caregiver.[2] Relationships with age mates develop gradually; close relationships with **same-sex friends** are common and usually become closer throughout childhood and into adolescence.[3] Friendships with members of the other sex tend to be less common at younger ages (note "other" rather than "opposite" sex, because males and females have many similarities). Cross-sex friendships become more common in late childhood, and **cross-sex relationships** usually become intense when romantic interests emerge during adolescence.[4]

## Human Sexuality, Attraction, and Intimacy

Beginning in adolescence, most people are romantically and sexually attracted to persons of the other sex; this is referred to as **heterosexual attraction**. A small minority of people are attracted to others of their same sex, which is referred to as **homosexual attraction**. Whether straight or gay, most people have a predominant and obvious **sexual orientation**, although a small proportion are romantically and sexually attracted to both males and females (**bisexual**).[5]

People who are straight and people who are gay are attracted to partners in similar ways. That is, there is something about the other person that is perceived to be romantically appealing or desirable. Although romantic attraction to same- and cross-sex partners occurs in similar ways, straight and gay people are members of majority and minority groups. The homosexual minority has been strongly stigmatized in the past (homophobia), being met with dislike, discrimination, and even violence. Because of this strong social stigma, many persons with same-sex attraction historically kept their sexual orientation secret,[6] or remained "in the closet," until adulthood.[7]

Human **sexuality** is multifaceted; it includes our sexual identities (as male or female), sexual orientations (hetero or homosexual), sexual attitudes and values, and sexual behaviors.[8] Some of these dimensions of sexuality are quite individualistic (like our sexual identities—our conception of being male or female), although other aspects of sexuality—especially sexual behaviors—are important components of close relationships with others.

## Intimacy

Given that humans are social creatures from birth, and that human closeness is imperative for survival during the early years of life, some people believe that there is an innate need for us to seek intimacy, belonging, or closeness with others.[9] Like bonding and attachment between parents and children, closeness with others in childhood and adolescence seems to fill emotional needs and psychological longings.

Relationships between parents and children often are very close and might be described as intimate. Same-sex friends also share many experiences in childhood and adolescence, and they can have secrets and develop deep feelings for each other; they often say that they would "do anything" for each other. Close same-sex friendships usually include sharing and support, and such friendships often continue throughout life.[10]

But parent-child closeness and long-term best friendships are different than intimate and sexual couple relationships. **Intimacy** can be defined as a particularly close interpersonal relationship that usually involves both physical and emotional closeness, including self-disclosure, trust, and sharing.[11] Romantic sexual partners *can* be friends (in spite of the famous line in the movie *When Harry Met Sally*), but romantic sexual attraction appears to be driven by biological forces that begin to be more strongly felt and expressed during the teenage years. The hormones that drive the development of secondary sex characteristics, and a growth spurt during adolescence, also stimulate cognitive and physical attraction to potential mates.[12]

**Physical intimacy** is characterized by romantic or passionate sexual attraction and behavior. The word "intimacy" sometimes is used euphemistically to specifically refer to sexual activity. It is possible, of course, for couples to share deep **emotional intimacy** without sexual or physical intimacy at all (as in cases of emotional and or spiritual closeness between lovers who are separated, or between aged partners). Conversely, it is quite common for some people to have sexual relationships without feelings of intimate emotional sharing and understanding (as in sexual activity with casual partners).

## Dating and Hanging Out

During the early to mid-teen years, most males and females in the U.S. spend increasing amounts of time observing, thinking about, and being around members of the other sex. In prior generations a formalized dating and courtship structure was common during adolescence and young adulthood. It began with group and double dating, proceeded through single and steady dating, and culminated in engagement and marriage.[13] When my mother died at age 88, I looked through some things she had saved from her teenage years in the 1930s, and found some "dance cards" listing the names of boys she had danced with during the night. In some subcultures in the U.S.A., a version of this traditional dating, courtship, and marriage process remains, but contemporary "dating" processes in the general population are much more casual and less formalized today. Contemporary "dating" is mostly "hanging out" with a partner or in small groups, and it occurs in more diverse and less organized ways than in the past.[14]

Middle schools and high schools provide settings and activities that allow many teenagers to check out potential partners in various situations. Kids see and relate to each other in school classes, but also during nonacademic school-related activities. Some couple pairing off is especially likely to occur among kids who have similar interests, around music, sports, debate, band, or whatever other school activities bring kids together in smaller groups. Similarly, young males and females form couple relationships based on their associations in groups as diverse as clubs and churches. Beyond these kinds of institutional means of "dating," teens seek out friendship groups in the neighborhoods where they live. Adolescents in the United States have always had a strong connection to cars, which provide the means for teens to leave their neighborhoods, their families, and other authorities, to associate with their peers in the youth culture. Regardless of how adolescent couples get to know each other, by the late teens and early twenties most of them have paired off with one or more partners in relatively serious, and usually exclusive, serial relationships.[15]

## Mate Selection

Someone once said that mate selection is "like a cake walk with a trap door," suggesting that partner selection is a random, unpredictable process. However, there is a well-established research tradition that seeks to understand and explain how partners find and select one another. From early on, research has shown that **assortative mating** occurs in highly predictable ways.[16]

Early explanations of mate selection included the idea that "opposites attract." This common-sense idea seems to be reflected in the old English proverb:

> *Jack Sprat could eat no fat.*
> *His wife could eat no lean.*
> *And so between them both, you see,*
> *They licked the platter clean.*[17]

The idea that opposites attract was formulated into the theory of **Complementary Needs** by Robert Winch.[18] It might seem logical that a dominant person would marry someone who was submissive, but such is not the case. Even with respect to personality types, the evidence shows that people are more likely to marry someone like themselves than they are to marry someone who is different, or their opposite. Simply put, partners tend to marry others like themselves, across a wide variety of characteristics.[19]

The tendency for marital partners to be like each other on specific social and even physical traits is termed "**homogamy**." For example, couples tend to be homogamous with respect to age, race, and social class. Partners even tend to be alike in height, weight, and IQ scores.[20] Of course there are exceptions, but it is unusual for partners to pair up if they are very different. Assortative mating usually comes into play so that people select and marry someone like themselves.

Mate selection operates like a series of filters that narrows down potential partners toward homogamy; this is partly because people of the same race and social class generally live in the same neighborhoods and attend the same schools. Marrying someone who lives nearby was recognized early on as a **propinquity** factor in mate selection.[21] Selection for social class is strengthened when some young adults drop out of high school and form a subgroup which tends to hang out together. Another subgroup is formed when those who graduate from high school attend local technical schools and community colleges. Similarly, still others go away to more expensive state or private universities. When this sorting by residence, education, and income level takes place during the late teens and early twenties, most young people form relationships and get married to someone of their same age group, race, and social class.

Whereas homogamy simply *denotes* similarities between marital partners, **endogamous norms** exert pressure for partners to marry within racial, ethnic, or religious groups.[22] So in a sense, endogamy *requires* marriage to occur within a group. In some geographical areas endogamous norms exert pressures less strongly than in other areas. For example, in Hawaii or New Mexico interracial marriages are quite common, because these areas have highly diverse racial and ethnic populations.[23] Conversely, interracial marriages are much less common in areas with smaller minority populations, both because of the stronger social stigma against such marriages, but also because there are relatively few minority group members to form interracial unions. **Exogamous norms**, requiring marriage outside one's own group, are less common. The most familiar exogamous norm requires marriage outside close kin relatives (siblings, cousins, and so on).

More complex theories of mate selection combine personality and "filter" theories of mate selection. The **Stimulus Value Role (SVR) theory** of mate selection is based on the premise that the earliest stages of attraction depend on getting past a "stimulus" level relationship that is defined by the filters described above; only then can potential partners learn whether or not they also share values and are compatible or complementary in their beliefs about future roles.[24]

Another multilevel theory of mate selection is Ira Reiss' **Wheel Theory of Love**.[25] Social cultural background and role conceptions filter potential partners and provide a mate selection context, but within this setting Reiss described a process that can lead to increasing closeness and intimacy. According to Reiss, **rapport** leads to greater closeness, which often leads to increased **self-revelation**, which builds up **mutual dependency** that (over time) brings about **intimacy need fulfillment**. These four elements of the process are interdependent and ebb and flow.

## Electronic Matchmaking

Online dating and matchmaking services are one of the most interesting recent innovations in the formation of contemporary relationships. Participant surveys, sometimes including several hundred questions, allow programs to match potential partners based on their stated goals, values, and personality profiles. Match.com and eHarmony.com are two of the largest services (businesses actually) that have millions of subscribers, and which use personality assessments to pair up potential dates.[26] Both of these systems target adult singles in general, whereas other services are more focused, such as Christian Singles and Ourtime.com, which target a religious subgroup and more mature singles, respectively. In fact, there are hundreds of internet dating sites that are specialized based on race, ethnicity, religion, and many other (and sometimes unusual) criteria. All such sites allow subscribers to remain anonymous unless two people want to communicate with each other, and then they might exchange messages or communicate with "virtual winks," or even exchange photos. Electronic dating services generally range in cost from about \$25–\$65 per month, but some are free, while others are very exclusive and expensive.[27]

As described by one review service, "With tens of millions of singles using online dating services each month, using one of the top dating sites is an easy way to expand your current dating options. If you're looking to get married, you'll want to choose a service with similarly marriage-minded singles, such as eHarmony or Chemistry.com. If you prefer casual romances or brief encounters you may also enjoy sites such as Spark that cater to singles that prefer more casual encounters. And, of course, if you just want to meet someone and see where things go, using a dating site with the largest possible user base, such as Match.com, will provide you with the best chances of success."[28]

Data show that increasing numbers of marriage partners first met each other on the internet. One source stated that about one-fourth (24%) of marriages in recent years are between spouses who met online.[29] This seems like a lot of electronic matchmaking, but it is plausible when considering that Match.com and eHarmony.com both have 15+ million users, and there are literally hundreds of smaller, more specialized online dating sites.

## Cohabitation

Cohabitation is another dramatic change from prior generations in the process by which contemporary young adults intensify their close relationships. The practice of unmarried people living together is not new, of course, but it is becoming much more prevalent in the United States. Living together before marriage was unusual in your parents' and grandparents' generation: just over 10% of people above the age of 24 were reported to have been cohabiting in the 1980s.[30] Cohabitation was even less common in prior generations. Consequently, cohabitation attracted a lot of interest when researchers studying the U.S. Census in the 1960s first noted the prevalence of unmarried couples who were living together.[31] They called cohabiting couples "POSSLQs" (Persons of Opposite Sex Sharing Living Quarters). A well-known commentator wrote:

> *There's nothing that I wouldn't do*
> *If you would be my POSSLQ*
> *You live with me and I with you,*
> *And you will be my POSSLQ.*
> *I'll be your friend and so much more;*
> *That's what a POSSLQ is for.*[32]

People who cohabited in earlier generations were notably different than their peers. Decades ago, those who lived together without being married were making a very nontraditional statement. Probably as a result, cohabiting before marriage was associated with lower marital quality and stability.[33] Very recently it has been noted that the negative relationship between cohabitation and marital instability lessened over time, and has now disappeared.[34] Today in the USA those who live together before marriage are in the majority (about 60% of marriages now are preceded by cohabitation). In two generations, cohabitation has become part of the normative pattern of forming close relationships in the United States.

# Marriage Ideals, Real Life, and Commitment

Most partners who are attracted to each other form a relationship because they expect their lives to be better together than apart. But real life is usually different than the ideal, and for many young couples relationships are highly idealized. Partners are not always considerate, beautiful or handsome, and every couple experiences differences of opinion and expectations. In some respects, regardless of how long partners have been together, everyone marries a stranger. It is probably wise to accept that most of life is finding a balance between idealized expectations and what happens in real life; all of us find ourselves making adjustments accordingly. Idealized images of married life will be short-lived for some, but for others their marriage ideals actually will be fulfilled.

Being **committed** to a person, and to the relationship, is an important factor in the stability and quality of that relationship.[35] A strong commitment to the marriage could be one of the reasons that arranged marriages tend to be more stable than love matches. It seems ironic, but love match partners, who freely choose to marry each other, are more likely to divorce than arranged marriage partners, who did not choose each other.[36] It seems likely that commitment to the relationship is a partial explanation.

## Getting Married Creates a Family

The act of marriage establishes a **family** according to the U.S. Census definition of "two or more people related to each other by blood, marriage, or adoption."[37] But a lot of marriage is working out how to do the stuff that has to be accomplished for you to survive—and hopefully to thrive—together as a couple.

As an independent single adult, or as a couple, you have to earn enough money to pay for food, clothing, transportation, and a place to live. These realities and necessities raise the fundamental issues of how you will earn money and how your work will be related to your marriage and family life. How will you choose an occupation and prepare for it? Most likely, your spouse or partner will be making the same kinds of decisions, and you might be at the stage of coordinating your decisions to try to make them fit together. You probably also will be deciding whether to have children, or when and how many children to have. How will the two of you coordinate your time and your resources to satisfy your work expectations and to fulfill your marriage and family goals together?

Dating, courtship, and mate selection historically culminated with engagement and marriage. Weddings are family-related events with significant financial implications. It has been said that every time a couple gets married, a hundred cash registers go "ka ching." For most weddings, there are lots of people to be notified and invited, arrangements and reservations to make, and lots of things to buy. Watching the movie *Father of the Bride* (starring Steve Martin and Diane Keaton) is one humorous way to gain some appreciation for the issues involved in planning for an upper-middle-class wedding. Some of you (as participants or parents) are very familiar with the many ways to spend money leading up to, and celebrating, a wedding. In 2012, the average wedding in the United States cost about $25–27,000.[38] Weddings do not have to be that expensive, because the cost is strongly related to the resources of the families involved, and the choices made by those being married. The bare essentials of a wedding officiator and marriage license can be purchased for around $100 in Las Vegas.

### The Martins

*One of the most interesting things about the Martins at this stage of their family life is that two of their three children are beginning to seriously explore future couple relationships. Matt, age 16, frequently hangs out with mixed-sex groups of friends, and he sometimes pairs off with girls who he likes the most. And Abbie, age 11, has started puberty, and she is obviously noticing and thinking about boys in ways that she didn't before. Luke is only 5, but for all of the Martin children (and their parents), the next 15 years will be a busy, complex, and important time for the kids to figure out long-term relationships. Choosing long-term and, potentially, life-time partners will help define central features of their future lives.*

## Summary and Conclusions

Years of dating or hanging out or searching online usually result in a pool of potential partners for single young adults in the United States today. Assortative mating occurs through mate selection processes, so that most young people will find a partner with whom they have many things in common (homogamy). Consciously or not, most young people will evaluate potential partners based on their sexual attraction, potential for intimacy, and compatible values, roles, and personalities.

Some of you will follow a traditional path into marriage, but probably with a shorter engagement than was typical in your grandparents' generation (who were likely to have been engaged for years). Others in the contemporary United States will eventually marry after cohabiting for some time (probably years) in place of engagement, or cohabiting while they are engaged. Some others are likely to gradually evolve into long-term cohabitating relationships that never become formalized by marriage.

Marriage and marriage-like relationships are the beginnings of family relationships. Partner selection might be based on several motivations or needs, including the need for human closeness and intimacy, the need to have a partner for practical economic and household reasons, and the need to have a partner to have and raise children together.

References

[1] Klaus, J. K. M. (1976). *Maternal Infant Bonding*. Mosby: The C V Mosby Co.

[2] Bowlby, J. (2008). *Attachment: Volume One of the Attachment and Loss Trilogy*. New York: Random House Publishing.

[3] Epstein, J. L. (1986). Choice of Friends Over the Life Span: Developmental and environmental influences. In E. C. Mueller & C. R. Cooper (Eds.), Process and outcome in peer relationships (pp. 129–160). San Diego, CA: Academic Press.

[4] Epstein, J. L. (1986). Choice of Friends Over the Life Span: Developmental and environmental influences. In E. C. Mueller & C. R. Cooper (Eds.), Process and outcome in peer relationships (pp. 129–160). San Diego, CA: Academic Press.

[5] Sexual Orientation. (2003). *International Encyclopedia of Marriage and Family*. Retrieved from http://www.encyclopedia.com/topic/Sexual_orientation.aspx

[6] Kimmel, M. S., Mahler, M. (2003). Adolescent Masculinity, Homophobia, and Violence. *American Behavioral Scientist*, 46(10), 1439–1458.

[7] Roffman, A. (2010). *Gay, lesbian and bisexual teens: Facing challenges and building resiliency*. NYU Child Study Center. Retrieved from http://www.aboutourkids. org/articles/gay_lesbian_bisexual_teens_facing_challenges_building_resilien ce?CSRT=7287789673103621532

[8] Hock, R. R. (2012). *Human Sexuality* (3rd ed.). New Jersey: Pearson Education.

[9] Baumeister, R. F., Leary, M. R. (1995). The Need to Belong: Desire for Interpersonal Attachments as a Fundamental Human Motivation. *Psychological Bulletin*, 117(3), 497–529.

[10] Griffin, E., & Sparks, G. G. (1990). Friends forever: A longitudinal exploration of intimacy in same-sex friends and platonic pairs. *Journal of Social and Personal Relationships*, 7, 29–46.

[11] Olson, D. H., DeFrain, J., Skogrand, L. (2011). *Marriage and Families: Intimacy, Diversity, and Strengths* (7th ed.). New York: McGraw-Hill, p. 253.

[12] Sisk, C. L., Foster, D. L. (2004). The neural basis of puberty and adolescence. *Nature Neuroscience*, 7(10), 1040–1047.

[13] Tang, K. (2011). *Dating Styles of the 20th Century*. Retrieved from http://www. ehow.com/info_7887898_dating-styles-20th-century.html

[14] CBS News. (2007). *Love in the 21st century*. Retrieved from http://www.cbsnews. com/2100-500164_162-614019.html

[15] W. Furman, B.B. Brown, & C. Feiring (Eds.), The development of romantic relationships in adolescence. Cambridge studies in social and emotional development. New York: Cambridge.

[16] Mare, R. D. (1991). Five Decades of Educational Assortative Mating. *American Sociological Review*, 56, 15–32.

[17] Greenaway, K. (2006). Jake Sprat could eat no fat, *Kate Greenaway's Mother Goose* (17). San Mariono, CA: Huntington Library Press.

[18] Winch. R. (1958). *Mate-Selection; a Study of Complementary Needs.* New York, NY: HarperCollins.

[19] Gyuris, P., Jarai, R., Bereczkei, T. (2010). The effect of childhood experiences on mate choice in personality traits: Homogamy and sexual imprinting. *Personality and Individual Differences*, 49, 467–472.

[20] Gyuris, P., Jarai, R., Bereczkei, T. (2010). The effect of childhood experiences on mate choice in personality traits: Homogamy and sexual imprinting. *Personality and Individual Differences*, 49, 467–472.

[21] Ellsworth, J. S. Jr. (1948). The Relationship of Population Density to Residential Propinquity as a Factor in Marriage Selection. *American Sociological Review*, 13(4), 444–448.

[22] Endogamy. (n.d.). In *Online Dictionary of The Social Sciences*. Retrieved from http://bitbucket.icaap.org/dict.pl?term=ENDOGAMY

[23] Jordan, M. (2012). More Marriages Cross Race, Ethnicity Lines. *The Wall Street Journal*. Retrieved from http://online.wsj.com/article/SB10001424052970204880404577226981780914906.html

[24] Murstein, B. I. (1970). Stimulus-Value-Role: A Theory of Marital Choice. *Journal of Marriage and Family*, 32(3), 465–481.

[25] Reiss, I. L. (1960). Toward a sociology of the heterosexual love relationship. *Marriage and Family Living*, 22(2) 139–145.

[26] Top 10 Best Dating Sites. (2012). *The Top 10 Online Dating Sites of 2012*. Retrieved from http://www.top10bestdatingsites.com/index.php?kw=dating%20service&c=9362800387&t=content&p=dating.about.com&m=&adpos=none&a=103&gclid=CJ-Vq6q5i7MCFQSCQgodh0YAdA

**Notes**

[27] Misadventures in Cleveland Dating. (2012). *Match.com vs. eHarmony vs. POF vs. OkCupid—Which online dating site is best?* Retrieved from http://thirtysomethingsingle.com/2012/01/16/best_online_dating_site/

[28] Consumer Rankings. (2012). *The 5 Best Dating Sites of 2012.* Retrieved from: http://www.consumer-rankings.com/dating/

[29] Stoddard, C. *Hooking up and connecting lives: Online dating and the economics of marriage search. Dissertation Abstracts International, A: The Humanities and Social Sciences*, 3263–3263. Retrieved from http://search.proquest.com/docview/61772642?accountid=14761. (61772642; 200933157).

[30] Thornton, A. (1988). Cohabitation and Marriage in the 1980s. *Demography*, 25(4), 497–808.

[31] Bunting, E. (1987). Will You be My POSSLQ? Harcourt Brace Jovanovich.

[32] Osgood, C. (1981). *There's Nothing That I Wouldn't Do If You Would Be My POSSLQ.* Holt, Rinehart, and Winston.

[33] Thomson, E., Colella, U. (1992). Cohabitation and Marital Stability: Quality or Commitment? *Journal of Marriage and the Family*, 54, 259–267.

[34] Copen, C. E., Daniels, K., Vespa, J., Mosher, W. D., Division of Vital Statistics. (2012). First Marriages in the United States: Data From the 2006–2010 National Survey of Family Growth. *National Health Statistics Reports*, 49.

[35] Rhoades, G. K., Stanley, S. M., & Markman, H. J. (2010). Should I stay or should I go? Predicting dating relationship stability from four aspects of commitment. *Journal of Family Psychology*, 24(5), 543–550. doi: http://dx.doi.org/10.1037/a0021008

[36] Xiaohe, X., & Whyte, M. K. (1990). Love matches and arranged marriages: A Chinese replication. *Journal of Marriage and the Family*, 709–722.

[37] United States Census Bureau. (2012). Frequently Asked Questions. Retrieved from http://www.census.gov/hhes/www/income/about/faqs.html

[38] Wedding Stats. (2012). Average cost of a Wedding. Retrieved from http://www.weddingstats.org/average-cost-of-a-wedding.html

# Chapter 8

# Marriage Expectations and Relationships

# Marriage Expectations and Relationships

When do you hope or expect to have a committed relationship? What about marriage, and what do you expect from your spouse/partner? What are your needs and expectations for communication? How important is closeness, intimacy, understanding, kindness? How do you feel about being in charge, or would you prefer to defer, or to make joint decisions? How important is it to have a lasting relationship? How sure are you that your marriage will endure? How important is permanance to you, and how committed are you? How strongly do you believe that marriage should be forever?

Almost all of us grew up with expectations that we would get married. For most people marriage is an especially important relationship, perhaps the most important relationship of all. For some people, marriage is a sacred religious sacrament that includes God, along with their partner. For many others, marriage involves at least strong social expectations from families and friends. In marriage, people expect (or hope) to find (or build) close, intimate, sexual and practical relationships that provide structure and meaning for their adult lives. Marriage traditionally was the way to begin a family, and to provide the couple environment for having and raising children.

About 90+% of adults in the United States eventually marry in their lifetimes.[1] Because marriage was so strongly expected and nearly universal, if someone did not get married in the past people wondered, why not? In prior generations, women who did not marry were referred to by derogatory terms such as "spinster" or "old maid," and their unmarried status suggested shortcomings or deficits; unmarried men were (and still are) just called "bachelors."

The percent of adults who have remained single well into adulthood has increased dramatically in recent decades. So, remaining single by choice—or at least delaying marriage—is more common nowadays, and "singlehood" is recognized by some as an emergent life style, without (or with less of) the negative connotations of prior generations.[2] The percent of adults who have never married has varied with economic and cultural conditions, so that singlehood was high during the Great Depression of the 1930s, but a lower percentage of people remained single during the years following World War II.[3]

# Norms

Norms are **expectations** about how people should act in various roles. **Marriage norms** define what marriages are expected to be like, or the ways we think about what husbands and wives should do. Sharing or holding the same or similar views (expectations) about marriage helps spouses understand each other and reduces conflicts between them. Understanding marital norms is important because married life can be smoother (or more difficult) depending on how much husbands and wives expect the same (or different) things from their relationships.

It has been mentioned that traditional norms in marriage were that the husband should protect and provide economically, and the wife should provide nurturance in relationships with husband and children. In the 1950s, these norms for husbands and wives were famously called "**instrumental**" roles for men and "**expressive**" roles for women.[4] The structural functional theory that characterized men's roles as "instrumental" and women's roles as "expressive" has been widely discredited.[5] Norms about marriage have changed immensely in recent decades, so that "bread-winner" husbands and "homemaker" wives are no longer the realities of life for the majority of Americans. The roles of men and women in marriage and society today are very diverse and often nontraditional.

There also are major subcultural differences in norms about marriage. Some religious or ethnic groups (e.g., fundamental Christians, Hispanics) hold more traditional norms, while other groups are less traditional. Norms about marriage in the United States also differ markedly from marital norms in other cultures. Think, for example, about how marriage is strongly husband-dominated (patriarchal) in Middle Eastern Islamic societies, as compared with relatively more **egalitarian** marriages in the United States and Europe.[6] In traditional Middle Eastern Muslim marriages, husbands average about 10 years older than their wives and men make all the major decisions. Education is limited for traditional Muslim females; they are expected to follow strict dress codes, and their roles in marriage, the family, and society are clearly prescribed.[7]

What about you? If you are female, would it matter if your husband didn't want to work full time, or didn't earn enough money to support the family? If you are male, would it matter if your wife didn't want to spend her time raising children? What if either partner didn't want to have children? What if one partner felt like they should make all the major financial decisions for the family? Maybe these scenarios would be okay, but maybe not. Whether or not marriages in the USA work out or don't work out depends heavily on both partners' expectations. Partner expectations about their marriage come from their own families of origin and, among other influences, from their ethnic, religious, and educational backgrounds.

*The Martins*

> *Rob and Maria's marriage is a strength in their lives. Like almost all married couples, there are times when they struggle to make things work, and their usually good communications sometimes break down. But they are fortunate to have a mostly open and assertive style of talking with each other that helps them manage upsets and coordinate their busy activities with the kids. Maria feels empowered to lead out with scheduling and keeping track of all the stuff going on in their lives, and in the lives of three children with different interests. Their marriage reflects their values and priorities that both partners should be involved parents.*

## The Core Norms of Marriage

One of the most obvious norms about marriage in the United States is the norm of **fidelity**. There is a generally held expectation of marital fidelity or exclusivity toward one's spouse. Most weddings include a pledge that husband and wife will be faithful to one another. Marriage partners are expected to hold a unique place with their spouse, unlike anyone else. This norm of faithfulness, loyalty, or fidelity is made vivid by the way people react when the norm is violated. Marriage partners normally feel jealous when their spouse shows inappropriate attention to someone else, and everyone understands a married person's hurt and anger if their spouse has an affair—an extramarital sexual relationship. "Cheating" is the common term for breaking the norm of marital fidelity. Adultery (having nonmarital sexual intercourse) was grounds for (or the basis of) many divorce proceedings in the past when divorce was fault based. About 25 percent of married men, and a lesser proportion of married women, are estimated to have had sex with someone other than their spouse.[8] Extramarital affairs continue to be one of the most common and most difficult issues for which couples seek marital therapy.[9]

Another norm about marriage is that it is expected to be **permanent**. This marital norm is communicated by the familiar phrase "till death do us part," which is repeated in most American wedding ceremonies. The expectation of permanence is core to the American conception of traditional marriage. The ideal of lasting relationships is, of course, in stark contrast to the reality that many marriages are not permanent, and for many reasons marriages don't last. Recognizing this fact, some couples "hedge their bets" by entering into prenuptial agreements to minimize legal hassles if (when) they split up. In reality, a small percentage of marriages are annulled or abandoned, but a substantial portion of marriages end through separation and divorce, so that about half of all first marriages in the U.S. are dissolved.

A less clear-cut norm of marriage is **kindness**—the expectation that spouses will be good to each other, seek the best for one another, and treat each other kindly. Marriages differ tremendously in the way that spouses treat each other and, unfortunately, this norm of marriage is also often contradicted by reality. That there is such a norm, however, is evident from the discomfort that is felt when a husband or wife belittles or is rude to their spouse in public. At the extreme, of course, there are laws against emotional and physical abuse in marriage. Law enforcement officers and legal professionals, unfortunately, are keenly aware that widespread domestic disputes and domestic violence violate the norm of kindness in marriage.

In summary, norms about marriage in the U.S. communicate societal expectations about how spouses should act toward one another, and what marriages should be like. In general terms, it is expected that marriage partners will be faithful to one another, attempt to remain together throughout their lives, and treat each other well. While being somewhat oversimplified, exclusivity, permanence, and kindness are general expectations or norms for marriage in the United States. Less general norms about marriage are always worked out by each couple, defining how they will treat one another, raise children, and make a living together.

## Communication

Communication is the process of conveying meaning, and as such, it is the fundamental dynamic underlying all human relationships.[10] Usually, we communicate by talking, but we also can communicate by a glance, facial expression, and by touching. Other nonverbal forms of communication include body movement, posturing, and silence. Think how satisfying (and unusual) it is when someone understands you completely or perfectly, and how frustrating it is when someone misunderstands you. Communication is a key to any relationship, and it is especially important in a close relationship like marriage.

Helen Keller wrote how she, as a young deaf and blind child, felt trapped inside herself with no way to communicate with those close to her. Her failures to make herself understood resulted in frustration and tears: "I felt as if invisible hands were holding me (back), and I made frantic efforts to free myself…I generally broke down in tears and physical exhaustion. If my mother happened to be near I crept into her arms, too miserable even to remember the cause of the tempest. After a while the need of some means of communication became so urgent that these outbursts occurred daily, sometimes hourly. My parents were deeply grieved and perplexed."[11]

Most of us don't face the communication challenges of a deaf and blind young child like Helen Keller, but all of us do experience times when our communications just don't work. Communication consists of sending and receiving messages, usually by speaking and listening. Communication is complicated by the fact that it occurs at several levels. There is the content of what someone says, but how did they say it (what was the tone of voice), and what did they really mean? After Helen Keller learned to speak, she noted that communication was more complex: "The deaf and blind find it very difficult to acquire the amenities of conversation. How much more difficult this must be for those who are both deaf and blind! They cannot distinguish the tone of the voice, or go up and down the tones that give significance to words; nor can they watch the expression of the speaker's face, and look is often the very soul of what one says."[12] Beyond the content of what is said, communications often are loaded with emotions, ironies, and multiple meanings.

People have different communication styles. Some people are direct in their communications—they say what they think without much filtering of the message for others. Or, some people are just the opposite—they have a very hard time saying what they really think or feel. Such partners might hold back because they are simply more private, or because they don't want to say something that could be offensive to others. What happens when two people who communicate so differently marry each other? One partner's direct communication style could be a problem if the other spouse is easily offended, or has easily hurt feelings. Conversely, it can be problematic when one spouse (or both!) has a hard time expressing how they really think or feel. And think about the possible dynamics when both are more alike than different in their communications.

Spouses usually hope to have good communication, open communication, clear communication, and to avoid misunderstandings or communication breakdowns. It is no accident that several of the most established and influential marital enrichment programs are based on improving couple communications.[13]

## Types of Marital Communications

Effective marital communication depends on partners sharing their feelings. Deeper level or intimate communication helps couples make decisions and solve problems with more complete understanding of one another.

One way of thinking about communication in marriage is to separate "**maintenance**" type conversations from deeper and more meaningful sharing. Maintenance communication is common or mundane, and probably constitutes the bulk of both everyday interpersonal and marital communications. Busy spouses find themselves just talking about what they need to get done, by whom, by when. Who is going to get the groceries, take care of the dog or the cat, fix the car (or maybe fix the cat!)? Effective maintenance communication is important for coordinating how spouses live together day to day. Effective maintenance communication becomes even more essential when there are additional family complexities, like major illnesses, financial stresses, and having and raising children. Although necessary, maintenance communication is not usually very fulfilling for the partners involved in a close relationship.

By contrast, **deeper communications** between intimate partners can satisfy their needs to feel close to each other, to be understood, and to share thoughts and feelings. This is the kind and quality of communication most often associated with young lovers deeply gazing into each other's eyes and touching one another. This type of communication also is seen among older partners who are deeply aware, trusting, and comfortable talking with each other.

It is important to remember that human communications are both verbal and nonverbal. Verbal and nonverbal messages are usually consistent, but not always. Sometimes a person's gestures, facial expressions, or body language are extremely important to gain understanding. This is why telephone or written conversations are usually considered to be less complete communication than talking with someone face-to-face. Sometimes what a person says is not what they really mean, and nonverbal messages can help to convey deeper feelings and emotions. It is well known in clinical work that conflicting verbal and nonverbal messages can cause serious problems in relationships.[14]

John Gottman and his colleagues developed one of the most intensive research programs about marital interaction in the world.[15] They interviewed spouses, observed couples in a home-like laboratory, recorded and coded their behaviors toward one another on videotape, and took physiological measurements (fidgeting, perspiration, heart rate). Based on these molecular studies of couple interaction over many years, Gottman identified the following four problematic communication patterns that he called the "Four Horsemen of the Apocalypse." *Criticism* is attacking the partner; *defensiveness* is denying one's own role and blaming the other; *stonewalling* is tuning out or shutting down communication; and *contempt* is insulting, putting down, name calling, or mocking the partner. Criticism tends to be more common among women than men, but the reverse is true for stonewalling (up to 85% of stonewalling is done by males). The important point, according to Gottman, is that regardless of how couples communicate, they must figure out how to resolve their differences and repair the disagreements that are inevitable in any close relationship.

## Power and Authority

**Authority** can be defined as legitimate power, or the right to exercise power, to make decisions.[16] Historically, men had authority in marriage, like they did in society more generally. The husband was traditionally recognized as the "head of the family," and he was expected to make major marital and family decisions. In a male-dominated era, adolescent boys and young men were expected to (and they did) initiate dating, make marriage proposals, decide where the family would live, manage the finances, and decide who would do what in the household.

You might have noticed the tendency for men to be more in charge (bossy) among the older generations of your own family. Although **patriarchy** was the traditional pattern for families in the United States, it always was the case that many families were different. In some marriages the wife is the more dominant personality, and in some marriages wives and husbands share more co-equal partnerships. Male authority also is a moot issue—or non-issue—in many single-parent families, except that overly dominant males could be a reason that the couple ended their relationship.

It is obvious that contemporary marriages are much more **egalitarian** now than in the past. This means that marriage partners today are more likely to do things jointly, based on both partners' interests and talents, and make decisions together, rather than playing out marital roles assigned by society. In this respect, modern relationships are much more about "role making" than "role taking" in the ways that power is shared.

Power is different than authority. Power and control might not be concepts that you usually associate with close relationships and marriage, but they are important nonetheless. **Power** is the ability to exert one's will.[17] Sometimes it is added that power is the ability to exert one's will, *despite resistance*.[18] Power is an important dynamic in all human relationships. It is important to know how decisions are made, who decides, or if there is a chain of command, especially if there are differences of opinion.

Power is important in relationships because couples have to make decisions. How couples decide is based on an interesting mix of personal characteristics and their larger social and cultural contexts. There is not necessarily an adversarial dimension to how spouses make decisions, but some spouses have greater influence over their partner because of experience, personality, or culture. The basis of power can be knowledge, expertise, or other factors.[19]

I remember hearing a story about a couple who were being interviewed at home by a professional. The husband, a large and gregarious man, was dominating the conversation with the interviewer, while the wife sat quietly in a chair off to one side. After a while, the interviewer had formed the opinion that the husband was clearly the person in charge of this family. Then the phone rang unexpectedly. The wife quietly said to her husband, "Answer the phone," which he did. This was an eye opener to the interviewer, who then realized that, despite the husband's overt talkativeness, the wife really was the person who gave orders in the marriage.

## Marital Benefits and Happiness

Among the most important dynamics of marriage is the satisfaction or happiness felt by the partners. There is a large research literature about what is correlated with marital satisfaction. Generally, researchers have asked husbands and wives how satisfied they are with different aspects of their marriages. Just comparing people who are married with people who are not, married people generally are happier about their lives than those who are single.

"Society has a large stake in strengthening marriages. Children should be our central concern and, in general, they do better when raised by two parents. Marriage also typically improves the health and economic well-being of adults, stabilizes community life, and benefits civic society."[20]

This bold assertion in favor of marriage is generally supported by research data. Linda Waite and Maggie Gallagher are among the most respected researchers who have summarized the research comparing married and unmarried adults. They conclude that the following are benefits of marriage: (1) healthier lifestyle in terms of eating, drinking, exercise, and avoiding harmful behavior; (2) longer life expectancy derived from emotional and economic support; (3) more frequent and satisfying sexual relationships; (4) greater wealth and economic assets based on increased income and sharing costs; (5) advantaged children from greater parental attention and better emotional adjustment and academic success.[21]

These general benefits of marriage are not experienced by everyone who gets married. For example, one study reported that black men usually derive some health benefits from marriage, but black women do not.[22] Further, some feminist scholars have asserted that traditional marriage makes some women sick.[23] In spite of these caveats, a loving relationship usually brings the partners great benefits and, on the average, married people appear to be happier and healthier than those who are single.

Gottman's detailed observation of couple communication and interaction was referred to previously. One of his interesting conclusions is that the balance of positive and negative interactions among partners can strongly predict the future of their relationship. Counting behaviors such as touching, smiling, paying compliments, and friendly looks as positives, versus name calling, ignoring, and rudeness as negatives, Gottman proposed that couples need a ratio of at least five times as much positive as negative interaction for their marriage to be stable.[24]

# Improving the Odds

So, what can be done to increase the probability that your marriage will be happy, stable, and fulfilling? One popular marriage and family textbook[25] summarized the following, based on research and clinical experience, as conditions that help maximize the chances for success in marriage:

1. Both individuals are *independent and mature*; in fact, age of the partners is the single best predictor of future marital stability.

2. Both individuals *love themselves as well as each other*; relationships do best if partners have good self-esteem, feel secure, and are self-confident.

3. Both individuals *enjoy being alone as well as together*; balancing separateness and togetherness is a sign of healthy individuals and couple dynamics.

4. Both individuals are *established in their work*; stable and satisfying jobs foster both financial and emotional well-being, so that there is more time, energy, and resources for the relationship to succeed.

5. Both individuals *know themselves*; partners can evaluate their own strengths and weaknesses, and not blame their problems on others.

6. Both individuals *can express themselves assertively*; being direct and positive and clear helps partners communicate more successfully.

7. Both individuals are *friends as well as lovers*; caring for the other, and focusing on the other's needs, tends to be reciprocated.

Keeping marriages strong over a lifetime can be a challenge. A major issue is taking marriage for granted while dealing with other concerns in life. Major competing priorities are likely to be jobs and finances and children and…(you name it). If partners do not engage one another to focus on their relationship, their natural tendency is to drift apart—not on purpose, but through neglect.

Bill Doherty, a well-known professional and advocate for marriage, wrote: "Ever since I moved to Minnesota, I have thought that getting married is like launching a canoe into the Mississippi at St. Paul. If you don't paddle, you go south. No matter how much you love each other, no matter how full of hope and promise and good intentions, if you stay on the Mississippi…you end up in New Orleans."[26]

Doherty has written about ways to maintain a vital marriage. He advocates reminding yourselves that your marriage is the foundation of your family, and that your marriage needs and deserves private focused time and regular dates to keep it vital. He also recommends the use of marriage rituals, such as kisses and hugs and affectionate names and sharing things that the two partners simply enjoy doing together. These marriage rituals occur every day when separating and joining, and in the cycles of weeks and holidays and celebrations together.[27]

### The Martins

*Rob and Maria benefit from being married. Being a couple provides them with emotional and sexual intimacy. They also like to do things that they both enjoy and share together. In more mundane ways, they manage a household and prod and remind each other to take better care of their health. Over their years of marriage they have tried lots of things and learned better food habits together, which they are trying to pass on to their children. Rob and Maria have strong commitments to each other, and to their marriage, and their focus on their couple relationship has been crucial to the success of their family.*

## Summary and Conclusions

Adults in the United States are expected to get married, and more than 90% say "I do." Norms of marriage include fidelity, permanence, and kindness, even though marital realities often fall short of these expectations. Traditional norms recognized the authority of husband-fathers (patriarchy), but contemporary norms are generally supportive of egalitarian (shared) power in marriage.

Communication is essential for human relationships. Marital communications are very complex, dealing with both verbal and nonverbal ways of expressing meaning. Communications are essential to get through day-to-day maintenance needs, but also to build and strengthen bonds of understanding and caring in relationships.

Positive marriage relationships have many benefits. Compared with single persons, the benefits of marriage include better physical and emotional health, longer life expectancy, better sexual relationships, improved financial assets, and advantages for children raised by two parents.

The probability of marital success is increased by: independence and maturity at the time of marriage; having positive regard for self and others; enjoying both autonomy and togetherness; having stable and satisfying work and income; being realistic and honest about oneself; communicating assertively and directly; and combining friendship and love.

References

[1] U.S. Census Bureau. (2005e). Marital status of the population by sex, race and Hispanic origin: 1990–2005. *Statistical abstract of the United States.*

Goldstein, J. R., & Kenny, C. T. (2001). Marriage delayed or marriage forgone? New cohort forecasts of first marriage for U.S. women. *American Sociological Review*, 66, 505–519. (Family & Social Policy textbook p. 221).

[2] Jayson, S. (2010). Free as a bird and loving it. In K. Gilbert (Ed.), *Annual edition: The family 10/11* (pp. 47–48). Boston: McGraw-Hill

[3] Olson, D. H., DeFrain, J., Skogrand, L. (2011). *Marriages and Families: Intimacy, Diversity, and Strengths* (7th ed.). New York: McGraw-Hill, 268–274.

[4] Bales, R., Bales Robert, E., Parsons, T., Talcott, B., & Olds, J. (1955). *Family, Socialization, & Interaction Process.* London: Routledge and Kegan Paul Ltd.

[5] Crano, W. D., & Aronoff, J. (1978). A Cross-Cultural Study of Expressive and Instrumental Role Complementarity in the Family. *American Sociological Review*, 43(4), 463–471.

[6] Alexander, A. C., & Welzel, C. (2011). Islam and patriarchy: how robust is Muslim support for patriarchal values? *International Review of Sociology*, 21(2), 249–276.

[7] Eposito, J. L. (2012). *Women In the Islamic World: Past and Present.* Retrieved from http://www.oxfordislamicstudies.com/article/opr/t243/e370

[8] Michael, R. T., Gagnon, J. H., Laumann, E. O., Kolata, G. (1994). *Sex in America: A Definitive Survey.* New York: Little Brown

[9] American Association for Marital and Family Therapy. (2010). Infidelity.

[10] Olson, D. H., DeFrain, J., Skogrand, L. (2011). *Marriages and Families: Intimacy, Diversity, and Strengths* (7th ed.). New York: McGraw-Hill, 92–93.

[11] Keller, H. (1990). *The Story of My Life.* New York: Bantam Classics, 9.

[12] Keller, H. (1990). *The Story of My Life.* New York: Bantam Classics, 16.

Notes

[13] Miller, S., Sherrard, P. A. D. (1999). Couple communication: A system for equipping partners to talk, listen, and resolve conflicts effectively. In R. Berger & M. T. Hannah (Eds.), *Preventive approaches in couples therapy* (pp. 125–148). Lillington, NC: Edwards Brothers.

[14] Utah State University Admin. (2005). Communication, Conflict & Commitment. Retrieved from http://ocw.usu.edu/family_consumer_human_development/ marriage_family_relationships/Communication_Conflict_Commitment_1.html

[15] Gottman, J. (1995). *Why marriages succeed or fail: And how you can make yours last.* New York: Simon & Schuster.

[16] Authority. (n.d.). In *Online Dictionary of the Social Sciences.* Retrieved from http:// bitbucket.icaap.org/dict.pl

[17] Power. (n.d.). In *Online Dictionary of the Social Sciences.* Retrieved from http:// bitbucket.icaap.org/dict.pl

[18] Barkan, S. E. (2011). *Sociology: Understanding the Changing Social World* (Brief Edition v. 1.1). Retrieved from http://catalog.flatworldknowledge.com/bookhub/ reader/4306?e=barkbrief-1.1-ch10_s01#barkbrief-1.1-ch10_s01

[19] French, J. R. P. Jr., & Raven, B. (1959). The Bases of Social Power. *Studies in Social Power* Retrieved from http://www.communicationcache.com/uploads/ 1/0/8/8/10887248/the_bases_of_social_power_-_chapter_20.pdf

[20] Estroff H. M. (1998, August 4). Debunking the Marriage Myth: It Works for Women, Too. *The New York Times.* p. 7.

[21] Waite, L., Gallagher, M. (2000). *The Case for Marriage: Why Married People are Happier, Healthier, and Better off Financially.* New York: Knopf Doubleday Publishing.

[22] Blackman, L. (2005). *The consequences of marriage for African Americans: A comprehensive literature review.* Institute for American Values.

[23] Bernard, J. (1982). *The future of marriage.* Yale University Press.

[24] Gottman, J. (1999). *The Seven Principles for Making Marriage Work.* New York: Three Rivers Press.

[25] Olson, D. H., DeFrain, J., Skogrand, L. (2011). *Marriages and Families: Intimacy, Diversity, and Strengths* (7th ed.). New York: McGraw-Hill.

[26] Doherty, W. J. (2001). *Take back your marriage: Sticking together in a world that pulls us apart.* New York: Guilford.

[27] Doherty, W. J. (2001). *Take back your marriage: Sticking together in a world that pulls us apart.* New York: Guilford.

# Chapter 9

## Parenthood— Having Children

# Parenthood—Having Children

Will I (we) have children? How many children will I (we) have? How much will it cost to have and raise them? Is it possible to make rational choices about having children? How will I do as a parent? How are parenthood issues related to marriage, and to other family concerns, and to work? Most of us think about the "we" versions of these questions, because partners usually try to answer these parental questions together.

This is a chapter about **parenthood**, or having children. Raising children, or **parenting**, is the subject of a later chapter. Because parenthood and parenting are common to the majority of adults throughout the world, these are not unique or unusual experiences. Most people take it for granted that they will have kids. Parenthood is, however, a long-term commitment and, if you have children, then parent-child relationships almost certainly will be an important part of your experiences throughout life. Alice Rossi famously said that "you can have ex-spouses and ex-jobs, but not ex-children."[1] So, having and raising children is a serious issue, because parenthood usually is a permanent, non-revocable commitment.

But parenthood is not just a personal, or even only a couple, issue. Reproduction also is critically important to society. Many societies develop norms and laws about childbearing partly because they want to identify a child's parents so that they can be held responsible for their child's well-being. Although unfamiliar to Americans, some societies literally attempt to plan and manage their population growth through policies about childbearing.[2] China is well known for its efforts to control **population growth** by establishing a policy that restricts each family to having only one child.[3] Conversely, at the opposite extreme of China's one child policy, some European populations have been in long-term decline because couples do not have enough children to meet **population replacement levels** (just over 2 children per couple, on average).[4] In some of these countries, social policies have been established to provide incentives that promote and reward childbearing.[5]

## Biological and Cultural Imperatives

Although it might seem incredible, many people do not make conscious decisions about having children. Why is this so? The most obvious reason for childbirth is the **biological imperative** that drives reproduction. People have children because conception and birth happen in the absence of taking deliberate preventative actions. Heterosexual couples have sex, conception occurs, and once pregnancy occurs a child will be born, unless there is a miscarriage (spontaneous abortion) or an induced abortion. So, many, many millions—perhaps the majority—of children around the world are conceived and born every year without any deliberate intention or plan on the part of their parent(s).

Besides the biological imperative that drives reproduction, there are also strong **cultural imperatives** about childbearing, children, and parenthood. In the United States various policies and laws support or favor parenthood, such as income tax deductions for dependents.[6] Many religions also promote childbearing, and "grand-parents in waiting" often are eager to welcome and spoil their children's children.

### The Martins

> Like other parts of their lives, Rob and Maria wanted to plan childbearing as much as possible. Early in their marriage they tried several forms of contraception, and eventually settled into Maria being on the pill, except during those times when they wanted to get pregnant. This worked out pretty well, and they were able to have children about when they wanted. But after Luke was born five years ago, in Maria's mid-thirties, she did not look forward to being on the pill for another decade. Rob and Maria talked through their options, and decided that one of them should be sterilized.

## Pronatalism and Religion

Specific teachings, encouragement, or social policies that favor having children are elements of cultural "**pronatalism**." Pro-birth pressures are not always obvious in specific policies or laws, but subtle influences still are reflected in continuing high rates of fertility among selected groups.

Most of the Americas, as well as many other cultures, have connections with Judeo-Christian teachings. As recorded in the first chapter of the Bible, God gave Adam and Eve the first commandment to "be fruitful, and multiply, and replenish the earth."[7] The cultural value of children is also directly reflected in the biblical statements that "Children are an heritage (gift) of the Lord,"[8] and "Children's children are the crown of old men."[9] Similar teachings valuing children and promoting parenthood are present in other major world religions.[10]

At one time, Catholics in the USA had high birth rates, probably related both to biblical teachings about having children, but even more related to the Catholic Church's opposition to any form of artificial birth control. Catholics in the United States no longer have high birthrates compared with other Christian religions,[11] but pro-childbearing messages still are reflected in the higher birthrates among people who belong to more literal or fundamental bible-based religions. Evangelical Christians and Mormons, for example, have higher than average birthrates.[12]

Mormons are a particularly interesting and unusual group in terms of childbearing and fertility.[13] At a Mormon blog spot recently, several persons wrote to address the question of why religious people tend to have more children. One person wrote that there are multiple reasons, including: doctrines command them to be "fruitful and multiply"; beliefs condemn birth control and abortion; doctrines sanctify human life.[14] In addition, religious faith allows religious people to believe in "happy endings" and fortifies their hope in the future. Another blogger wrote that some religious persons might be less concerned about overpopulation, species extinction, nuclear proliferation, or global warming, based upon their belief that these problems don't exist, human innovation will always be able to solve these problems, or the state of the world is less important than their religious beliefs that promote childbearing.[15]

A female blogger who is also a Mormon mother wrote:

> "For me, getting married and having children were both promises to commit my life regardless of future circumstances. That's a very scary prospect. If I felt I was doing it alone, it would be even scarier. In that way, my faith enables me to have a larger family. And I thank God every day for my family because it establishes a daily praxis of self-sacrifice and devotion to others. Since this is the stuff my faith is made of, my family facilitates my faith. I tell my children that you become an adult when you can take care of yourself but you don't finish the transition until you dedicate your life to taking care of others. I find that faith and family has helped me with that transition."[16]

As mentioned in the introduction, I grew up in Utah, which is over 60% Mormon—the largest religious majority in any state.[17] When I was in middle school I rode a bus every day to school. It was quite a long bus ride, and the bus driver always played the radio on the same local station. Every morning at a certain time the radio announcer would broadcast the birth announcements from the previous day. More than 50 years later, I still remember the jingle that was played to introduce the birth announcements:

*Across the street and a few houses down*
*A tiny little baby has come to town*
*To brighten up the household, and make two hearts so glad,*
*The sweetest little baby, just for mom and dad!*

Such pronatalist sentiments, and religious imperatives to bear children, seem to be fading influences of the past. People with a secular, nonreligious view of the world could easily think of religious influences on fertility as being quite outdated, naïve, or even misguided. However, a religious blogger recently wrote: "As a university educated man (Engineering and Mathematics) married to a university educated woman (Mathematics), I take umbrage at the allegation that religious people are uneducated…. My wife and I have children to express our faith that there will be a future…. People with faith tend to be happier…. It is probably that happier people worry less about the future, so they can take the leap of faith that is parenthood."[18]

Evangelical Christians, Mormons, and those of Latin heritage are likely to feel strong pressures to have children, and in some cases not to use contraception. Recently a group called "Quiverfull"[19] was formed in the United States, based on the rejection of all birth control and the value of having as many children as Providence provides. Some of this group's central teachings, and its name, comes from the Bible.[20]

*Lo, children are an heritage of the LORD:*
*and the fruit of the womb is his reward.*
*As arrows are in the hand of a mighty man;*
*so are children of the youth.*
*Happy is the man that hath his **quiver full** of them.*

At the same blog spot referred to above, there was an interesting exchange about why religious people might have more children than those who are less religious, or those who claim no religion:

**Male guy A:** "Religious people have larger families because Western religions encourage having children. Further, as a general proposition (there are, of course, exceptions), religious people tend to place a higher emphasis on altruism, whereas secular people tend to be more self-focused. Thus, for a religious person, children provide the opportunity to nurture and benefit other human beings. For many secular people, however, children merely consume time and resources that otherwise could have been devoted to their own amusement."[21]

**Male guy B:** "I am appalled by this sentiment…I am an atheist who teaches instead of working in a field where I could easily make quite a bit more money. I choose not to have children, not because I am selfish, but because I do not believe that bringing a child into a world as broken as ours is currently responsible. I, like many secularists I know, give more money to charity than my religious friends, treat people with more respect and care a great deal about every person on the planet. It's about being human, not about believing in beings that may or may not exist."[22]

Data show large differences in fertility by religious affiliation and orthodoxy.[23] Regardless of how religion and culture influence you, it is important to recognize that you have some control over the reproductive decisions in your life. Should you have sex with this person? Should you use contraception? If pregnancy occurs, what do you do? Is having children an expected part of your marriage and family plans? Are you ready to be parents and provide a good (happy, stable, fun, fulfilling) life for your child(ren)? Is the timing right for you to have this child? These are some of the most weighty and important life decisions that you will ever make.

## Decisions about Having Children

The first fertility-related decision is whether or not to have children. For many people, this is not a question at all, because they were raised with strong expectations that—like marriage—they would have children. Parenthood is taken for granted by most of us. Most people think about having a child—or children—as an expected part of their life's experiences.

On the other hand, some adults are ambivalent about having children, and a minority of adults are clear that they DO NOT want to be parents. People decide not to have children for various reasons, like the blogger noted above who thought it would be socially irresponsible to bring children into this messed-up world. Others might be deterred by the daunting and permanent responsibilities of parenthood, and the costs (financial and otherwise) of providing for children. It is currently estimated that, based on the median family income, raising a child to the age of 18 in the United States costs about $235,000.[24]

Beyond the financial costs of children are the time commitments and responsibilities of parenthood. A mommy blogger wrote: "Our society expects so much more of parents…something as small as seat belt laws reflect society's changing expectations for parents. Fifty years ago parents weren't expected to keep their children safe from all potential dangers. Kids played in their neighborhoods unattended, walked to school by themselves, and rode in the car on their parents lap. Those may seem like little things but when parents have to watch their children every minute of every day and drive them to everything from school to a visit to a friend's house a block away, the burden gets to be overwhelming."[25]

For various reasons, about 20% of women in the United States reach the end of their childbearing years without having children.[26] Some of those women made deliberate *choices* not to have children (they successfully remained **childfree**), some were ambivalent (maybe yes, maybe no—okay,…no) and others were celibate, sterile, or otherwise *unable* to have children (they ended up **childless**, but often not intentionally).

Almost all people (couples) in the United States who *do want* to have children still have family planning decisions to make. An exception to this statement might be the small minority who believe that they should not "play God" by regulating their own fertility. Some traditional and religious people believe that the timing and number of children that they will have depends on fate, or what God decides for them. Some Christian groups who marry at young ages and practice no birth control achieve an average of about 11 births per woman, sometimes referred to as the level of "**natural fertility**."[27]

In recent years the "Duggars," an evangelical Christian family, have received considerable media attention because the husband and wife have had 19 children together (a 20th child was miscarried in 2011).[28] If you are a young person contemplating having children in the future, you have to think about the implications of having that many offspring to support.

Leaving fertility in the hands of God was common historically, especially before people had the understanding and technology to plan for or prevent conception. If the decision is not to have children, or to suspend or defer a decision, parenthood can be avoided by **abstinence** (not having sexual intercourse), by consistent and accurate **contraceptive use**, by **sterilization**, and by **abortion**.

At the present time in the United States, not attempting to control fertility seems inconceivable to most people, but leaving conception and birth up to God is considered their religious duty by others. Not using contraceptives is common among highly orthodox people of certain religious groups, and among others in the poorest economic circumstances.[29]

More than 100 years ago, Margaret Sanger led a movement to promote family planning.[30] The campaign to accept birth control gradually gained momentum, became allied with women's suffrage, and later merged with the Planned Parenthood Federation of the United States.[31] Today, Planned Parenthood is the largest organization providing family planning education and services in the United States and, through an international federation, around the world. The organization is devoted to the ideal that births can be planned so that every child is a wanted child.[32]

Among its many global health initiatives in recent years, the Gates Foundation sponsors a campaign to increase the availability of birth control around the world.[33] This Gates initiative points out that more than 1 billion people use birth control, mostly without hesitation, and "They do it because they want the power to plan their own lives, and to raise happy and healthy families when they are ready to do so. There is no controversy around this routine fact of everyday life."[34] The campaign to agree that there is "no controversy in contraceptives" includes a pledge that: "I believe that every girl and woman deserves the opportunity to determine her own future."[35]

## Conception and Contraception

Growing up, most young people probably assume that they will be able to have children when they want. The reality is that many pregnancies occur unexpectedly, and sometimes couples cannot become pregnant when they want. These realities are the reason that I stated earlier that people have *some* control over the reproductive events in their lives.

Fertility is much more complex than might first be imagined. "Most American families want two children. To achieve this, the average woman spends about five years pregnant, postpartum or trying to become pregnant, and three decades—more than three-quarters of her reproductive life—trying to avoid an unintended pregnancy."[36]

Some level of effort, consistency, and planning usually are required to prevent conception. "Two-thirds of U.S. women at risk for unintended pregnancy use contraception consistently and correctly throughout the course of any given year; these women account for only 5% of all unintended pregnancies. In contrast, the 19% of women at risk who use contraception inconsistently or incorrectly account for 43% of all unintended pregnancies."[37]

"About half (49%) of the 6.7 million pregnancies in the United States each year (3.2 million) are unintended. An *unintended* pregnancy is one that was either mistimed or unwanted. If a woman did not want to become pregnant at the time the pregnancy occurred, but did want to become pregnant at some point in the future, the pregnancy is considered **mistimed** (29% of pregnancies). If a woman did not want to become pregnant then or at any time in the future, the pregnancy is considered **unwanted** (19% of pregnancies). An *intended* pregnancy is one that was desired at the time it occurred, or sooner."[38]

Unintended pregnancy is most likely to happen when young couples don't use contraception at all, or because they were using contraception inappropriately or inconsistently. "Unintended pregnancy rates are highest among poor and low-income women, women aged 18–24, cohabiting women and minority women."[39]

For most people in the United States, decisions about whether and when to have children are made jointly between partners. Before reliable contraceptives became widely available, people tried to prevent conception in whatever ways they under-stood. Male **withdrawal** before ejaculation, and **condoms**—the oldest "barrier method"—were historically used to prevent sperm from being deposited inside the vagina where they could fertilize the egg. **Natural family planning** methods also were used, based on avoiding intercourse during the most fertile time in a woman's 28-day cycle (the midpoint between her periods, about the 14th day) when she is most likely to conceive.

**Birth control pills**, first introduced in 1970, revolutionized family planning. Although condoms remain the most common method of contraception among teen-agers in the United States (and among those who have sporadic sexual relations), "the pill" has become the contraceptive method used by many women who are married, or who are in long-term relationships.[40] There are many other contraceptive methods being used, especially in developing countries, like **intrauterine devices** (IUDs) and hormonal **implants** (Norplant). For most people in the United States, the major decisions about contraception are based on the method's effectiveness, cost, and ease or convenience of use.

It takes effective communication and ongoing effort for most sexually active couples to avoid conception during their fertile years. "Some groups—including higher-income women, white women, college graduates and married women—are comparatively successful at timing and spacing their pregnancies. For example, higher-income white women experience unintended pregnancy at one-third the national rate (17 vs. 52 per 1,000)."[41]

Most of us know couples who unexpectedly became pregnant at the end of their childbearing years (40–45 years of age for most women). Because of increasing rates of **sterilization** among both men and women, however, it is less common now to have a "surprise" baby in the later childbearing years after the couple thought they were finished having children. After people have had as many children as they want, sterilization (vasectomy for males, tubal ligation for females), has become common in advanced societies.[42] Because it is essentially 100% reliable, and does not require taking precautions with each act of intercourse, or daily pills, or monthly planning, those who think they have finished childbearing often seek to be surgically steril-ized if they are still at risk of becoming pregnant.

# Infertility

Among those who assume that they will be able to have children when they want, many couples are unsuccessful when they try to conceive. **Infertility** is defined as not conceiving during one year of having regular sexual intercourse without using contraception.[43] Infertility is more common than most people think, affecting about one in five couples in the United States. Infertility is becoming more common because couples now wait longer to have children, and infertility increases with age. About 60% of couples who are unsuccessful after trying to conceive for a year are eventually able to conceive, so they are "less fertile" rather than "**sterile**" (unable to have children).[44]

Sometimes the cause of infertility is present in the male, sometimes in the female, sometimes both, and occasionally the cause remains unknown. About 40% of the time, infertility is due to the male's low sperm count, or his sperm being defective. The most common causes of infertility among females are failure to ovulate normally (so no egg is present to be fertilized), or blockage of the fallopian tube(s) so fertilized eggs cannot pass into and attach to the uterus. About 15% of the time when couples are infertile, both partners have one or more of these problems.

Being the infertile "odd-one-out" can be disconcerting to a person who lives in a culture that places high value on having and raising children. Infertility can be especially painful for a woman whose identity has been shaped by years of expectations and training to become a mother. Imagine how it would feel not to be able to become pregnant in a culture where motherhood is the central woman's role, and especially when most of your friends are celebrating their good news as they get pregnant and become parents. Unknowing family members also might ask why you are waiting to have kids. Months and years of infertility could be painful as parental hopes and dreams remain unfulfilled.

**Infertility testing** takes time and it is not always conclusive. Male sperm count and motility analysis can be done quickly, but female fertility testing takes longer. Most female tests, or each new intervention to increase the chances of conception, require another monthly fertility cycle.

I grew up in a family of four children in a culture that highly values families, so I always expected to have children. My wife came from a larger family in the same area, with deep extended family ties, so having children was a core expectation for her too. When we got married and expected that we would become pregnant, we were disappointed. After trying to become pregnant for a long time, followed by years of fertility testing and interventions, my wife and I realized that we probably never would conceive. Some remaining options were experimental (not covered by insurance) and expensive at the time; we could have spent $10,000 for in vitro fertilization, and still had a low probability of conceiving. So, we decided that our parenthood dreams would best be fulfilled through adopting children.

**Adoption** is also more complicated than most people think. At first we hoped to adopt a healthy same-race infant, but that was not possible through the public agencies where we lived. We were about to move, so we tried to get on a private agency waiting list that would keep us in their queue after we moved to a different state. About two years after starting with the agency, we adopted our first child, a boy, and two years after that we adopted our second son. Given that we had been childless for six years before our first adoption, after adopting two sons I thought we were probably through having children. Then a friend called to tell us about a little girl who soon would need a home, so we arranged for her private adoption, and completed our family.

### The Martins

*Having children always was an expected part of Maria and Rob's expectations. Parenthood was so mutually important that it was one of the core values that attracted them to each other. They also wanted there to be time for each of their children to start out life as an individual, so they planned several years between Maria's pregnancies. Having children ages 16, 11, and 5, if they maintained the same spacing, now would be the time to have another child. But the thought of starting over with new parent responsibilities for an infant was not the least bit appealing. Maria and Rob enjoy each of their children, but they also realize the commitment of time, energy, and money required to raise them. Maria and Rob felt that their family was complete with three children, so they decided not to have any more.*

## Summary and Conclusions

Having children: If? When? How many? In what kind of relationship? These decisions used to be left to fate or God, but increasingly young people and couples make these decisions themselves, still influenced by both sacred and secular forces. Some people remain childfree or childless, and people who do have children are having fewer children than in the past. Why is this so? One blogger wrote: "We have fewer children because we can. It's not expected, it's not needed, and there are practical reasons for having fewer… Where it was once practical to have many children, now it is practical to have fewer."[45]

The increasing percentage of women having no children, the steep rise in nonmarital childbearing (above 40% of all births in the United States occur outside marriage), and the decline in family size (a two-child norm) is truly amazing. In just a few generations, having children has changed dramatically in the United States. These momentous major life decisions now are up to you.

References

1 Rossi, A. S. (1968). Transition to Parenthood. *Journal of Marriage and the Family*, 30, 26–39.

2 *World Population Control—U.S. Strategy and UN Policy Program.* (2012). Retrieved from http://fathersforlife.org/health/population_control.htm

3 Rosenberg, M. (2012). *China's One Child Policy.* Retrieved from http://geography.about.com/od/populationgeography/a/onechild.htm

4 Craig, J. (1994). *Replacement level fertility and future population growth.* Retrieved from http://www.ncbi.nlm.nih.gov/pubmed/7834459

5 Wong, D. (2004). Singapore unveils incentives to halt falling birth rate. *Financial Times.* Retrieved from http://www.ft.com/cms/s/0/2301654e-f6fc-11d8-a879-00000e2511c8.html#axzz2E1fqnfve

6 *Tax Credits & Tax Deductions for Parents with Children or Dependents.* (2012). Retrieved from http://www.efile.com/tax-deductions-credits-for-parents-with-children-dependents/

7 Genesis 1:28

8 Psalms 127:3

9 Proverbs 17:6

10 Natalism. (n.d.). In *Ask Define Online.* Retrieved from http://natalist.askdefine.com/

11 Hayford, S. R., Morgan, S. P. (2008). *Religiosity and Fertility in the United States: The Role of Fertility Intentions.* Retrieved from http://www.ncbi.nlm.nih.gov/pmc/articles/PMC2723861/

12 Hayford, S. R., Morgan, S. P. (2008). *Religiosity and Fertility in the United States: The Role of Fertility Intentions.* Retrieved from http://www.ncbi.nlm.nih.gov/pmc/articles/PMC2723861/

13 Heaton, T. B. (1986). How Does Religion Influence Fertility?: The Case of Mormons. *Journal for the Scientific Study of Religion*, 25(2), 248–258.

14 Mormon blogger 1

15 Mormon blogger 2

[16] Cody. (2008). Faith Equals Fertility. [Web log comment] Retrieved from http://moreintelligentlife.com/story/faith-equals-fertility

[17] Canham, M. (2012). *Census: Share of Utah's Mormon residents holds steady.* Retrieved from http://www.sltrib.com/sltrib/home3/53909710-200/population-lds-county-utah.html.csp

[18] Faith Equals Fertility. (2008). [Web log comment] Retrieved from http://moreintelligentlife.com/story/faith-equals-fertility

[19] Falsani, C. (2011). *A Quiver Full of Controversy.* Retrieved from http://www.huffingtonpost.com/cathleen-falsani/quiverfull_b_861283.html

[20] Psalms 127:3–5

[21] Hanoack. (2008). Faith Equals Fertility. [Web log comment] Retrieved from http://moreintelligentlife.com/story/faith-equals-fertility

[22] Faith Equals Fertility. (2008). [Web log comment] Retrieved from http://moreintelligentlife.com/story/faith-equals-fertility

[23] Hayford, S. R., & Morgan, S. (2008). Religiosity and Fertility in the United States: The Role of Fertility Intentions. *Social Forces*, 86(3), 1163–1188.

[24] Lino, Mark. (2012). *Expenditures on Children by Families, 2011.* U.S. Department of Agriculture, Center for Nutrition Policy and Promotion. Miscellaneous Publication No. 1528–2011.

[25] Gee, G. (2007). Mormon Family Shrinkage. [Web log comment] Retrieved from http://mormonmatters.org/2008/02/10/mormon-family-shrinkage/

[26] Walker, E. (2011). *Complete Without Kids: Seven Reasons Choosing to Be Childfree Is on the Rise.* Retrieved from http://www.psychologytoday.com/blog/complete-without-kids/201111/seven-reasons-choosing-be-childfree-is-the-rise

[27] Epsenshade, T. J. (1971). A New Method for Estimating the Level of Natural Fertility in Populations Practicing Birth Control. *Demography*, 8(4), 525–536.

[28] Dube, R. (2011). *Michelle Duggar, mom of 19, miscarries.* Retrieved from http://today.msnbc.msn.com/id/45603597/ns/today-today_health/t/michelle-duggar-mom-miscarries/#.UKZ_acXA98E

[29] *Facts on Unintended Pregnancy in the United States.* (2012). Retrieved from http://www.guttmacher.org/pubs/FB-Unintended-Pregnancy-US.html

[30] Chelser, E. (2000). *Margaret Sanger, Birth Control Pioneer.* Retrieved from http://www.prb.org/Articles/2000/MargaretSangerBirthControlPioneer.aspx

[31] Chelser, E. (2000). *Margaret Sanger, Birth Control Pioneer.* Retrieved from http://www.prb.org/Articles/2000/MargaretSangerBirthControlPioneer.aspx

32 Planned Parenthood. (n.d.). *Mission.* Retrieved from http://www. plannedparenthood.org/about-us/who-we-are/vision-4837. htm

33 Doughton, S. (2012). *Gates Foundation's birth-control initiative could fire up its critics.* Retrieved from http://seattletimes.com/html/localnews/2018631466_birthcontrol08m.html

34 Gates, M. (2012). *Why Contraception? Why Now?* Retrieved from http://www.unfoundation.org/blog/why-contraception-why-now.html

35 *There is No Controversy In Contraceptives.* (2012). Retrieved from http://www.no-controversy.com/

36 *Facts on Unintended Pregnancy in the United States.* (2012). Retrieved from http://www.guttmacher.org/pubs/FB-Unintended-Pregnancy-US.html

37 *Facts on Unintended Pregnancy in the United States.* (2012). Retrieved from http://www.guttmacher.org/pubs/FB-Unintended-Pregnancy-US.html

38 *Facts on Unintended Pregnancy in the United States.* (2012). Retrieved from http://www.guttmacher.org/pubs/FB-Unintended-Pregnancy-US.html

39 *Facts on Unintended Pregnancy in the United States.* (2012). Retrieved from http://www.guttmacher.org/pubs/FB-Unintended-Pregnancy-US.html

40 Jones, R. K. (2011). *Beyond Birth Control: The Overlooked Benefits of Oral Contraceptive Pills.* New York: Guttmacher Institute.

41 AGI In Brief, January 2012

42 Bartz, D. (2008). Sterilization in the United States. *Rev Obstet Gynecol,* 1(1): 23–32. Retrieved from http://www.ncbi.nlm.nih.gov/pmc/articles/PMC2492586/

43 Infertility. (n.d.). In The Mayo Clinic online. Retrieved from http://www.mayoclinic.com/health/infertility/DS00310

44 Merck & Co. (2009). *Merck manuals online medical library, home edition for patients and caregivers.* Infertility.

45 Martin, B. (2008). Mormon Family Shrinkage. [Web log comment] Retrieved from http://mormonmatters.org/2008/02/10/mormon-family-shrinkage/

# Chapter 10

# Work and Family Issues and Conflicts

# Work and Family Issues and Conflicts

What kind of job or career do you want? What will you need to do to prepare or qualify for it? How important is having a job that you really enjoy? How important is money to you? How much income is enough? What do you expect from your partner's work and income? Will your work life complement or be a hassle with marriage and parenthood? How will you achieve a satisfying—or at least an acceptable—balance between your work and family life?

Employment and careers, marriage and parenthood—these are among the most important dimensions of most people's lives. In this book, Chapters 1–5 focused mostly on work and finance-related topics. In Chapters 6–9, the focus was mostly on marriage and family-related issues. This chapter takes a deliberately more integrative approach, and discusses how work and family—two major domains of our lives—intersect, connect, and sometimes conflict with each other.

### The Martins

*The simultaneous challenges of providing childcare for young children and earning income were resolved by Rob and Maria through their decisions to have Maria be a stay-at-home mom, and have Rob be employed full time. This has worked out, with the children being well cared for, and the family having adequate financial support. But now that the children are older and don't require as much of her attention, Maria is thinking seriously about the years ahead of her as a working adult. She wonders about retooling for a job with more opportunities for advancement. Maria was employed before having children, but in a job that was not career-oriented. Her educational preparation and primary work experiences as a CNA reflected her choice of work in a field (nursing) that remains one of the most highly gender segregated. It has been 11 years since she stopped working—a long time to be out of the labor force. There will be some catching up to do, but she is looking forward to the challenge, with occasional trepidation.*

## Historical Context

Family members have always had to earn a living while meeting one another's needs as spouses and parents and children. Traditionally, being an adult male was most closely associated with employment (working for money) outside the home, and men tended to subordinate their family-related roles of husband and father. Conversely, women's work-related employment outside the home was secondary; women traditionally were mostly focused on wife-mother roles and relationships within the home, especially emphasizing childrearing.

My wife and I followed traditional gender roles in work and family life. She graduated from college before me, and was employed as a public school teacher and held other jobs when I was in graduate school. After our unexpected delay to begin parenting, when we had our first child she quit income-earning jobs to provide the large majority of childcare, and manage our kin keeping, our finances, and our household. Her full-time and time-consuming work at home complemented my full-time faculty career.

I had a traditional faculty research and teaching career and, except for classes and required meetings, my schedule was very flexible. University teaching faculty typically work nine months (like primary and secondary school teachers), and they often structure their office time to meet with students around the courses they teach, which might be Monday, Wednesday, and Friday, for example. At research universities, however, most tenure track faculty members also have research roles in addition to teaching, and their research projects are usually demanding every day and year round; that certainly was the case for me.[1]

My wife and I followed the common pattern of our generation in Utah, in which many mothers stopped their employment when children were young, but some mothers remained employed part time, and others went back to work full time after the children were in school, or after they had left home. Traditional work and family roles worked well for us, although different ways of balancing work and family also work well for others. Nontraditional work and family roles are becoming the new normal, as the economy and population changes.

## Major Demographic Changes

One recent analysis[2] pointed to three major demographic shifts in American society that have put increasing pressures on America's working families. These are: (1) the continuing high labor force participation of mothers, which highlights a need for alternative childcare; (2) high divorce rates, and high—and still rising— nonmarital birth rates, which intensifies time pressures for working single parents; and (3) the unprecedented increase in the elderly population, which poses challenges for working families who often help care for older relatives.

The authors summarized: "These three demographic changes, intertwined with the movement for gender equality and the imperative of women's work, have all but eclipsed the once traditional view of males as breadwinners and females as homemakers. Women still spend more time than men keeping house and tending children, but the division of responsibility both inside and outside the home is becoming more equal and seems likely to continue moving in that direction. Work-family tension promises to be a permanent feature of American family life, one that affects men as well as women."[3] These three major demographic trends form the structure of this chapter about work and family life.

## Employment of Mothers

Mothers have always worked—by the very definition of being a mother. But they were not always employed and paid for working to the extent that they are now. In the contemporary United States, young women are much more likely than their mothers and grandmothers to be part of the paid workforce. "Because women work to create a career, to maintain a middle-class lifestyle, or to avoid poverty, most mothers want to work or believe they must work."[4]

There has been a dramatic increase of mothers entering the labor market for paid work in recent decades. In 1975, 47% of mothers with children under 18 were employed, but by 2007 that proportion had risen to 71%.[5] Over two-thirds of mothers in their thirties with a young child at home are in the labor force.[6] Infants and young children cannot be left alone, so when families have young children and their mothers are employed, someone else needs to take care of them. Childcare might be provided by a spouse or partner, by an older sibling, by a grandparent or other relative, by non-relative home care, or by nonrelatives in group care.

One of the more unusual ways of adapting to a full-time working wife-mother is for the husband-father to become a **stay-at-home dad**, as mentioned in Chapter 4. I remember the first family I met who were like this; she was a university faculty member, and his major responsibility was taking care of their children. He also dabbled with running a small antique store on the side. Decades ago when I met them, this couple had decided to divide their roles in nontraditional ways, with the mom earning most of the money for their family, and the dad being the primary caregiver for their children. It worked for them.

The model involving a full-time working mom and an at-home dad is becoming more common. The Boston College Center for Work & Family reports that stay-at-home dads now often make a conscious choice to be home with their children, not just as a result of an unexpected job layoff.[7] When this choice is made, it appears that having dad take care of the home and children could benefit their families, their wives' careers, and their own personal fulfillment. The preceding sentence seems to be much like what once was said about their supportive stay-at-home wives by older generations of career men.

Not surprisingly, having a stay-at-home husband-father is reported to greatly enable and facilitate the career of a working wife or partner. It reminds me of the saying that I used to hear from hard-working and competitive female colleagues—that they needed a wife. Having an at-home husband enables some contemporary women to pursue their own careers in a much more assertive fashion, with fewer conflicts and limitations of the kind that were commonly faced by working mothers in the past.[8]

## High Divorce Rates and Nonmarital Childbearing

When spouses separate and their marriage splits up, divorce almost always leads to two households. Not only does it cost money to get divorced (about $14,000 on average)[9], ex-spouses usually both have to work to support themselves (and their children when they are present) after they form separate households. If divorcing spouses have children the process is complicated, because the best interests of the child(ren) must be considered in planning custody and childcare arrangements. Whether custody is solely with one spouse, shared, or joint custody with both parents, childcare often is an issue because it is hard for single parents to work and provide constant care for their child(ren), without the support of others.

In earlier generations there were very strong stigmas against unmarried women having children. In your grandparents' or great grandparents' generation, births to unmarried women were termed "**illegitimate**," and before that children born to single women were referred to by the strongly negative term "bastards."[10] This level of derogatory social stigma is difficult to comprehend in modern times.

Consistent with the negative stigma that was so pervasive, it was rare for women to have children if they were not married. To avoid being shamed by negative reactions, some unmarried pregnant women moved away to hide their situation, and after giving birth they relinquished their newborn babies for adoption. Many women sought abortions if they were pregnant but not married. Because having a child outside of marriage was made to be very undesirable, it occurred infrequently.

One of the most striking trends affecting American families in recent decades is the rapid increase in **nonmarital childbearing** (formerly "illegitimacy"). Less than 5 percent of all births were to unmarried women in earlier decades, and remained at that low level throughout the 1960s. By 1970, about one birth in ten was to an unmarried woman, and by the early 1980s, 20% of all births were nonmarital. Rates of nonmarital childbirth continued to increase through the 1990s, rising more sharply after about 2003; currently over 40% of all births are to unmarried women.[11]

Whether women with dependent children become single through divorce or through giving birth without a partner, single mothers share the dilemma of how to care for children while earning a living. Single parents, especially single mothers, are likely to turn first to relatives for help with childcare.[12] Relative care most often involves grandparents, adult siblings, or other more distant kin. Sometimes friends help provide care for children, especially when there are no family members living nearby.

## Growing Elderly Population Spurs the Need for Elder Care

The older population—persons 65+ years of age—numbered about 40 million in 2010, and they represented 13% of the U.S. population, about one in every eight Americans. By 2030, there will be about 72 million older persons, more than twice their number in 2000.[13]

The proportion of older people in the U.S. population has been gradually increasing as a consequence of declining birth rates and increased longevity. Persons over 65 constituted less than 10 percent of the population in the middle of the 1900s, and just over 12% of the population in the year 2000. Their proportion will increase more rapidly as the Baby Boom generation ages, and are expected to be 19% of the population by 2030.[14]

The pertinent issue is that work and family pressures and conflicts often increase when middle generation adult children, in the prime of their working years, need to provide more help for their aging parents. Childcare and elder care both take time. Family obligations to care for elderly parents are sometimes not easily reconciled with the demands of the workplace, and sometimes elder care requires unexpected or urgent actions.

When my parents were in their 70s, they moved away from their adult children to live along the Oregon Coast. My siblings and I, living in Utah, liked to visit our parents in Oregon, but we also were concerned about what we would do when our parents' health declined. About a decade later, after mom had a stroke, and both of them were in somewhat poorer health, our parents moved to southern Utah to be closer to family. Having our parents, then in their 80s, less than a six-hour drive away made it more feasible for us "kids" (ages 55 to 65) to help care for them.

It is difficult to describe the number and types of things with which aging parents usually need help. The time will come when aging parents are no longer able to drive themselves, or make their way alone to do activities of daily living. When a parent falls, develops dementia, or has any number of chronic health conditions, they need someone to help them. Usually that help comes from children in their 50s and 60s, who are often at the height of their own careers. Frequently the middle-aged adult children who try to help their parents are also launching their own young adults. Hence the classic term, the "**Sandwich Generation**," in which the middle generation is pulled between the needs of their young adult children and their aging parents (and maybe feeling like they are being bitten into, or chewed on!).

# Work and Family Stresses and Conflicts

The major demographic changes noted above suggest that childcare and elder care, traditionally provided by families, often come into conflict with work. As more and more women are employed and remain employed after having children, or become single parents through nonmarital childbearing or divorce, some reasons for work-family conflict have become clearer.

Joan Williams wrote that "…the key problem for women…is that workplaces still are designed around an ideal worker who starts to work in early adulthood and works, full time and full force, for forty years without a break, taking no time off for childbearing, childrearing or anything else. The result is a clash of social ideals. The ideal worker norm clashes with the norm of parental care."[15] Stated more succinctly, the "**ideal worker**" is defined as always available for work, and the "**good mother**" is defined as always available to her children.

For both women and men, work-family conflicts are often encountered when their job demands conflict with, or deny them, the flexibility needed to care for children, or for family members with special needs at any age, including aged parents.

Williams believes that the solution is to reshape workplaces around the values needed for children and families. In a better reshaped workplace, schedules would be more **flexible** so that parents can be with children or their aging parents as needed, and career breaks would not spell career doom.[16]

What are some of the other most likely stresses and conflicts between work and family life? Anne-Marie Slaughter's article "Why Women Still Can't Have It All" in *The Atlantic* addresses why it's difficult for women to hold high positions in the workplace, given the delicate balance between work and family.[17] One specific work and family conflict is the "**face time**" needed, or expected, in many jobs. Slaughter questions the effectiveness of required office hours, and suggests that changing the default rules of "**presentism**" in the office would help workers to more successfully combine careers and families. In some cases, a solution could allow people to work when and where they need to, so long as the work gets done (well).

But it is a challenge to reduce face time in some jobs. For example, in retail businesses, employees must be there to work directly with the public, manufacturing requires hands-on work with equipment and products, and financial services and health care are based on meetings with clients and patients. Likewise, management in any of these occupations demands the physical presence of most managers and support staff. A nine-month teaching contract, or the flexibility of faculty work schedules, is not common throughout business and industry.

To some extent, changes are taking place as workplaces become less rigid. People increasingly are allowed **flexibility** by employers to alter their work schedules to make them more compatible with childcare needs, such as getting the kids off to school or coming to work very early so that a parent can be there when children arrive home after school. Innovations provided by **flexible work schedules** and **telecommuting** are making a positive difference for families. When seeking these types of accommodations, where they have not been in place before, it is suggested that a worker proposing an alternative work schedule and/or place should emphasize "HOW I will get the work done, vs. WHY I need to work this way."[18] This results-oriented approach to allowing greater flexibility makes employers more willing to let employees adjust their work styles, as long as they still get the job done.

One observer noted that young women sometimes tend to "**lean back**" even before they have children because they think that—after they do have children—they won't be able (or want) to be constantly available to their employers.[19] She also stated, "If you won't be constantly available it doesn't mean you're worthless. You may not even be *worth less*: After all, what should matter is whether you can do high-quality work, not whether you can do it constantly."[20] Further, Williams says, "It just doesn't make sense to lean back before you have children, because the best advice is to work really, really hard before you have children so that you have the skills—and the bargaining power—to continue your career on your own terms after you have children."[21]

In my university vice president position someone was needed to market (to publicize and tell the story about) the good things that were happening with faculty and student research. There had been no marketing position before, and there was little budget for it, but we searched through university channels to find the most promising candidate for the job. We hired a lower division undergraduate with great recommendations and lots of potential. She worked half time for us while completing her degree, and her creativity and quality of work were outstanding. When she graduated we enthusiastically offered her a full-time position. She continued to do excellent work, and soon earned a reputation as one of the most talented marketing people at the university. After a few years she became pregnant, so we talked about future scenarios. She loved her work and didn't want to quit, and we didn't want to lose her. But she would soon have a newborn baby to take care of, and her role as a mother was also very important to her. She suggested a short-term maternity leave, after which she would work 75% time, mostly from home and at night, instead of working in the office. She and I both took a risk to change her working arrangements. She continued to produce the most creative marketing at the university, and giving her the flexibility she needed to balance her work and family roles was well worth it to everyone.

Speaking of the "**mommy wars**," Slaughter advised women to stop judging each other. "Ideal worker women often preach to younger women who want to take longer leaves, career breaks and work part time: 'You just don't understand what it means to succeed in this career.' And the younger women snap back: "We don't want your pathetic lives. You just turned into men."[22] Williams wrote that mommy wars can be so bitter because both groups' identities are at stake. On the one hand, ideal-worker women need to prove that their children are fine although they weren't always there with them. On the other hand, ideal-mother women who settled for a lesser career (or no career), need to prove that their compromise was necessary or worth it, for the good of their families.[23]

In a recent blog about women's issues, it was noted that "We often think of a career path as being a ladder: start at the bottom, and work your way to the top. This complicates matters for women who want to have children. A woman can either delay her start up the ladder, or jump off somewhere during the climb. Instead, we should think of a career path as irregular stair steps, with periodic plateaus (and even dips) when they turn down promotions to remain in a job that works for their family situation…"[24] This is exactly what happened with our university marketing expert, who cut back on her "face time" and her time at work after she had a baby. By allowing employees to focus their efforts on attaining results—as opposed to spending time in the office—even the stair-step career path can be altered. It may not be necessary to step off the path at all if employers can reduce face time requirements or expectations.

Some workplaces are becoming more progressive and more productive by moving toward a **Results-Only Work Environment (ROWE),** in which the culture is reshaped to manage the work, not the people. "ROWE makes it easier to manage all areas of my life, including being a mother, wife and career-oriented person. I feel like I am better at all these roles I play since I can manage them all as I need to."[25]

The need to change the structure of work and careers has been receiving significant national attention. "Two prominent, influential women are talking—a lot and influentially—to two different audiences about the same problem. Young women, listen to Sheryl Sandberg. Corporations, listen to Anne-Marie Slaughter. And let's bring men into the conversation."[26]

The increasing involvement of fathers with their children was noted earlier in this chapter in connection with the discussion about stay-at-home dads. Men apparently are feeling that they have more freedom to alter the ideal-worker norm. This is seen in the Boston University center's two earlier reports—*The New Dad: Exploring Fatherhood within a Career Context* and *The New Dad: Caring, Committed and Conflicted*; the latter study finds that the roles of men and women in relation to the workforce continue to change.[27] As gender roles change, fathers are increasingly likely to experience more active caregiving for children. As fathers become more involved with caregiving, employers will need to adapt their policies and actions regarding who needs support to provide family care—it is not only a women's issue anymore.

It is remarkable to see the extent to which contemporary young fathers are engaged in childcare, compared with prior generations. Baby changing stations are provided in men's restrooms, and dads are expected to be there at back-to-school night. More parenting and childcare is still provided by mothers than fathers, but among young couples, especially among well-educated dual career couples, the lopsided imbalance has shifted substantially.

### The Martins

> Rob's work has provided income for their family, but with little flexibility to be with the kids as much as they would have liked. He can see that there is potential for him to have greater career advancement and higher pay if he is willing to travel more and take on more responsibility. But both Maria and Rob are hoping that he will be able to spend less time at work in the coming years, and spend more time with the kids while Maria is restarting her work career.

> Meanwhile, Maria and Rob's parents are still living and in relatively good health. But after another decade or so, chances are that the inevitable process of their parents' aging will require Rob and Maria to make some decisions about how they will be involved in their parents' elder care. About a decade from now, Maria and Rob will also be launching their own children as young adults, into college, careers, marriage, and starting families of their own. These changing and dynamic situations are what balancing work and family life is all about.

## Summary and Conclusions

In earlier generations men tended to be employed and women tended to be family-centered. The old fashioned terminology was that men were "**breadwinners**" and women were "**homemakers**." But the relationships between families and employment—work for pay—have changed dramatically in recent decades, mostly as a result of the ways that marriages and families have been changing.

Three large scale demographic changes with major work-family implications are underway. First, women in unprecedented numbers are preparing for careers and remaining employed after having children. Secondly, there are major needs for childcare if mothers are single because of nonmarital childbearing, or if they become single mothers through divorce. Finally, the rising older age population in the United States is increasing the need for family members to provide elder care in the later years of life.

These changes collide with traditional workplace expectations, including being always present on the job (face time). In light of the obvious tensions between work and family needs, there have been increasing signs of flexibility and other changes in the workplace. Some of these accommodations include flex time, telecommuting, and Results-Only Work Environments (ROWE). Fathers also have become more involved with family needs than in the past, especially with childcare, but not to the extent that mothers have entered and remained in the workforce.

---

### References

[1] Miller, B. C. (2002). Mountains, Mormonism, marriage and family: Life and career reflections. In S.K. Steinmetz and G.W. Peterson (eds). *Pioneering Paths in the Study of Families*. NY: Haworth Press.

[2] Haskins, R., Waldfogel, J., McLanahan, S. (2011). *Work-Family Conflict: Look to Employers and Communities for Solutions.* http://futureofchildren.org/futureofchildren/publications/docs/21_02_PolicyBrief.pdf

[3] Haskins, R., Waldfogel, J., McLanahan, S. (2011). *Work-Family Conflict: Look to Employers and Communities for Solutions*, p. 1–2. http://futureofchildren.org/futureofchildren/publications/docs/21_02_PolicyBrief.pdf

[4] Haskins, R., Waldfogel, J., McLanahan, S. (2011). *Work-Family Conflict: Look to Employers and Communities for Solutions*, p. 1. http://futureofchildren.org/futureofchildren/publications/docs/21_02_PolicyBrief.pdf

[5] Galinsky, E., Aumann, K., & Bond, J. T. (2008). *2008 National Study of the Changing Workforce: Times are changing—Gender and generation at work and at home.* New York, NY: Families and Work Institute.

[6] Lavery, D. (2012). More mothers of young children in U.S. workforce. Population Reference Bureau. Retrieved from http://www.prb.org/Articles/2012/us-working-mothers-with-children.aspx.

[7] Harrington, B., Deusen, F. V., Mazar, I. (2012). *The New Dad: Right at Home.* Retrieved from http://www.bc.edu/content/dam/files/centers/cwf/pdf/The%20New%20Dad%20Rightf%20at%20Home%20BCCWF%202012.pdf

[8] Harrington, B., Deusen, F. V., Mazar, I. (2012). *The New Dad: Right at Home.* Retrieved from http://www.bc.edu/content/dam/files/centers/cwf/pdf/The%20New%20Dad%20Rightf%20at%20Home%20BCCWF%202012.pdf

[9] Olson, D. H., DeFrain, J., Skogrand, L. (2011). *Marriages and Families: Intimacy, Diversity, and Strengths* (7th ed.). New York: McGraw-Hill, 227–228.

[10] Macfarlane, A. (2002). *Illegitimacy and illegitimates in English history*. Retrieved from http://alanmacfarlane.com/TEXTS/bastardy.pdf

[11] Ventura, S. J. (2009). *Changing Patterns of Nonmarital Childbearing in the United States*. NCHS data brief, no. 18. Hyattsville, MD: National Center for Health Statistics.

[12] Boushey, H. (2003). "Who Cares? Child Care Choices of Working Mothers." Data Brief 1. Washington, DC: Center for Economic and Policy Research.

[13] United States Department of Health & Human Services. (2012). *Administration of Aging* [Older Populations by Age Group: 1900 to 2050 with Chart of the 65+ Population]. Retrieved from http://www.aoa.gov/aoaroot/aging_statistics/future_growth/future_growth.aspx

[14] United States Department of Health & Human Services. (2012). *Administration of Aging* [Older Populations by Age Group: 1900 to 2050 with Chart of the 65+ Population]. Retrieved from http://www.aoa.gov/aoaroot/aging_statistics/future_growth/future_growth.aspx

[15] Williams, J. C. (2012). *Slaughter Versus Sandberg: Both Right*. Retrieved from http://www.psychologytoday.com/blog/family-friendly/201206/slaughter-versus-sandberg-both-right

[16] Williams, J. C. (2012). *Slaughter Versus Sandberg: Both Right*. Retrieved from http://www.psychologytoday.com/blog/family-friendly/201206/slaughter-versus-sandberg-both-right

[17] Slaughter, A. (2012). Why Women Still Can't Have It All. *Atlantic Monthly* (10727825), 310(1), 84–102.

[18] Lepore, M. (2011). *Is Asking For Work Flexibility Career Suicide?* Retrieved from http://www.thegrindstone.com/2011/11/02/career-management/flexible-work-life-balance-success-389/

[19] Williams, J. C. (2012). *Slaughter Versus Sandberg: Both Right*. Retrieved from http://www.psychologytoday.com/blog/family-friendly/201206/slaughter-versus-sandberg-both-right

[20] Williams, J. C. (2012). *Slaughter Versus Sandberg: Both Right*. Retrieved from http://www.psychologytoday.com/blog/family-friendly/201206/slaughter-versus-sandberg-both-right

21 Williams, J. C. (2012). *Slaughter Versus Sandberg: Both Right*. Retrieved from http://www.psychologytoday.com/blog/family-friendly/201206/slaughter-versus-sandberg-both-right

22 Williams, J. C. (2012). *Slaughter Versus Sandberg: Both Right*. Retrieved from http://www.psychologytoday.com/blog/family-friendly/201206/slaughter-versus-sandberg-both-right

23 Williams, J. C. (2012). *Slaughter Versus Sandberg: Both Right*. Retrieved from http://www.psychologytoday.com/blog/family-friendly/201206/slaughter-versus-sandberg-both-right

24 Ressler, C., & Thompson, J. (2012). Our Answer to "Why Women Still Can't Have It All." Retrieved from http://www.gorowe.com/blog/2012/06/29/work-culture/our-answer-to-why-women-still-can-t-have-it-all/

25 Ressler, C., & Thompson, J. (2012). Our Answer to "Why Women Still Can't Have It All." Retrieved from http://www.gorowe.com/blog/2012/06/29/work-culture/our-answer-to-why-women-still-can-t-have-it-all/

26 Williams, J. C. (2012). *Slaughter Versus Sandberg: Both Right*. Retrieved from http://www.psychologytoday.com/blog/family-friendly/201206/slaughter-versus-sandberg-both-right

27 Harrington, B., Deusen, F. V., Ladge, J. (2010). *The New Dad: Exploring Fatherhood Within a Career Context*. Retrieved from http://www.bc.edu/content/dam/files/centers/cwf/pdf/BCCWF_Fatherhood_Study_The_New_Dad1.pdf

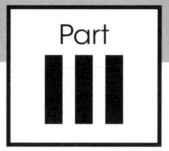

# Part III

# Balancing Work, Family, and Parenting Responsibilities

# Introduction

Welcome to Part III of the book. My name is Kaelin Olsen, and I'm excited to introduce you to important parenting and child-guidance concepts. I have four children. At the time of this writing they are all young, and that presents me with some unique and interesting views on balancing work and family, such as trying to figure out maternity leave, as well as issues when my children are sick or attending half-day education programs. I teach child-development and parenting classes at Utah State University, and I am associated with the Child Development Laboratory at the University. While my personal life has led me into the area of balancing work and family, I have been intrigued as I have watched hundreds of families associated with our laboratory program work towards achieving a balance between work and family responsibilities.

A big part of helping children succeed is recognizing that childhood is a different state than adulthood. Children need time to explore and process information so they can understand their environment. They learn by moving and doing rather than by sitting and listening. Children also need adults to help them navigate the trails of life. Respecting and protecting those differences can help parents achieve a level of balance between work and family responsibilities. When you recognize your children's need to spend time with you in both playful and teaching moments, you also find joy in your parenting journey. Taking time to balance work and play, not only for children, but also for you, can help as you work to maintain the state of childhood.

In Part III of the book, we will explore skills and knowledge that can help parents understand their child(ren) better. As our understanding of child development increases, so does the ease in which parents can make thoughtful and beneficial decisions for their children. Parents that have a higher level of self-understanding tend to feel more confidence in the decisions they make for their families.

*Kaelin Olsen*

# Chapter 11

# The Speed of Slow— Setting a Parenting Pace

# The Speed of Slow—Setting a Parenting Pace

Parenting is an amazing journey. Raising children can be a most exhilarating experience and often frustrating, as well. Parents can feel that one minute they really understand their children and have the ability to take care of them, and the next minute feel like they don't recognize anything about their children or their behavior. The demands can seem never-ending, and then one hug from little arms can make any irritation melt away.

This chapter will introduce, define, and explain how families are raising children within a social context, and how childrearing is driven by a personal value system. The idea of being busy and being hurried will be addressed, and finding a family pace. Relationships and attachments that connect us to each other can help us find the joy in a busy life. The topics will create a framework, or lens, for exploring practical parenting approaches.

### The Martins (Maria)

*I have always loved being a mom. There are moments I struggle, but I love being with my children and watching them grow. I have learned over the years that when I am out and about in the community, I really like to watch other parents. I learn so much by seeing what other parents do. I have also picked several families in my neighborhood that I watch because I like their family interactions and how their children behave. I have noticed over the years that what works for other parents, doesn't always work for me, but I love looking for new ideas. Rob teases me about this, but I think it helps me become a better mom.*

## Parenting in a Social Context

Parenting is a dynamic role that changes with the needs of the child or the adult in the parent–child relationship. Parenting also requires a complex skill set. Some of the skills parents utilize include empathy, communication, teaching, sharing, organizing, and planning. Parents are required to determine what roles they play and what skills are important to put into practice. Therefore, parents must define which parenting behaviors are acceptable, and which are not. For example, parents might ask themselves if they will spank their children. Do they buy a treat for good behavior in the grocery store? Most parents make these role decisions based upon the model they have seen used by their own parents.

Throughout my childhood my mother made us pick up and put away 21 personal items around the house every night before bed. (Amazingly, she called this 21 pick-up!) It was important to my mother that my siblings and I take responsibility for the toys and items we had used during the day and not put away. I dreaded this nightly call to arms. I can't tell you how many nights I said (under my breath of course!) that I would never make my children play 21 pick-up. Now I have to smile when I tell my children that it's time for 21 pick-up, and I hear my daughter say, "When I'm a mom, my children will never have to do this!" It's easy to fall back on practices that are familiar to parents as they raise their children. If parents wish to make changes in parenting practices, they must thoughtfully consider their behaviors.

Historically, parenting has been viewed as a "sacred cow," meaning that extended family members and individuals in society didn't intervene in a parenting relationship.[1] It was assumed that adults learned how to parent within the family system, and that families knew what was best for their children. This assumption meant that research within the family structure wasn't valued and there was nothing new to learn about families because everyone had all the answers. Newer, more contemporary views on the family rely on education and research to improve family functioning. Individuality is another strong contemporary component in today's family. Individuality is important for both parents and their children.

Neighborhoods, friends and associates, places of employment, economic factors, historical timing, and personal experiences all influence how people make decisions about parenting. Collective efficacy defines how a neighborhood functions. In a neighborhood with collective efficacy, the neighbors know each other and interact.[2] They rely on each other for help, support, and even fun. Neighbors look after each other and provide the assistance they can. In such neighborhoods, there are programs and community assistance that families can use in times of crisis or need. Children and families in these neighborhoods also have a sense of belonging and understanding about how they can work with each other. In neighborhoods where collective efficacy is lacking, families may feel more lonely and isolated, and without a support group in times of trouble and need. Families may feel like they must rely on themselves to solve problems, or may simply give up because they feel overwhelmed.

The idea of collective efficacy shows how a family or individuals in a family are influenced by society. A cohort is a group of individuals that grows up within the same time frame. A cohort has generally experienced the same events that may influence value judgments. For example, my cohort experienced high school in the 1980s. We can define ourselves by neon-colored clothing and hair styled in "high" fashion. My cohort could probably sing you a song by Huey Lewis and the News, but might not recognize something by Coldplay. We view the world through a cohort-driven lens. Can you think of an experience that ties you to your cohort?

## Parenting with a Personal Value System

Parents bring their own personal history and knowledge of life and child development into the parental relationship. They must seek to balance their own life's experiences with their partner's. When my husband and I were first married and discussing (we should've done this before we were married!) what was important for our future children, we realized we didn't hold the same beliefs about after-school activities and involvement. We spent a lot of time talking about our experiences from childhood in comparison to our hopes for our future children. We learned through our communication that we wanted to have a similar approach to discipline. Our conversations about our children help us maintain consistency. We've realized that it's crucial for us to adjust discipline according to each child's needs and make any adjustments for each child's personality fit and daily needs.

Keeping all of this in mind can be overwhelming. Sometimes it's hard to be flexible and to adapt to emotions, personalities, and situations that can occur in families. Personal biases are also going to affect what parents consider important. Some are going to emphasize their own personal values as they teach their children. It's what they know and understand. For example, if parents want their children to excel in school, homework completion is going to be important. If they want their children to play a musical instrument, then lessons and practicing will follow. If they want a clean home, then their children will have jobs or chores to complete. Values influence the relationship between parents and children.

### The Martins

*Maria is involved with many different community programs. Often, she has to take Luke with her to meetings because kindergarten isn't a full day of school. Maria feels better when Luke behaves well, and she becomes very anxious if Luke misbehaves or interrupts the flow of her work. One day, when Maria was meeting with Abbie's school principal, Mrs. Larsen, Luke got out of hand. Luke starred crawling under the principal's desk. Maria was embarrassed and became mad at him. She stopped talking to Mrs. Larsen, got down on the floor to pick up Luke, and told him he needed to change his behavior. Luke didn't understand what Maria meant. When she sat him in the chair, he quickly slid off the chair and started to explore under the desk again. Exasperated, Maria again pulled him off the floor and told him to change his behavior. Mrs. Larsen was uncomfortable with the interaction, and wanted to help. She handed Luke a piece of paper and told him she needed to talk with his mommy for five more minutes. She then told him to fold the*

*best paper airplane he could, and when their work was done, they would
take the airplane to the playground and fly it. Luke excitedly worked with the
paper until it was time to go outside to fly it.*

Maria felt that Luke didn't listen to her because she lacked authority. Her desire to
get him to listen to her and obey became increasingly stronger. It's a common desire
for parents to want their children to behave well. Maria wished for Luke to behave
and wait as she completed her work. What Maria lacked in the above situation was
the ability to translate her value into actualized behavior. Mrs. Larsen was able to
work with Luke by providing him with knowledge about the situation, what was
acceptable behavior while he waited, a reference to how long he would have to wait,
and the next activity they would do together. This may seem so simple, but many
parents are easily wrapped up in what has to be accomplished that they don't take
the time to help children understand what is going on around them.

Working to make our verbal (explicit) and nonverbal (implicit) messages convey
the same thing can help our children succeed. For example, slowing down, taking
a few minutes to help children understand what is going on, and then letting them
know what to expect empowers them and helps them feel important. When children
experience these feelings, they are more likely to work with their parents. Regardless
of how parents and children work together, parental values are conveyed. Maria
might value her involvement in the community, or the importance of education,
or even how to act when talking with other adults; however, the message that was
sent to young Luke was different. The actual message looked more like this: "Adults
have more important things to do than spend time with children"; "I can't help
you"; or, in an extreme case, "I don't love you." As people make conscious decisions to parent and focus on the needs of our children, values can be communicated
in more appropriate ways. Children can be sensitive to the emotional content in
what parents say. They get the messages that are generally implied, and if parents
are not careful and thoughtful about what they say and how they say it, they may
send children the wrong message.

## Always Busy, Always Hurried

Because people are all so busy, daily responsibilities sometimes seem to get in the
way of parenting. Often, it's easy for parents to take the perspective that after this
project, or after that class, or when the children are in school, there will be more time
to focus on what the children need or how to improve parenting skills. Some parents
learn quickly that life happens in the midst of this chaos. Others may struggle with
this balancing act for years. The following vignette illustrates how many parents
may feel overwhelmed by their responsibilities.

### The Martins (Maria)

*I remember when I was working that things seemed to get out of hand as we
tried to get out the door in the morning. My day started at 5:30 a.m. I would
quickly shower and get ready for work. Then the race would really begin!
By 6:00 I would multitask as I sorted laundry, checked overnight emails, and*

*started breakfast for the family. At 6:45 I would make sure that Matt and Abbie were up and getting ready for school. While I would move the laundry to the dryer I would remind Abbie to practice the piano and have Matt feed the dog. I would double-check backpacks for the day while Rob was making lunches for everyone and unloading the dishwasher that ran through its cycle the night before. We would all sit down to eat breakfast at 7:45 and try to take a few minutes for conversation and synchronizing schedules. I would give out last minute reminders about after-school activities and we would figure out the logistics of comings and goings. At 8:00 I would hurry and fold the load of laundry and pull something out of the freezer to thaw for dinner. At 8:20 we would run out the door to make it to school and work on time. When I would get to work at 9:00, it sometimes felt like the first time I could take a break for the morning.*

## The Pace of Life

It may seem that Maria and Rob were making life harder than it needed to be, and for some parents this scenario just wouldn't work for them. I think people can relate to the need to keep moving and doing and how, despite giving their best effort, still feel like they are 10 minutes behind on everything throughout the day. This "hurry, do this, hurry, do that" attitude definitely affects the stress level of the household in the morning (or any other time of the day!). The question becomes how to address the problem (stress, need to get things done) without adding more hours to the day. This may seem overwhelming to some people. Maybe that's how every day feels to them. People experience different responsibilities, and different reactions to those responsibilities. The key to balancing work and family successfully is to explore the pace of family life and how to best meet our needs and the needs of children.

Why is it that families feel stretched or struggle to find a balance between their work and family responsibilities? Recent research shows that work hours have increased 10 hours per week since 1977.[3] Some employees also report that they struggle with the boundaries of the office moving into their homes because they are electronically (cell phones, e-mail, and Blackberries) available 24 hours a day.[4] Interestingly, time at work is not the only factor affecting families. Cultural shifts have increased time devotion to parenting practice as well. There is an expectation that parents spend time with their children and be more purposefully involved in childrearing.[5] Time spent at work and with children has decreased the amount of time that most adults have for themselves or their own hobbies.[6] The resulting effect of time demands, physical and emotional exhaustion, and lack of personal time is role overload.[7]

I have to admit that there are many times that I, too, feel overwhelmed and experience role overload. I have a hard time saying no to things. Taking a healthy approach to what can be done and how much can be done is crucial (and hard) for me. These are decisions that are important to every member of the family. Therefore, parents need to communicate about what they can do, and what children can contribute by easing the workload around the house. When time restraints occur, children notice the example set by parents about what can be reasonably accomplished. As families work and communicate together, they can find the pace that is right for them.

This pace families set may be used to describe the personality of the family. For example, my family likes to work in the morning and play in the afternoons. This concept is interwoven through our family fabric and creates our family personality. As a result, we make lists for shopping, clean up before bed, and, in general, eat our vegetables before sweets. Our personality and pace also defines the flow of energy throughout the day. I know, for example, that my pace is faster and more efficient in the morning and slows down throughout the day. Defining the pace and flow of energy can help families recognize time for work and time for play in daily schedules. This balance is important for families to establish healthy relationships.

## The Speed of Slow

A typical morning in the Martin household is rushed and a little chaotic. There are some positive and negative things that occur within their daily routine, but it seems that the Martins are experiencing role overload. On the positive side, the housework is being maintained; the parents are working together to accomplish the morning routine; there is a little time for connection at breakfast; and there is time taken to make sure all the family members have what they need for the day. Some of the negative aspects might include Maria having to awake so early, both Maria and Rob taking a lot of the children's personal responsibility on themselves by checking backpacks, preparing lunches, etc., leaving little time for having simple conversations with each other, and making only quick connections.

Taking time for a deep breath can eliminate a lot of frustration and feelings of being frazzled. Deliberately thinking about the things that need to be accomplished and developing a plan, and consciously deciding not to rush, can prevent the frustration and stress from creeping in and taking over a situation. I have found that if I feel a little frazzled, I generally am getting caught up in trying to get things done. During these moments, if I can take a deep breath and look at the big picture I can generally find a better approach. Let me share with you a personal example of what I mean. One morning my son was performing in a city 80 miles away. My husband woke early to take my son to the bus. I thought it would be nice to take my other children to the performance, and then we could spend the rest of the day together at the zoo. This required an early morning start, and I had a lot to do to get out the door. I needed a diaper bag, packed with a few more essentials than usual for the baby, things to entertain my girls on the road, snacks and water for the day, and directions printed off the Internet. I know this doesn't seem like a lot to get done, but the little extra was just enough to put me over the top.

I awoke a little bit early to get everything together, thinking I was fine; however, as the morning progressed I realized that we were running late. I found myself getting more and more frustrated and couldn't figure out why things that were usually done, or didn't take so long to do were not getting accomplished. I could feel my frustration rising. Soon, the baby was crying, the girls were running around, and I was getting little accomplished. I had to pause for a minute and take a deep breath because I didn't want to start the day feeling this way, and I didn't want to cause my children to feel frustration on this "fun" day.

What I learned that day was important. I hadn't been teaching all my children the skills to help them succeed. My oldest son is five years older than the rest of my children. I have taught him well how to help me and his siblings get ready in the morning. His efficiency masked the fact that I hadn't taught his younger siblings the same skills. We were a little later getting out the door that day, but I was able to take the time to teach some self-help skills, like gathering materials and packing a bag to my younger children. Later, I also took time to talk with my son and convey how much I appreciated his help, and that it was also important that everyone in the family learn the jobs required for our family to succeed. Daily jobs have run more smoothly since that time because the responsibility is distributed between all the family members.

## Points of Thought

Do you think there is something that could make the Martins' overwhelming morning routine better? Yes! The Martins could make some changes in their daily routine that might make things better for them. Taking time to thoughtfully establish a routine or family pace could bypass the feelings of disorder or chaos that might be created from a lack of planning. What do you think those changes should involve for the Martins? What would work best for you?

## Family Pace and Relationships

Balancing the workload, finding time to spend together, and using effective communication are tools that help parents in daily interactions and can reduce role overload. These interactions are the building blocks used in the relationship between family members. Taking time to focus on relationships in the family is an essential part of family success. For example, getting to know a new infant is a fun and tiring experience. Parents often struggle through the transition, figuring out how to meet the physical demands of the child. Once they reach a comfort level with their infant, they can more readily focus on meeting the infant's emotional needs. The creation of a secure attachment is one of the best gifts parents can bestow to their children. A secure attachment is the end product of balancing work, family interaction, and communication with our children. Some specific strategies to build a secure attachment follow.

### The Martins (Rob)

*The day we took Matt home was so wonderful. Matt was a good baby. He quickly set a schedule for sleeping and eating. He was relatively easy to take care of because he was so predictable. After I adjusted to waking up every 3 hours to feed Matt, I was able to focus on different things. I started to notice how he would turn his head every time he heard Maria or me start to talk. I noticed how he would work so hard to look into our faces. I loved to hold him, and I wondered what I could do to ensure Matt's success in the future.*

## The Parent–Child Relationship

The relationship between parent and child is a bidirectional relationship built upon interactions back and forth between the parent and child. A perfect example of this occurs while watching a mother play with her young infant. The mother looks at her baby and says, "Oh, you are so cute!" The infant looks at the mother and smiles back. This is all the feedback a mother needs to continue the conversation! "I am so lucky to be your mom!" This time the infant "coos" back and the interaction circle grows stronger and stronger. These sweet connections continue day after day forming a foundation that parent and child use to start a lifelong relationship. When these positive interactions occur often, children are more likely to learn that their parents are going to meet their needs. When parents quickly and consistently respond to their infant's cries of distress, that constancy helps children learn about their environment. Infant's learn that when they need something, and they cry, parents come to help. Trust is built through simple daily interactions: changing a diaper, dressing and feeding infants, and comforting them in times of distress.

## Creating a Secure Base and Attachment

A major goal of all parents should be to promote a secure attachment with their children. Attachment is an emotional bond that one person forms with another person. Attachments form in infancy and usually remain throughout our lives.[8] These attachments encourage people to seek each other out and to be near one another. It's built on foundations of trust in our bidirectional interactions. Infants and children manifest this by following parents, reaching to be held, and watching them during play activities. In turn, parents encourage attachments by keeping a watchful eye on infants and responding affectionately and sensitively. The interactions in the relationship parents have with their children establish the type of attachment bonds they form. Parents that take the time to create and build positive interactions with their children establish a secure base for children to explore the world.

Several built-in biological behaviors promote secure attachment. Research shows, for example, that adults like to look at infants. Infants' large eyes and small noses draw adults to them. The smiles and cries of infants also encourage people to take care of them. Parents adjust their behaviors to match their infants' rhythms and tempos. Infants also like to look at their parents, and they like to hear the singsong way parents talk with them through "infant-directed speech." Parents that establish this sensitivity and consistency in their interactions with their infants form a secure attachment. These children are comfortable and confident in their relationship with parents. This basic trust generalizes to others as well as the environment, helping children feel secure in more independent exploration of their environment.[9]

The quality of the attachment bond is affected by the reassurance and predictability of the parental relationship. Parents' anxieties, anger, depression, and other disruptive behaviors can affect the attachment bond. Children often reflect or mimic the behavior in relationships to others. If parents ignore their children, children often respond likewise. If parents are manipulating the situation, children express those same behaviors. These types of interactions are indicative of insecure attachments.

In a study done several years ago to determine what parents can do to encourage a secure attachment, hospitals provided parents of newborn children with a snugli (a soft infant carrier that a parent wears and places the infant on their chest) or an infant seat (like a car seat to be used in the house).[10] Where the normal attachment rate is about 30%, parents who had been given snuglies were found to have strong attachments with their infants at a rate of 70%. Parents who were using the infant seats were found to have secure attachment rates less than half of normal. The study was never completed because the initial findings were so compelling that researchers felt that depriving infants of a snugli put them at extreme risk. The message learned is that being close physically helps parents become aware of their infant's needs earlier so they can help them. In other words, physical closeness often leads to emotional closeness.

Why does this matter? Infants with secure attachments have parents who are sensitive to them, responsive to their requests for help, and available to their infants. These infants in turn are comfortable with their parents; they are sad when their parents leave, but happy when their parents return. They are more independent, social, and persistent in task completion. They enjoy exploring their world, and know they can trust their parents to help them. Infants who lack a secure attachment may ignore their parents, be clingy, and/or alternate between wanting the parent and pushing the parent away.

## Attachment and Working Parents

Children of working parents can have secure attachments with their parents. Sometimes it may feel like it's too much work, because employment cuts into the amount of time parents can physically spend with children, but it's possible. Just like any other parent, working parents must be aware of their children's strengths and weaknesses. They must try to get to know their children's like and dislikes and what is really important to them. They must also make a conscious effort to connect with their family whenever they can throughout the day.

Children have a sense of what their parents are feeling. They may not understand the emotion; however, they are aware of how it makes them feel. Anxiety is something that infants can feel; they can pick it up from parents, as well. When parents come home from work feeling stressed or upset about the day, they don't even need to say anything; when they pick up their infants, the anxiety is felt. Infants may respond by crying or fussing. They may want to be held, or want to be away from us.

As parents prepare for work, or come home after work, they can use good parenting practices to reduce the spillover from work into our family life. Relaxation techniques to help disconnect from work can be effective. Listening to music may help on the way home from work. I have found that when I take a few minutes to refocus on the way home from work, I can pay better attention to my children. I enjoy hearing about my children's day, and I know that my children are most likely to give me that information as I walk in the door. If I have taken time to transition into the next part of the day, I feel that I am a better parent.

Establishing a connection ritual can be helpful, as well: your child running to greet you as you enter the door, or maybe playing a quick game of hide and seek, an activity that both parent and child can look forward to at the end of the day.

## Quality vs. Quantity Time

The last thing for parents to understand is that it really isn't a matter of quality time versus quantity time. Children need both. Parents need to have special interactions with their children that focus on communication, fun, learning, and connection. They also need to have these times often. Children simply need parents, and the more they are together enjoying the company of one another, the stronger the likelihood of a secure attachment.

My baby is a happy, easy-going child. My husband and I quickly discovered that he really responds to music and singing. He also loves to snuggle, and needs to have time hugging and playing with us. As he plays, he likes to be near someone. We find that if we are singing, touching his arm as we walk by him, saying his name often, he is calm during the busy parts of the day. Now part of our family habit is to sing as we are getting ready in the morning or as we cook dinner. My baby responds quickly and happily to the music and smiles and plays as we work. We learned to meet his needs, and he learned that we are there and he can trust us.

## Finding Joy in Raising Children While Working

Sometimes talking about letting the stress of the day go as you head home is easier said than done. As parents work to succeed at home and in their employment one thing is certain; there will be times when parents feel overwhelmed. There are a few things that parents can do to avoid the frequency and intensity of these times. Parents who know their day's schedule are better off. Knowing what things have to be accomplished, and when, can help parents plan out their day and follow through on those many responsibilities they face. The schedule doesn't have to be followed minute by minute, but knowing when important times are can help parents also know if there is any flexibility in the day, what can be let go if need be, and what is crucial for family goals. Multitasking is a natural thing that a lot of individuals do. Ironically, multitasking needs to have a balance if it's going to be more of help than a hindrance.

Having a child help with dinner preparations while you talk about the good and sad points of their day is a great way to multitask. It also creates the opportunity for a connection between parent and child. Starting dinner, catching up on returning phone calls, and paying the bills may be too much, and spread parents' focus too thinly. Self-awareness about capabilities helps individuals know what they can reasonably accomplish with the right amount of attention. Pushing the limits will eventually catch up to someone and the outcome could be devastating.

I have a tendency to multitask more than I should. In our family, we have what we call the great pea incident. It was one of those days I just knew I could get so much done. I woke early, started laundry and cleaning my storage room. I was getting so much done! I sent my older two children out the door to their piano lessons, and my preschooler and baby were playing right outside the storage room in close proximity to me. I got to a point where I needed to work in the kitchen washing some containers so I moved the children upstairs with me. The children were playing, life was good, and then the phone rang. While I was talking on the phone, my preschooler started playing in our sensory table. This is a big tub on legs that I fill with peas, macaroni, shaving cream, water, etc., for the children to explore. That day we filled it with dried split peas. With a measuring cup, my preschooler decided to scoop out the peas and started taking the peas to the sink and dumping them down the drain. She made sure to turn on the water and wash them down. I knew she was putting them in the sink, but I didn't realize how many she got down the sink before I redirected her to put them in a container. I ended my phone call, and finished washing the containers I had. The three of us quickly went back downstairs and finished the storage room cleaning. My older children came home, and I began to clean the fridge while all my children played for a few minutes. I found cabbage salad that had lived its life, and dumped it down the disposal. If you think about this for a minute, you can guess what happened. The dried split peas soaked up the water in the disposal, and expanded. When I added the cabbage salad (and yes, it had to be cabbage!) and turned on the water, there was a *glub* sound, and then an explosion! I had peas and cabbage everywhere! I sat there with cabbage and peas in my hair, on my clothes, my floor, walls, and ceiling, and all I could do was laugh. My children came running when they heard the weird sounds coming from the kitchen. When my preschooler saw me she started to cry, saying, "I'm so sorry!" over and over. I was glad that I was laughing! My preschooler would've felt horrible if I yelled at her that day. The great pea incident taught me that sometimes too much is too much! I had got a lot done that day, my list of things was being whittled down quickly, but at what cost? I needed to give my children more time. Having them play while I spent the day working wasn't a bad thing, but I could've slowed down, included them in the cleaning, talked with them instead of on the phone, and avoided deep cleaning my kitchen, which wasn't on the agenda. (Yes, I did have to take the pipes apart to clean out the peas, and before it was all done the kitchen smelled amazing!)

One of the most important things for all parents to establish at some point is what they consider to be the key values for the family. Some families feel that a home-cooked meal shared at the end of the day is crucial to their happiness, while another family may feel it's the time they spend riding bikes together at the end of the day. If families are aware of what they feel is important, it's easier to make sure it gets done. Naming those important values helps all family members work together to make it happen.

Organization is something that is truly essential for working families. Having a place to put backpacks, papers that need to be signed, and written communications about location and activities are some of the basic things families need. Children's rooms can be organized so they can more independently and successfully take care of their own needs. Pinpointing stressful times of the day, and why they are stressful, can help. Maybe stress occurs in the morning because children can't find homework or check for school lunch. One thing that might help is packing the backpacks the night before to eliminate the run-around in the morning.

Parents can also create a calm environment by taking a "working with" approach to interactions with their children rather than a "doing to."[11] Avoiding the "hurry and" mentality can reduce pressure on children, increasing their ability to think through and then do what is needed. The extra pressure of telling your child to hurry may in fact slow them down. Awareness and sensitivity can help parents work with their children.

### The Martins

*Maria has learned that the environment around her affects her family. This can be something as simple as watching other parents and mimicking their behaviors, or more complex, as she recognizes the collective efficacy in her neighborhood. Just like scaffolding used to create a building, social constructs establish a foundation of values for families. Awareness of the environment, as well as future goals for children, can help parents direct their families toward favorable outcomes.*

*Rob is on the right track. The awareness he noticed with Matt when he was an infant was something that was real, and it helped him create a better bond with his son. By being sensitive and responsive to his infant, Rob established a secure attachment that made it more likely that Matt would turn to Rob when he needed help. When Rob held Matt and comforted him when he was upset, he was helping Matt develop trust. Taking time to talk and share ideas helps to maintain the secure attachment through life. It may seem simple, but the back and forth interactions with parents build the strongest foundations for young children.*

### References

[1] Bigner, Jerry J. (2006). *Parent-Child Relations: An Introduction to Parenting.* Seventh Edition. Pearson Merrill Prentice Hall, New Jersey.

[2] Berger, K. (2006). The developing person through the lifespan.

[3] Bureau of Labor Statistics. (2005). Women in the labor force: A databook (USDL 05-849). Washington, DC. Available at http://www.bls.gov/cps/wlf-databook-2005.pdf.

[4] Presser, H. B. (2003). *Working in a 24/7 economy: Challenges for American families.* New York: Russell Sage Foundation. And Bond, J. T., Thompson, C., Galinsky, E. & Pronttas, D. (2002). *Highlights of the national study of the changing workforce.* New York: Families and Work Institute.

[5] Bianchi, S. M., Robinson, J. P., & Milkie, M. A. (2006). *Changing Rhythms of American Family Life*. New York: Russell Sage Foundation.

[6] Whitehead, D. L. (2008). Historical trends in work-family: The evolution of earning and caring. In K. Korabik, D. S. Lero, & D. L. Whitehead (eds), *Handbook of work-family integration: Research, theory, and best practices* (pp. 13–35). Ontario, Canada. Academic Press.

[7] Duxbury, L., Lyons, S., & Higgins, C. (2008). Too much to do, and not enough time: An examination of role overload. In K. Korabik, D. S. Lero, & D. L. Whitehead (eds), *Handbook of work-family integration: Research, theory, and best practices* (pp. 13–35). Ontario, Canada. Academic Press.

[8] Ainsworth, M.S. (1974). *The development of infant-mother attachment. A final report of the office of child development*. Office of Child Development, Washington DC.

[9] Ainsworth, M.S. (1979). Infant-mother attachment. *American Psychologist*. 34(10), 932–937.

[10] Anisfeld, E., Casper, V., Nozyce, M., & Cunningham, N. (1990). Does infant carrying promote attachment? An experimental study of the effects of increased physical contact on the development of attachment. *Child Development* (61), 1617–1627.

[11] Kohn, A. (2006). *Unconditional Parenting: Moving from rewards and punishments to love and reason*. New York, New York: Atria.

# Chapter 12

## Parents in Transition

# Parents in Transition

Parenthood is defined by transitions. Parents learn one set of skills to raise their infants and toddlers, and then they realize those change with their preschooler. Adjustments are made throughout middle childhood, and then as their child reaches adolescence, parents find a new set of rules are needed to succeed. This ever-changing dynamic makes parenting challenging to say the least!

### The Martins (Rob)

*I remember when Matt was born. I was truly terrified to even hold him. I felt like he was so small and fragile. Maria was good to show me how I could hold Matt and how strong he was, but still it was hard for me to feel confident in my parenting skills.*

*Matt was so much fun when he was in elementary school. I was his coach when he played baseball, and I really enjoyed teaching him about the sport and watching him learn and grow. Those years were easier for me to parent Matt. It seemed that we could talk about everything, and he really wanted to know my opinion.*

*Matt is older now, and things are different. Sometimes he seems moody, but I know that he has a lot on his mind. He is making so many decisions about his life, and I am sure he is overwhelmed. We talk sometimes, but I know that he wants opinions from others, as well. I love watching him grow into the man he will become; I just hope he thinks I did okay as a parent.*

I think that these changes and challenges can make parenting exciting. It's fun to see a new developmental stage with my children and wonder if I can be the type of parent I want to be as well as the best parent for my child. Each parent experiences different transitions. In this chapter I will discuss the transition to parenthood, variations in parenting beliefs, and making the decisions to work and parent.

## Transitions to Parenthood

Having a child is one of the biggest events in the life of a family. The impact of the change is felt on many different levels, sometimes even in daily interactions like changing a diaper, wiping a nose, making a meal, setting up play dates, and in general terms the psychological changes that occur through the lifelong interdependent relationship. The work structure that a couple has established changes to accommodate the child. Couples must create a new balance of expectations and redefine "who does what" in the relationship. How do couples react to these changes and how does this important transition affect their relationship?

### The Martins (Rob)

*I think that Maria has always wanted to be a mother. After we were engaged, Maria started to talk about our children and what she wanted to name them, how she hoped they had my eyes, and how she wanted a boy first. I was really scared when she started to talk that way. I was still getting used to the idea of marriage, and she had already made us parents! I really questioned my abilities to become a father. I wasn't sure I could do it.*

# From Partners to Parents: The Decision

I understand Rob's feelings about parenthood. It's scary and overwhelming to think about taking care of someone else all the time. I am sure that Rob is not alone in his feelings about parenthood. It's human nature to question one's capabilities, and I know as a parent that I wonder if I do more damage than good on a daily basis.

During the course of a day I am a chef, chauffeur, therapist, sociologist, teacher, tutor, housekeeper, encyclopedia, nurse, social director, financial advisor, and mom. (The list could go on and on!) I am skilled in some of these roles, adequate in some, and poor in the others. I have to admit that I wasn't completely aware of the challenges I would face as a parent, but learning new skills and working with my husband to foster success in the lives of our children has been delightful. When couples make the decision to become parents, it should involve many discussions about complex issues. There are many reasons that couples decide to become parents.

## Adult Developmental Task

People may consider having children and caring for them to fulfill a major adult role. Successful childrearing is a goal of many adults, and many people look forward to becoming parents. Erikson's[1] theory provides an explanation about becoming parents. He believed that as individuals reach adulthood, there are psychological, social, and physical triggers that create a sense of generativity. Generativity is an attitude of productive work that creates meaning, usually through employment or parenthood. Without a sense of generativity, Erikson's theory states that life is empty and purposeless and adults stagnate.

I have found that I really like to cook and clean with my children. The time I have with my children while we complete these daily tasks allows me to teach them skills they will need in the future, but we can also talk about our day and strengthen our relationship as well. These moments help me to feel accomplished as a parent, but also as an adult.

## Cultural Influences

Cultural beliefs that people hold influence the decision to become parents. For example, in Native American families, children are viewed as treasured gifts. Adults are responsible to observe children and learn about their unique characteristics that will one day contribute to the tribe. Children are taught to be in tune with the surrounding nature, and aware of others' needs.[2]

The expectations of children's behavior, how parents intrinsically think about, and eventually treat children, are all influenced by cultural beliefs. Individualist cultures emphasize the importance of individuals over the group. This is practiced in much of the United States, where independence, competition, production, and personal responsibility are stressed. Collectivist cultures emphasize cooperation and interdependent relationships over individuality. Latino and Asian cultures value cooperation and the process rather than the product. The individual is responsible for maintaining the harmony and well-being of the group and putting aside personal interest.[3]

These values and basic belief systems are passed on to children through their earliest interactions with others. This is crucial for helping infants and children learn how to become members of the greater community. Cultural interactions become scripts for development and socialization, forming foundations for perception, motivation, affect regulation, and social behavior.[4]

## Economic Factors

Many couples talk about financial issues and carefully consider many different aspects related to the economic cost of raising children. Because our finances dictate our lifestyle, some couples postpone parenthood for a time to meet the costs of raising young children.[5] As you read in Chapter 9, for a child born in 2011, the total estimated cost of raising that child to the age of 18 is $235,000.[6] Family expenditures include items like housing, childcare, transportation, and food. Parents must also consider health care, insurance, clothing, and other miscellaneous expenditures as well.

Couples must seriously consider their employment status and if both partners are going to remain in the workforce after the child is born, or whether they will make changes. The increases or decreases in cost must be considered when making the decision to become a family.

## Emotional Factors

These factors take into account the attitudes couples have toward parenting. The decision to have children is more socially and psychologically driven today compared to a more economically based one in the past.[7] Research conducted by Cowan and Cowan found that couples approach pregnancy and parenting in different ways.[8] In their study, they found about 50 percent of the couples were *Planners*. These couples talked about their feelings related to becoming parents, and came to a mutual decision about the timing of the pregnancy. About 15 percent of their recruited couples were *Accepting Fate*. Couples in this category didn't discuss parenting, or they stopped using contraception, leaving the decision up to fate. These couples became parents accidentally, but willingly accepted the consequences. *Ambivalent* couples made up about 17 percent of the sample. These individuals were not sure what they wanted to do about the pregnancy and parenting. The remaining 17 percent of the sample were placed in the *Yes-No* category. One partner was excited about parenting, and the other partner did not feel ready to parent but felt they had to go along with their partner to maintain the relationship.

The *Planners* transitioned to parenthood very well, maintaining a stable marital satisfaction level while tracked for two years. The *Yes-No* couples experienced marital dissatisfaction that continued to decline from late pregnancy to the child's 18-month birthday. When these couples were tracked to the child's entrance to elementary school, it was found that about 75% of them had divorced.[9] Couples that take time to communicate their feelings about parenthood, including their desires concerning parenthood, the timing of becoming parents, and expectations for parents and children, seem to accept the demands and roles of parenting easier.

# Becoming Parents: What Changes?

When do transitions to parenthood occur? For some individuals it happens early in life. They might be playing "house" in preschool or taking care of their dolly when they just know they want to be a mom or a dad someday. Others might start to think about parenting in high school as they daydream about the children they might have with their current crush. For others it might not happen until they are married and start to discuss children with their spouse. Still, some might never feel ready to transition to parenthood, even when they are holding their newborn.

### The Martins (Maria)

*Abbie enjoyed playing "house." I loved watching her when she didn't know I was looking. I spent so many hours playing with my dolls when I was young. I loved being the mom and taking care of all my dolls. I envied Abbie and her play because she didn't have to worry about the bills or responsibilities that go along with parenting. She would sing to her babies and dance with them. Abbie would carefully feed them and puts them down to bed. Seeing her play reminded me that I need to take time and just be with my children. It is up to me to take the time to be with them and love them. I have such a wonderful opportunity to get to know them and discover their personalities. It really is an amazing journey when I take time to think about it!*

## Parents in Transition

It's so fun to see how much growth happens the first few weeks in the life of infants. They quickly become social, interactive individuals. At the same time, many changes are taking place within parents. These changes might not be as noticeable as the infant; however, they are just as important. As adults make the transition to parenthood, the changes can be profound and life-altering.

Becoming a parent is a big decision, and one that will affect couples for the rest of their lives. It affects the individuals as well as the dyadic relationship (a dyadic relationship is a relationship between two people in which both individuals influence the other). Parenthood is unique to each individual, providing personal meaning and consequences that affect couples. Cowan and Cowan found that parenthood permanently changes the roles and relationships between partners.[10] There are several domains that change when couples become parents.

## Changes in Identity and Parental Role Arrangement

Starting in pregnancy and continuing through the first 18 months of the infant's life, parents have been found to define themselves more as parents and less as partners or lovers. Couples start from a more similar place at the beginning of pregnancy—they are a couple, or maybe a worker or a student. As the pregnancy progresses, Cowan and Cowan's research found, women are more likely to define themselves as parents than partners and men are more likely to define themselves as workers or students than women are.[11]

Influences from an individual's family of origin may also affect how parental roles are arranged. Some people change the perceptions of their family of origin. Some view their parents in a more positive light, with a better understanding of their parenting practices. They also accept and adopt many of their parents' practices as they raise their children. Others associate negative feelings with their own upbringing and wish to change many of the practices their parents used.

The division of labor within the household shifts after an infant joins a couple. Typically, household tasks and responsibilities become more traditionally shared, even if the couple were equal sharers before parenthood and expected to continue that pattern after the delivery of their child.[12] Baxter, Hewitt, and Haynes found that transitions to parenthood include an increase in the amount of time that women spend doing housework each week (up to six additional hours each week).[13] With each subsequent birth, the hours spent completing household tasks continue to increase for women. Fatherhood doesn't seem to increase the amount of time men spend in completing housework. Current research hasn't investigated the amount of time men and women spend in childcare activities. Couples may equally share the time involved in taking care of their children; however, there is a gender gap in time spent in housework.

Taking time for communication and experience-sharing changes with the arrival of an infant as well. The lack of time creates higher levels of conflict, and couples usually argue about "who does what."[14] Sleep deprivation and emotional exhaustion from the constant care of a newborn can make any adult irritable and on guard.[15]

It seems that nine months is a lot of time to transition to role changes within the family. When a pregnancy is planned and the child is greatly anticipated, many families can start to establish healthy lifestyle changes. The couple might take a prenatal health class together or read parenting books. They may even choose to take a parenting class and try to learn more about the changes in their upcoming family. This is an ideal situation, where the couple plans, communicates, and even takes time to dream about their future family.

## Variation in Parenting

It seems that every parent has his or her own parenting philosophy about how one should raise children and what is the most important thing to teach children. There is so much variation in parenting and raising children that one can easily get overwhelmed with advice and instructions shared by those around them. Why does so much variation exist? Because there are so many influences on family functions.[16] These include childhood experiences, personal attitudes, and current circumstances. Specifically, variations are seen with beliefs about family membership and marriage, parents' abilities to communicate and solve problems, amount of money made, education level, and relationships with friends and neighbors that might provide a social support network.

Christoph Heinicke also identifies three psychological qualities that impact the parenting atmosphere created by individuals.[17] They include (1) parents' feelings of self-esteem; (2) their capacity for positive, mutually satisfying relationships with others, especially with the partner; and (3) their capacity for flexible problem solving. These traits help parents provide optimal care to their children once they are born. This research coincides well with my own personal philosophy of good parenting. I feel the foundation of strong, positive relationships with our children is based upon how well we know ourselves, how well we know our children, and how well we make decisions based upon that knowledge. For example, I know I want my children to play a musical instrument. My children are engaged in lessons throughout the week that take time. I also know that I don't like to wait around, and my children have picked up this trait as well, and it makes them anxious if they have to wait for me and wonder if everything is okay. This may seem like a contradiction, but it's up to me to solve this dilemma. The way I have solved this problem is to carry a bag with me at all times with a book, notebook, pencil, maybe a few papers to grade, so that I can be productive while I wait for my children. I don't feel like my time waiting for them is wasted, and my children don't have to worry about why I am late. This way when they come running to me at the end of their lesson, I am there with a smile, instead of a frown.

Along with personal attitudes, influences from family of origin and social construct ideologies affect the way adults construct their parenting beliefs and practices. "Ideologies are patterns of beliefs, ideas, opinions, and values that are used to create meaning."[18]

## Parental Ideology

Women and men generally view their parenting responsibilities in different ways. Women tend to be more permissive and protective of their infants and toddlers. Their attitudes are child-centered.[19] Men perceive themselves as a playmate rather than a caregiver.[20] These differences lead to conflict in the couple relationship. The discrepancies in childrearing attitudes can create tension, especially as the child grows older and it's perceived by the parents that the child needs limits. Couples must begin to make decisions together to create limits.[21]

## Becoming a Mother

A study conducted by Myra Leifer found that mothers experience a lot of changes and problems.[22] Mothers report (1) feelings of tiredness and exhaustion, (2) a loss of sleep, especially in the first couple months of their infant's life, (3) concerns about ignoring their husband's needs, (4) feelings of inadequacy as a mother, (5) an inability to keep up with the work around the house, and (6) feelings of being tied down. Mothers also reported that they did not anticipate all the ways having an infant would change their lives. They also underestimated the amount of work involved in caring for their infant. Women with higher self-esteem, who identify with the mothering role and who easily adapted to the pregnancy experience ease into parenthood more smoothly.[23]

Johnston and Swanson interviewed 95 women about their mothering expectations.[24] Mothers were free to answer the open-ended questions that were asked of them. The results varied between at-home mothers, part-time employed mothers, and full-time employed mothers.

At-home mothers defined a good mother as being at home and available for their children. This availability was explained as a constant and physical accessibility. A need for patience was a common theme in their parental descriptions. They experienced psychological stress associated with always making themselves available for their children, and always putting their own needs last on their to-do list. At-home mothers reported high levels of happiness, but they also felt lonelier than other mothers. At-home mothers easily identified their role and how they had constructed their beliefs and practices.

Just as at-home mothers did, part-time employed mothers defined a good mother in terms of physical accessibility and addressed issues of keeping their temper and seeking patience. Their responses varied from both at-home mothers and full-time employed mothers because they emphasized communication and an emotional openness and connection in their relationships with their children. The sense of balance part-time-employed mothers feel is associated with their reportedly highest levels of happiness. When asked about how they separate work and family, part-time employed mothers reported that they did experience tension, but most resolved it by compromising their career for family.

Full-time employed mothers explained good mothering in different terms than the other mothers. Psychological and emotional accessibility were emphasized over physical availability. Full-time employed mothers addressed ideas of nurturing such as love, affection, laughing together, playing, self-esteem, and responsiveness more frequently than at-home or part-time employed mothers. Most also commented that if they had more time, they would be better mothers. In terms of happiness, full-time employed mothers fell between part-time-employed mothers on the high end and at-home mothers on the low end. Full-time employed mothers stated that the unhappiness they felt was associated with the lack of time they had with their children, and with the knowledge that their children were learning life skills from a childcare provider. Mothers with full-time employment had a hard time separating work and family responsibilities. Many full-time employed mothers reported that they wanted to do everything and do it well, but they also knew it was impossible.

Mothers, regardless of their status at home or engaged in paid work, do have ideologies of good mothering. It seems that mothers choose their work status based on these ideologies, but that their work status does influence the development of their ideologies. Mothers that can achieve their ideology consistency (their beliefs match their practices) are going to be happier with their employment status.

## Maternal Employment

Most employed mothers report being happy and satisfied.[25] This *does* depend upon whether they want to work or not. Mothers who want to work report they are happy with their roles, but they do feel stretched. Women who are satisfied with their work role, whether it's outside of the home or staying at home, interact better with their families. Mothers who want to work outside of the home, but can't, show more signs of depression. Women who work outside of the home, but don't want to, show more anxiety about leaving their children.[26]

One controversial finding is that sons and daughters of working mothers are treated differently when both parents work.[27] Daughters tend to benefit from dual-working parents because they help more around the household. They learn more skills associated with meal preparation and cleaning because of the expectation for them to help out. The help that daughters offer in the home also leads to positive treatment from the parents because of the help provided by the daughter. Independence is also fostered, as well as seeing different role models in their working mothers. Sons usually experience a disadvantage because they have less time with their parents. One behavior that was noted in the study was that if sons have a lot of energy, they are encouraged to go outside, or play in a different room while parents complete a task so they won't interfere or slow down the task completion. There is also a tendency for less nurturing parenting for sons of working parents. This may be associated with the stress parents feel with a lack of time to complete their many responsibilities.

## Becoming a Father

Mothers are not the only individuals to experience changes because of the birth of a child. Fathers report changes as well, such as a (1) loss of sleep, (2) the need to adjust to new responsibilities, (3) disruptions in their daily routines, (4) ignorance about the amount of work an infant requires, and (5) financial worries.[28]

Men who adjust better to parenthood have more knowledge about child development, and better relationships with their wives than men who have trouble adjusting to parenthood.[29] Father involvement in their infant's care affects working mothers. When newborn infants were left with their fathers compared to infants in other care situations, mothers reported less anger, depression, and anxiety.[30] Fathers are competent caregivers, especially with the mother's encouragement.

Mothers become the "gatekeepers" that determine how much a father is involved with the child. Mothers who are more traditional in their view of family life tend to hinder father involvement. The father's prenatal predictions of how successfully they will parent are also a big factor in determining future involvement. When fathers are encouraged to attend prenatal health check-ups with the mother, especially when an ultrasound is completed, and they are active in the birth process, they are more likely to feel a connection with the child from birth.

A good father is critical to the optimal development and well-being of a child. Father's roles are more than being an economic provider; contemporary fathers are expected to nurture, engage in caregiving, and create emotional support in both obvious and subtle ways. Successful fatherhood correlates strongly with many attributes of children successfully growing up. Fathers that actively participate in their children's lives increase the healthy, normal development of self-esteem, peer social interaction, and appropriate gender-identity development. (Boys are helped to understand masculinity, and girls formulate appropriate roles of a relationship.) Children who are lucky enough to have their father involved in their lives are also more likely to succeed in school and to avoid substance abuse and delinquent behaviors in adolescence.

## Paternal Employment

Men also experience difficulty in weaving together work and family. Men often report in surveys that they are not as involved in their families as they would like to be because of the cultural expectation that work comes first. Many men feel society would rather them work longer hours to provide for their family, and that if their spouse is working, they must not be a good financial provider for the family.

When men are involved with their family, and they help to accomplish the family work in the home, it raises their self-esteem and life satisfaction. Many men report they are happy when they can spend time with their family. Many also report that they think it's important for them to be involved in their children's lives and attend performances, sporting events, school meetings, etc., as part of that involvement.

### The Martins (Rob and Maria)

*It was hard transitioning from being married adults to being parents. When we went from a "duet to a trio," we didn't realize how complicated the harmonies could become. We had some struggles trying to figure everything out, but the one thing that saved us was how we learned to communicate with each other. We could talk about our hopes and dreams—that was the easy part. But we could also talk about the things that were frustrating us, and what we hoped to change. These conversations were building blocks for that change. When something was wrong and we couldn't work it out between us, we turned to books, trusted friends, and our parents. We created the working system that allowed the melody of our family to resonate throughout our home.*

## Transitions Back to Work

After a baby comes, some decisions are easy—picking a car seat, buying a mobile. Some require a little bit of conversation, but are made relatively quickly like feeding habits, color of paint for the bedroom. Other decisions are hard and require thought and lots of talking, such as, what to name the baby, what doctor to take the infant to, and to work or stay home. This section discusses points of consideration for couples as they make these complicated choices.

*The Martins*

Notes

> *When Matt was born, the Martins were just starting out. Money was tight, and so the decision was made that Maria would keep working to help out financially. Maria felt like she was tired all the time. It was hard to keep up at home because she was so tired when she got home from work that all she could do was take care of Matt. Rob was frustrated because he felt like he was expected to do so much more around the house, but he never knew how to help out. They were also both concerned about Matt and if his childcare was good. After Abbie was born things went from bad to worse. Maria felt so pulled to do well in her job, have a perfectly maintained house, and well-behaved and educated children. The pressure was overwhelming. Rob tried to help, but when he would ask what he needed to do around the house, it was common for Maria to explode and tell him he should just know and do it. The childcare costs skyrocketed with two children in care. When Matt was diagnosed with a language delay, Maria and Rob took a serious look at the costs and benefits of having one parent at home. They decided that the money didn't compensate for the lost time at home, and Maria decided to quit her job. Staying home wasn't as easy as a transition Maria thought it would be. She enjoyed working, and it was hard to go from being needed as a busy CNA to completing work at home for which she often wasn't thanked. It was also a struggle to find enough places to cut costs to meet the lost income. Maria never regretted the move though, because she was able to be with her children and help them and direct their learning in a more complete way.*

## Making the Decision to Work

The decision for both individuals in a partnership to work is a complicated process. Many social and cultural factors come into the mix, as well as future goals and expectations for the children. The decision-making process takes time, and most couples need to talk through different possibilities and options.

Often parents make the decision to become a dual-working couple because of financial concerns. The market in the United States is flat.[31] It's hard for individuals to find employment that will rise with the cost of inflation. The job market is different; many jobs exist now that didn't a generation ago, and technology creates and changes jobs constantly. The decline of unions and a robust manufacturing sector in the United States has in many ways changed or eliminated many jobs that existed previously.[32] Work that women do has absorbed a lot of the changes in men's work and salary loss of the last few years. In many families the woman's salary is not optional—it's crucial for survival. One factor that isn't always recognized is that some women want to work and strongly desire to succeed in a career. Women recognize their strengths and may see a good fit with a career and have a strong desire to complete training or education to work in that field. They may feel more complete as they work and fulfill those personal dreams.

Sometimes the tipping factor in creating a dual-working couple is that only one partner works in a field or has the opportunity for economic opportunities that strengthen the family such as health care or retirement options. A paycheck is not the only financial compensation received from employment, and the savings in health care payments may warrant keeping a job, or taking a different job. The knowledge that children can go to the doctor, have braces, attend high-quality childcare, or have money put away for their future education may make the decision easier to work or stay home.

The other factor that comes into play is similar to the choices adults make when deciding to have children. Some adults may feel personal growth knowing they are contributing to the social economic ladder. Some people may also receive personal fulfillment in their employment that may help them reach the generative stage and connect with their community.

It's easy to see why couples and families can feel so torn apart about what to do with employment. "Should I go back to work after I have my baby?" It isn't an easy yes/no question. Couples must consider beliefs, ideologies, finances, and figure out what's best for their family. Many families struggle with these questions, even after they feel they have made the right decision.

## The Transitions Back to Work After Childbirth

Once the decision to work or stay home has been made, the choices are far from over. In fact, they are really just beginning. Should both partners work full-time, what about part-time work, and should both partners work the same shift? This section addresses those issues.

*Family Leave: A Dad's Perspective, by Matthew Hendel*[33]

*When we had our first son, I was encouraged to take family leave: four weeks off when he was born, and four more weeks when he was two months old after my wife went back to work. During that time, I was the one who changed his diapers, determined when he needed to be fed, put him to sleep for naps, and played with him. Even when both parents work similar hours, the cultural myth persists that moms know how to care for children, and dads do not. The act of being my son's primary caregiver put me on equal footing with my wife in terms of how we raised him. It helped pull me out of the mindset of asking my wife for everything, and instead relying on my own intuition in how to care for my child.*

*Sadly, few father receive any paid time whatsoever when a child is born. Perhaps more insidiously, even when fathers are given leave, we are often discouraged from really taking the time off. Sure, you can be on leave, our companies tell us, as long as you keep up with e-mail and come to important meetings. In my experience, workplace evaluations also ignore time spent with a new family member when considering workload and goal achievement.*

*Family leave is not a women's issue. Without family leave for fathers, everybody loses: fathers don't get one-on-one time with their children; mothers become overworked and over-burdened with parenting decisions; and most importantly, our children do not receive the full participation of both parents.*

Many times the first major decisions that must be made after a couple decides to continue as a dual-working couple with children is maternity and paternity leave. In the United States it's not required that employers provide maternity and paternity leave for their employees. Many employees that make the decisions to stay home for a time after an infant is born do so without pay.

Most working Americans are not guaranteed paid family leave to spend time with a new child. Parents are left to their own devices to patch together some type of leave on their own using sick days and vacation time or taking time off work without pay. Very few states offer paid family leave. California and New Jersey do offer family leave, but it is limited to 6 weeks of time or less. Research has shown that 25% of what are called "poverty spells," or times when a family's income slips below what is needed to cover basic needs, begins with the birth of an infant.[34] As published by the National Partnership for Women and Families, there is a strong correlation between paid parental leave and healthier children. Infants receive better prenatal and postnatal care as well as having a greater likelihood that they will be immunized. There is also indication of stronger bonding between parent and child.[35]

The Family and Medical Leave Act of 1993 insured that parents could take time off to be with a newborn infant, or a family member (including children), during a time of illness for up to 12 weeks time without pay. If parents opt to take this option, they are guaranteed a position of equal compensation, benefits, and responsibility if their job is no longer available. This allows families to take time, but the financial loss inhibits many individuals from considering this opportunity.

The next decision that a couple may face is how they want to work, or need to work. Family typologies exist that explain the division of labor and financial contributions and how they differ between spouses.[36] In high-status families, the couple both work high level jobs and earn higher income. They report higher levels of stress in balancing work and family, and have lower rates of marital satisfaction. Couples in low-stress families work lower level jobs such as manufacturing and earn a lower income, but they tend to report happier marriages and better balance between work and family. Main-secondary families have one partner working a high level job (usually the father), and one partner working part-time or a low level job (usually the mother). These couples generally report their marital happiness between high-status and low-stress families, and still struggle with balancing work and family responsibilities.

There are other patterns of working and parenting that also affect the family work and happiness. Parents need to determine a pattern of how they will share the family work and rates of earned income, and hours spent in paid employment. Depending on whether couples choose to be equal sharers, 60-40 couples, 75-25 couples, or alternating shifters will determine the differences between work responsibilities. Couples must communicate to create a sense of working together and determining what common goals are most important for the family. These patterns can change depending upon the needs of the individuals, couple, children, and family during any particular time in the family development (young children vs. adolescent children) and social time frame (early career vs. established career).

When couples and partners look at the pros and cons of working full-time or part-time, or who will work full-time or part-time, many different components enter into the equation. Both partners working full-time is going to take away time for the things that need to get done around the house, and meeting the needs of the children, but the financial gain may be necessary. Having a partner work part-time may free up time to meet household obligations and help in child development, but the lack of benefits and extra finances may create problems. When making the decisions about hours worked in a week individuals must consider family needs, employment expectations, and employment flexibility. Some couples feel the best option is to work different hours. While this often seems like a win-win situation, it's hard to maintain over time. One parent can be 100% parent and then 100% employee throughout the day completing the tasks at both home and work as they arise. However, the loss of family togetherness and time for couple communication takes its toll and can hurt a marriage relationship.

Another interesting cultural phenomenon is that working women, and how much they work, is really an emotionally charged decision. Many women try to make the decision based upon what is best for themselves and their families, and then feel like they have to justify that decision to the world. The wall between women is very much real; on one side, mothers in paid employment, and the other, at-home mothers. One way is not better than another, but criticisms go back and forth over the wall. It would be more effective if society could support the decisions women and couples make about their family and economic differences with programs and benefits for all families.

## Work and Family Spillover and Work Conditions

Family life shapes the work environment, and the work environment shapes family life.[37] Employees can have a bad day at work because they had an argument with their spouse on the way to work, had to miss their child's afternoon soccer game because of a staff meeting, and was frustrated by the lack of benefits received from their employment. On the other hand, a parent might come home and yell at the dog because the manager was in a bad mood, be short-tempered with children while helping them to finish homework, and burn dinner because their mind is still on work concerns. This back and forth interaction between work and family is called **spillover.**[38]

Spillover is affected by the family social status, interpersonal skills, friendships and other social supports, and flexibility of their employment. These factors can affect the degree of spillover between work and family, as well as how individuals recognize the spillover and change it if necessary. Families face many challenges as they balance work and family. Some factors that can contribute to family stress include: long work hours, inflexible work hours, and having an unsupportive supervisor. Working conditions are an important part of employment that is easily overlooked.

When employers try to be "family friendly," they find that spillover from family is lessened, and work production and satisfaction increases among employees. Family-friendly employers emphasize flexibility and personal responsibility for their employees. Most family-friendly companies allow employees to set their own schedule as long as they can accomplish their work and complete any collaborative work with colleagues. Other benefits family-friendly companies may offer include, but are not limited to the following: fitness centers, internet services, health care benefits, retirement plans, tuition/book reimbursement, on-site childcare, and childcare reimbursements.

### The Martins

*It's a struggle to learn the ropes of parenting. Transitions can create tensions and stresses in a relationship, and transitions and change seem to define parenting more than consistency in situations. Knowing yourself and your values is an important part of making decisions that help you deal with parenting transitions. Rob and Maria will have less struggle in their life if they can communicate and share in the decision-making process. As they work together to negotiate the division of household labor, financial contributions, and child care responsibilities, they can find happiness and joy with their lives and their children.*

References

[1] Erikson, E. H. (1963). *Childhood and society* (2nd ed.). New York: Norton.

[2] Hildebrand, V., Phenice, L. A., Gray, M. M., & Hines, R. P. (2000). *Knowing and serving diverse families* (2nd ed.). Upper Saddle River, NJ: Merrill/Prentice Hall.

[3] Keller, H. (2002). Culture and development: Developmental pathways to individualism and interrelatedness. Online readings in Psychology and Culture. Available from the Center for Cross-Cultural Research, Western Washington University, Bellingham, WA (http://www.ac.wwu.edu/~culture/contents_complete.htm).

[4] Keller, H. (2002). Culture and development: Developmental pathways to individualism and interrelatedness. Online readings in Psychology and Culture. Available from the Center for Cross-Cultural Research, Western Washington University, Bellingham, WA (http://www.ac.wwu.edu/~culture/contents_complete.htm).

[5] Markus, H.R., & Kitayama, S. (1991). Culture and the self: Implications for cognition, emotion and motivation. *Psychological Review, 98,* 224–253.

[6] Lino, M. (2012). Expenditures on children by families 2011. U.S. Department of Agriculture, Center for Nutrition Policy and Promotion. Miscellaneous Publication No. 1528–2002. Washington, DC: U.S. Government Printing Office.

[7] Lino, M. (2012). Expenditures on children by families 2011. U.S. Department of Agriculture, Center for Nutrition Policy and Promotion. Miscellaneous Publication No. 1528–2002. Washington, DC: U.S. Government Printing Office.

[8] Bigner, J. (2006). *Parent-child relations: An introduction to parenting.* New Jersey: Pearson Prentice Hall.

[9] Cowan, C. P., & Cowan, P. A. (1997). Working with couples during major life transitions. In S. Dreman (Ed.), *The family on the threshold of the 21st century* (pp. 17–48). Hillsdale, NJ: Erlbaum.

[10] Cowan, C. P., & Cowan, P. A. (1997). Working with couples during major life transitions. In S. Dreman (Ed.), *The family on the threshold of the 21st century* (pp. 17–48). Hillsdale, NJ: Erlbaum.

[11] Cowan, C. P., & Cowan, P. A. (1992). *When partners become parents: The big life change for couples.* New York: Basic Books. Republished by Lawrence Erlbaum Associates, Fall, 1999.

[12] Cowan, C., Cowan, P. A., Heming, G., Garrett, E., Coysh, W., Curtis-Boles, H., Boles, A. J. (1985). Transitions to parenthood: His, hers, and theirs. *Journal of Family Issues, 6*(4), 451–481.

[13] Goldberg, W., Michaels, G., & Lamb, M. (1985). Husbands' and Wives' Adjustment to Pregnancy and First Parenthood. *Journal of Family Issues*, 6(4), 483–503. Retrieved March 22, 2008, from Academic Search Premier database.

[14] Baxter, J., Hewitt, B., & Haynes, M. (2008). Life course transitions and housework: Marriage, parenthood, and time on housework. *Journal of Marriage and Family* 70, 259–272.

[15] Cowan, C., Cowan, P. A., Heming, G., Garrett, E., Coysh, W., Curtis-Boles, H., Boles, A. J. (1985). Transitions to parenthood: His, hers, and theirs. *Journal of Family Issues*, 6(4), 451–481.

[16] Gottman, J. M., & Gottman, J. S. (2007). *And baby makes three: The six-step plan for preserving martial intimacy and rekindling romance after baby arrives*. New York, NY: Random House.

[17] Susman-Stillman, A., Appleyard, K., & Siebenbruner, J. (2003). For better or worse: An ecological perspective on parents' relationships and parent-infant interactions. *Zero to Three*, 23(3), 4–12.

[18] Heinicke, C. M. "The transition to parenting," in *Handbook of parenting*, 2nd ed., ed. Marc H. Bornstein, vol. 3: *Being and becoming a parent* (Mahwah, NJ: Eribaum, 2002), 363–388.

[19] Johnston & Swanson. (2006). Constructing the "Good Mother": The experience of mothering ideologies by work status. *Behavioral Science*, 54(7–8), 509–519.

[20] Cowan, C., Cowan, P. A., Heming, G., Garrett, E., Coysh, W., Curtis-Boles, H., Boles, A. J. (1985). Transitions to parenthood: His, hers, and theirs. *Journal of Family Issues*, 6(4), 451–481.

[21] Goldberg, W., Michaels, G., & Lamb, M. (1985). Husbands' and Wives' Adjustment to Pregnancy and First Parenthood. *Journal of Family Issues*, 6(4), 483–503. Retrieved March 22, 2008, from Academic Search Premier database.

[22] Cowan, C., Cowan, P. A., Heming, G., Garrett, E., Coysh, W., Curtis-Boles, H., Boles, A. J. (1985). Transitions to parenthood: His, hers, and theirs. *Journal of Family Issues*, 6(4), 451–481.

[23] Leifer, M. (1980). *Psychological effects of motherhood: A study of first pregnancy*. New York, NY: Preager.

[24] Feldman, S. S., & Nash, S. C. (1984). The transition from expectancy to parenthood. Impact of the first-born child on men and women. *Sex Roles*, 11, 61–78.

**Notes**

Wente, A., & Crockenberg, S. (1976). Transition to Fatherhood: Lamaze Preparation, Adjustment Difficulty and the Husband-Wife Relationship. *Family Coordinator*, 25(4), 351. Retrieved March 22, 2008, from Academic Search Premier database.

[25] Johnston & Swanson. (2006). Constructing the "Good Mother": The experience of mothering ideologies by work status. *Behavioral Science*, 54(7–8), 509–519.

[26] Johnston & Swanson. (2006). Constructing the "Good Mother": The experience of mothering ideologies by work status. *Behavioral Science*, 54(7–8), 509–519.

[27] Johnston & Swanson. (2006). Constructing the "Good Mother": The experience of mothering ideologies by work status. *Behavioral Science*, 54(7–8), 509–519.

[28] Stuckey, F. M., McGhee, P. E., & Bell, N. J. (1982). Parent-child interaction: The influence of maternal employment. *Developmental Psychology* 18(4), 635–644.

[29] Leifer, M. (1980). *Psychological effects of motherhood: A study of first pregnancy*. New York, NY: Preager.

[30] Feldman, S. S., & Nash, S. C. (1984). The transition from expectancy to parenthood. Impact of the first-born child on men and women. *Sex Roles*, 11, 61–78.

Wente, A., & Crockenberg, S. (1976). Transition to Fatherhood: Lamaze Preparation, Adjustment Difficulty and the Husband-Wife Relationship. *Family Coordinator*, 25(4), 351. Retrieved March 22, 2008, from Academic Search Premier database.

[31] Vandell, D. L., Hyde, J. S., Plant, E. A., & Essex, M. J. (1997). Fathers and "others" as infant-care providers: Predictors of parents' emotional well-being. *Merrill-Palmer Quarterly*, 43, 361–385.

[32] Clarke-Stewart, A., & Allhusen, V. (2005). *What we know about Childcare*. Harvard University Press.

[33] Hochschild, A. (2003). *The second shift*. New York, NY: Penguin Group.

[34] Hendel, M. (2006). Family leave: A dad's perspective. In. J. Blades & K. Rowe-Finkheiner (Eds.), *Motherhood Manifesto* (pp. 22–23). New York, NY: Nation Books.

[35] Blades, J., & Rowe-Finkheiner, K. (2006). *Motherhood manifesto*. New York, NY: Nation Books.

[36] Crouter, A. C., & Manke, B. (1997). Development of a typology of dual-earner families: A window into differences between and with families in relationships, roles, and activities. *Journal of Family Psychology* 11, 62–75.

[37] Crouter, A. C. (1984). Spillover from family to work: The neglected side of the work-family interface. *Human Relations*, 37(6), 425–441.

[38] Crouter, A. C. (1984). Spillover from family to work: The neglected side of the work-family interface. *Human Relations*, 37(6), 425–441

# Chapter

# 13

# Childcare and What Matters Most

# Childcare and What Matters Most

No matter the family structure—if there is an at-home parent, both parents involved in paid work, or a single parent—all parents have a need for non-parental care of their child, at least on occasion. I can't imagine any parent who doesn't hope for high-quality and nurturing care that ensures that children are safe and loved.[1] I know that I spend time wishing for Mary Poppins to swoop in to my rescue!

### The Martins (Maria)

*The first few years after I went back to work following the births of Matt and Abbie were some of the hardest years for me. I wasn't happy with the childcare situation, but I didn't feel like we could afford a better placement. I wasn't even sure what better placement would look like. I have learned so much since then, and when I need help with Luke now, I know the things that make the both of us comfortable. I need to know that Luke won't be ignored, even if he demands a lot of time. I want to know that he won't just be placed in front of the television and ignored until I get back. Luke wants to have something to do, and he loves to have friends to play with.*

## Childcare 101

Ironically, it's hard to give an accurate number to the children in childcare in the United States today. The estimate is anywhere between 60–80%. Some children are cared for in homes of friends, family members, or a mishmash of different situations that are informal and unregulated in the United States.[2] This complicates the ability to generate data and provide concise information.

Social changes in the United States over the last half-century have affected families. The need for high-quality childcare has grown faster than the ability to supply it.[3] The fastest growing need for care is for infants and toddlers. More mothers are returning to work before their infants are one-year old. This increased need is also tied to different licensing standards for children under the age of two. There must be higher ratios of adults to children, and licensing associated with infants and toddlers is more restrictive to meet health standards than for older children.[4]

Another social trend that has increased in the last several decades is that young families are more geographically isolated from their extended families. Where families might have used grandparents or aunts to help provide care for children, now they must look for other options because they are not near family members.[5]

The continued emphasis on early education and school readiness has also fueled the need for quality childcare. As headlines tout the importance of the early years for brain development, many public service announcements also promote enrolling children in preschool programs. Families with a stay-at-home parent are also seeking out opportunities for their children to attend an early education experience.[6]

## Types of Childcare

There are several types of childcare used in the United States today. One type is care for the child in the child's home. If childcare is provided by a relative it's usually the most economical and stable care. If a hired non-relative provides childcare and that individual is trained in early childhood education, this can be expensive. Care by a non-relative in the child's home (nanny care) is uncommon in the United States because of the prohibitive costs.

A family childcare home is a care arrangement in which an adult cares for a small group of children in his or her own home. This care is usually located close to the child's own home. This type of care is generally the least expensive, and can operate with or without a license, though it's recommended that parents use providers with a license. Typical family childcare providers have graduated from high school, but have not received training in early childhood education. They are less likely to provide structured, organized, or educational activities. However, parents often choose this type of care for their infants and toddlers because they feel the home atmosphere is more reflective of the experience they would have with a parent. Parents often comment on the need for a nurturing and loving environment when they choose family childcare options.

Childcare centers are the most visible option parents have to make childcare arrangements. Childcare centers are more likely to provide school readiness activities, and provide children with opportunities to play with peers. Most childcare center providers have received some training that is ongoing in early childhood education. They tend to have less flexible hours of operation and are more expensive than family childcare, but not as costly as in-home nanny care.

Families make all different kinds of decisions about childcare and how it will work for them. There isn't a set formula that helps parents determine the most ideal situation for their child. The following case studies show how families take care of their children while they are working.

### Laura

I was lucky. When I had my children, I didn't want to leave them for extended periods of time while I worked. I approached my boss and proposed bringing my infant to work until she became mobile. When she could crawl, then I would find an appropriate childcare center for her to explore and learn in. I was able to work, and because I wasn't worried about my daughter at childcare, I was able to be more productive at work. This situation worked so well for me with my first child I was able to do this with my second child. It was a good situation that worked well for me and for my family.

### Alison

I knew I wanted to be with my new baby as much as possible, but we needed my income to make ends meet. When I discovered I was pregnant, I approached my employer about working from home a few days a week. I was surprised when they agreed and helped me work out a schedule that took me to the office only once a week for six hours. I have to work consistent hours at home, and sometimes that is hard when my baby cries and I am trying to get a project finished up, but for the most part, it works. I have also loved the convenience of working in sweats. The only problem with working at home is that it's hard to leave it alone. When I have a big project, I seem to work 24 hours a day. It's hard when the office is a place you never leave.

### Lisa

I have a demanding job, and I like to be involved in the community. I have a busy schedule, but it works for me as long as I keep everything structured. I looked into having someone come to my house. I thought it would be convenient, but I soon discovered this wouldn't work for me. I always came home to a messy house, and waiting for someone to come so I could leave made me feel out of control. I opted to take my infant to a childcare center. This has worked out beautifully. I know what to expect when I come home every evening, and I control when I leave the house in the morning. I have been frustrated with the number of teachers my child has had, four in ten months. I would have hoped for more consistency to help him attach. I guess that you just can't have everything.

### Ellen

I looked at every center in my area, even some that would have been inconvenient to get to, but I couldn't find the right placement. I wanted to see someone snuggling and loving the children, and I never saw that. I was talking with a neighbor one day, and they suggested family childcare. I was a little leery, but started looking around. The first home I visited was just perfect. There was time for loves and stories, just the things I would *be doing with my child if I were home. Both my child and myself have felt comfortable and taken care of. I also love the flexibility of having my daughter stay an extra thirty minutes so I can run an errand on the way to pick her up.*

### April

*It sounds crazy, but to cut costs and ensure that my son was being taken care of, we developed a combination of care. My husband works 10-hour days and is off on Friday, so he takes care of my son on Friday. Then I wanted my son to have a preschool experience so on Tuesday and Thursday mornings he goes to preschool and my mom picks him up and takes care of him in the afternoons. My neighbor offered to help on Monday and Wednesday. So between my husband, my mom, preschool, and my neighbor, we have put together a good fit. It does get crazy remembering where my son goes every day, but people who love him surround him.*

### Nancy

*When we decided to have me go back to work after having the twins, it was a matter of finances. We needed every penny we could earn. Childcare for two children was so expensive! We really felt the only way to keep the most income was to work different shifts. I work swing shift, and my husband works the day shift. We have a crossover of about 2 hours when my twins go to a childcare center. I hate never seeing my husband except on weekends, but we are able to keep the most amount of money. I hope we don't have to do this forever though!*

## What Is Quality and Why Does It Matter?

Research over the years has shown that if a child attends a high quality program, there is not a negative effect on development. However, the key to this is quality. If children do attend low quality childcare and it's paired with poor parenting, children do have negative outcomes. When parents are selecting childcare for their children, they need to look for quality to ensure a better child outcome.[7]

The greatest single indicator of quality in a childcare setting is the ratio of caregivers to children. The lower the ratio, the more likely children are to receive the care they need. The staff should be well trained in early childhood education and have experience with children. They should also be consistent in the classroom, with low staff turnover. The staff should work to provide ample opportunities for educational and social stimulation. There should also be effective communication between parents and childcare providers. This communication should happen often so parents are aware of their child's activities, accomplishments, and areas of weakness.[8]

## But Will Childcare Hurt Them?

Many parents and educators are concerned about outcomes of childcare as they relate to a child's cognitive, social, and emotional development. So the burning question becomes: will childcare hurt children? The results from the National Institute of Child Health and Human Development (NICHD) study which followed 1,364 healthy newborns from infancy through elementary school showed that child outcomes were better when children attend care that more closely met quality standards.[9]

Specifically, children had higher language comprehension, fewer behavior problems, and rated higher on school-readiness scales.

There are risks associated with childcare as well. Children that start in childcare at young ages (in infancy) and attend programs for thirty hours or more each week do show unfavorable outcomes as do children attending low quality care.[10] If parents can carefully place their children in quality care situations, with individuals who are responsive to them, for less than thirty hours a week children are more likely to be competent and caring.

## Childcare—It's Not Just About Non-Parental Care

Parents are responsible for the care and growth of their children. The need for non-parental care when parents are away from their children is one aspect of childcare; however, parents also need to nurture their children. What are the best ways to do this?

I love my children so much and want them to be happy and to reach their potential. Sometimes the lines blur between what is happiness and what my children are capable of. I project my thoughts and expectations on my children. When I catch myself doing this, I find that I have taken the joy out of life's journey for my children. They are working to please me instead of themselves. How can parents help facilitate learning and development without extending their parental responsibilities? How do parents encourage their children to take advantage of opportunities without adding pressure? And how do parents know when enough is enough? These questions can get complicated as children grow.

*The Martins (Maria's Thoughts)*
> *As I think about what I want for the children when they leave the house, I want happiness for them. I guess that is a natural reply, but I know that if they are happy, they will do better in life. I know that when I have been happy with what is going on around me, I am more likely to support others and reach out to them. Who doesn't want that for their children? Sometimes when the house is chaotic and the children are fighting or bickering, I wonder if they will ever be happy. They seem to get on each other's nerves so often. I also wonder if the things they say to each other in the heat of the moment will affect them forever. When I was little I loved to sing, and now I don't because my older brother made fun of me. Will Matt scar his younger siblings? Will Abbie feel like Luke is always bothering her? How can I help Luke maintain his raw enthusiasm for life? How can I help them love each other and see the good in themselves and each other?*

## Self-Concept vs. Self-Esteem

Self-concept and self-esteem are two terms that are commonly used interchangeably; however, they have different meanings.[11] **Self-concept** is our idea about who we are. Children learn this information from infancy, and it's based upon our social, emotional, and personality attributes. Self-concept can be broken down into different dimensions.[12]

1. **Physical self:** the way people view themselves based upon their physical looks. Physical skills are also a part of this dimension. Athleticism, or the lack of it, contributes to ideas about body image.

2. **Social self:** the way people define themselves according to race, ethnic background, culture, and religious self. How people interact with others and friendships are a part of this dimension.

3. **Academic self:** the self as viewed in the child's mental abilities and aptitudes. School success or the lack of it fits into this dimension.

4. **Self-esteem:** the evaluation process used to define self-concept. In healthy situations, people use self-esteem to compare their actions to what their own ideal outcome is. When they lack self-esteem or have a negative self-esteem, they compare their actions to the ideals of others.

Looking at the above information, it might seem that there is still little difference between self-concept and self-esteem. They both involve evaluation and understanding of the self. Self-concept is more of a cognitively constructed idea, whereas self-esteem is emotional evaluation of self, based upon the respect people have for themselves. While both ideas change throughout life, self-concept is more likely to remain constant, and self-esteem can change more frequently and radically.

## Resiliency and Self-Esteem

It almost seems like children are born with relatively good self-esteem, and through experience and comparison, they negatively impact their self-understanding. I remember a story I heard on the radio a little while ago. It was a *Focus on the Family* minute put together by Dr. James Dobson.

*"John McKay, the great football coach of the University of Southern California and the Tampa Bay Buccaneers, was being interviewed on television when the subject of his son's athletic talent was raised. That year John McKay Jr. was a successful player on his dad's college team. Coach McKay was asked to comment on the pride he must feel over his son's accomplishments on the field. His answer was most impressive: "Yes, I'm pleased that John had a good season last year. He does a fine job, and I am proud of him. But I would be just as proud if he had never played the game at all."[13]*

Coach McKay was saying, in effect, that John's football talent is recognized and appreciated, but his human worth does not depend on his ability to play football. Thus, his son would not lose respect if the next season brought failure and disappointment. John's place in his dad's heart was secure, independent of his performance. I wish every child could say the same.

As I listened to that story I quickly thought about my children and their life experiences. Thinking about my children in the context of their self-esteem and pondering all their different stages in life (from infancy to adolescence), I was really struck by how self-esteem changes over the years. I watch my infant, and he is so confident in his abilities! He thinks he can walk. He pulls himself up on the couch and then turns to someone in the room and gives the biggest smile! Then when you smile back, he moves away from the couch and toward you. He places one foot away from the couch, lets go, and is immediately down on the floor! It doesn't stop him though—he crawls over to the couch and starts again. Using learning to walk as an analogy, there are times when my adolescent has fallen down on the floor. I have to smile at him and encourage him so he will venture out of his "negative evaluations" and try something new. I wish there was a magic pill that I could use to inoculate my children against losing self-esteem!

When children are given a strong foundation in emotional intelligence, they are better able to maintain good self-esteem.[14] When children melt down and are in tantrum mode, parents can respond with coaching and validation, helping them learn about their feelings and appropriate responses to them.

Resiliency is a set of protective mechanisms that modify a person's responses to risk situations. Children who have learned this resiliency can navigate successfully through our complex society. They have learned to bounce back after a setback has occurred in life.[15]

Can parents teach their children to be resilient? Maybe, maybe not. Resiliency is not a fixed personality trait. It's more a set of protective factors that children may or may not use during stressful or negative points in their lives. Children are resilient in some situations, but not in others. Parents may not be able to specifically teach resiliency; however, they can increase the likelihood of our children becoming resilient by encouraging certain skills and attitudes.[16]

First, parents can teach children **heightened sensory awareness.** Help children see the beauty in the things around them. If they are looking for bad or negative traits, they will always be there, likewise with positive outlooks. The child who looks for happiness is the child who finds it. Point out birds in the trees or how blue the sky is when going for a walk. Tell them that their smile lights up your day, or that watching them learn and grow makes your life more meaningful. They will understand what you are saying and look for the good themselves.

It may seem a little corny to point out the positive, and I sometimes take a "love everything" approach to this, which can become overbearing! The important thing to remember is that parents want their children to enjoy their life journey, and part of that is looking for happiness.

Children who are surrounded by adults that have **high, positive expectations** of their abilities are more resilient. Research has found that children have higher levels of motivation to complete a task if they know an adult believes in them.

My son will quickly tell you that I expect him to get good grades. He will also explain that I expect him to get good grades so he can get a scholarship and go to college. The part that is missing in that high expectation is that I want him to love learning, organize his work, set goals and accomplish them, and respond openly to others' ideas. If he can learn these traits, I know that the good grades will follow. I just hope that in all the teaching and talking about school, he gets the message that I care about him.

**A clear and developing understanding of one's strengths relating to accomplishment** is crucial for future success. In elementary school, children start to look beyond themselves and compare their abilities to others. This can be devastating if they feel they never measure up. Children need to know about their abilities and have some recognition for those to maintain positive feelings about themselves. When they can find positive personal attributes, it builds their self-concept, and helps support a more positive self-esteem.

Another thing that can help children develop resiliency is **developing a sense of humor.** Children should cultivate humor to help them keep perspective. Finding the humor in a situation can help relieve the tension and stress associated with it. Children who can find the humor in different situations, without laughing or making fun of others, are children others seek to be around.

One important note about humor: Sarcasm is a pervasive type of communication in our society. Children don't always understand sarcasm and the subtle humor that is associated with it. One day as I was watching a preschool class at our university lab school, I saw a little girl gluing various materials to wood, seemingly engrossed in the process of creating. A teacher came over to sit with her. The teacher sat down and asked the little girl, "What are you making?" The little girl replied, "This." The teacher, either offended or unsure of herself, didn't know what to do. She started talking about everything, giving this little girl a play-by-play of what was happening around the room. At one point the teacher said, "Everyone is busy, and no one needs me to help them. I am the teacher, and I don't need to teach! LOL!" The little girl curiously looked at the teacher and then went back to her work. She didn't get the underhanded humor of the teacher, nor did she understand the texting phrase, LOL.

This teacher did what many parents commonly do: she forgot the child. Children don't need the sarcasm because they don't understand it. What they do need is someone to be there and share time with them, point out good things, and enjoy genuine happiness with them. I wonder what would've happened in this situation if the teacher had been more open to the little girl. Do you think the little girl would've responded differently if the teacher had said, "Tell me about your work," and then listened?

## Why Is Self-Esteem Important?

Children with higher levels of self-esteem are able to act independently, assume responsibility, and take pride in their own accomplishments. They are more likely to tolerate frustration and attempt new tasks and challenges. These children also handle positive and negative emotions and offer empathy and assistance to others. When adults communicate to children that they are interested in what they are doing, thinking, and feeling, children develop a healthy self-esteem. When adults show that they are committed to children by giving them boundaries that are understandable and developmentally appropriate, children know adults care. Being a positive role model and teaching children coping strategies such as sharing, managing anger, conflict resolution, and dealing with stress can see them through the tough times.[17]

## Building Confidence

When children are given the illusion of fear, and are then able to conquer that "fear," they gain confidence. That same confidence is crucial for children to become risk takers. Everything that people do in life—learning to read, riding a bike, marriage, or parenting— requires that they take a risk and try. Children who are so focused on the outcome and scared to try are those children who struggle. Creating situations that help children overcome this illusion of fear is so important.[18]

One of the first steps parents can take toward creating an illusion of fear is what they say to children. When parents tell children to "be careful," they are actually teaching fear. Using the words "pay attention" will help children develop awareness, but without the fearfulness. Awareness is a great concept for children. It helps children understand their environment and have knowledge about what is happening without the caution that fear creates.

Parents can also cultivate experiences for children to try things at their own pace even in moments of fear. Our family enjoys skiing, and I remember that one of my daughters was scared to ride the chair lift. We spent countless Saturdays on the bunny hill using the towrope to get back up the hill. As her abilities and confidence grew, her desire to ski down the bigger hill overtook the feelings of fear she associated with the chair lift. The first time she went on the chair lift, she covered her eyes and held her breath! But each time it got easier for her. Now she is confident to get on the lift and ski down the hill. These memories help make her more likely to take a risk again!

## Talking with Your Child

Understanding that parents are the best teachers for their children makes communication that much more vital. Children respond best when they learn from parents in a trusted environment and not the media, computer, or friends.[19] I have learned that when I give my children a little bit of information at a time and let them process what they are hearing, they are more likely to talk. I want them to come and ask me about things they hear at school or from the television. Parents should always follow the lead of the children. Watch their attention span; give them a little information at a time, building upon what they know. Having a positive attitude helps children build confidence about what they are learning, and makes it more likely they will ask the questions they have.

Parents need to be aware as they think about when to have these discussions. Driving to school in the morning may not be the best time for some children, but it may be the best for others. I like to look for times that are quiet and allow for dialoguing. I have found that I need to be open and aware of when my children like to talk. For example, one of my children really likes to talk right after school, and they are more willing to open up at that time. Another child likes to talk right before bedtime. Learning those open times can facilitate communication. Also, big things need to be discussed at many different intervals. Lots of small conversations are more effective than one big talk, which can easily turn into a lecture. Children need time to process what is being said.

### The Martins (Rob's Thoughts)

*One thing I have picked up with Matt and Luke is that consistency always helps. I have to work hard to let Abbie know I am there for her. My actions, words, and interactions with her must show her that I want to listen, that I will listen any time, and that I want to help. Abbie is at such a crossroads of life, wanting to be a little girl because that is what she knows, but stretching her wings at the same time. I can help her see the fun in life by encouraging her to set goals and reach for them, make friends, and finally talk to me when she has concerns. It really is just putting my love for her into practice.*

## Going to School

When children grow enough to attend school, it's a milestone, not only for children, but parents as well. Parenting responsibilities change, the children's responsibilities change, and the cultural influence in the home changes. This is one of the first times that children will be able to compare the things that go on in their home with the things that go on in other homes. Children learn these differences by spending time in the homes of their friends, but also through talking and interactions at school.

### The Martins (Maria)

*I remember the first day of kindergarten for each of my older children. It's such a magical moment where children go from being little to making progress toward meeting their goal of "being big." I have been surprised how it seems that my children physically grow to match the emotional maturity that happens during this time. I sometimes wonder about Luke. I think he feels as big as Matt sometimes, and I wonder if kindergarten is ready for him! I just hope he gets a teacher that will work to understand him.*

*It's interesting sometimes to think about one child just starting his school career and one child ending his. Matt and Luke are on opposite ends. I have decided that ending the school career is more apprehensive for me. I guess I really don't know what to expect. How will my parenting change? Will Matt still need me? I think he is looking forward to graduating so he can leave the family home. I'm not even sure if he'll stay in contact very often. I sure hope so. I don't think he realizes how much Luke looks up to him! I guess this is just one more hill (and probably valley) that we will travel in life.*

## Parents as Teachers

One of the most empowering thoughts for parents is to recognize that they are their children's first teachers. The learning that takes place in the home in the first years of life is foundational to the learning that happens outside of the home in later years. Most parents don't understand the importance of this role, and society doesn't always promote this idea. Parents are very influential over their children and the activities and interactions that lead to their future learning.[20]

Whether parents are working outside the home or not, parental attitudes about education have a powerful effect on children from birth. Research has followed some children who succeed in the school setting, and some common parental characteristics were found. Some of those characteristics, not surprisingly include:

reading to children, having books available (near the bed with a lamp is one of the best ways to do this), talking with children, planning television watching, and providing stimulating interactions with children.[21]

When parents have higher educational expectations, they tend to encourage children to achieve more in school. Parents can also influence children's education by going to the school that the children attend and helping when they can. This can be hard for working parents, but staying in touch with teachers through e-mails or notes back and forth can help. I also like to offer my help with big projects that require "take-home" work. Teachers can send home cutting, grading, or other needed items with my children, and I can complete them and send them back to school. The message that is being sent is, "I care about my children's education and I want to be involved." The other message that is sent to your children is that education is important and I will do what I can to help you succeed.

It's also important for parents to know that a lot of ideas associated with success in school form in the early years of life. They manifest themselves through secure attachments, authoritative parenting, and playful interactions. When parents get down on the floor and play with children, they can model and show children many things such as sharing, helping, and negotiation. These are the first things children need to learn before they go to school. The outcome for children with these skills is higher than children without these skills, or those children that must learn these skills at school. Play is the strongest foundation we can build in preparing children for school. Children build their attention spans, incorporate problem-solving skills, and gain awareness through play.[22]

## Types of Parental Involvement

Families whose children are doing well in school usually exhibit the following characteristics:

1. **Establish a daily family routine**—including a time and place for completing homework, giving children household responsibilities, having a set bedtime (and routine), and eating dinner together as a family. These types of behaviors empower children and help them know what to expect. It also communicates to them what they should be doing so they are aware of the expectations placed on them.

2. **Monitor out-of-school activities**—this not only includes the time children spend away from the family house, but also activities in the home such as television watching and video games. Children are more likely to succeed when parents set limits on television and video games, and are active in monitoring their children. Parents who ask questions like, who will you be with, where will you be, what will you be doing, are parents that are helping their children succeed.

3. **Model the values of learning, self-discipline, and hard work**—communicating with children and listening to them can help them gain self-confidence and understand that their ideas are appreciated. Children succeed when parents help them find information to their questions and support their educational inquiries. Demonstrating that achievement comes through hard work is also something parents can teach their children. Parents can recognize a job well done and convey the importance to children through everyday conversations.

4. **Express high but realistic expectations for achievement**—helping children learn to set goals and achieve them gets them on the right path. Noticing children's special talents and informing family members about them can help children feel special. Be careful of how this is done, so embarrassment isn't the emotion felt by the child.

5. **Encourage children's development or progress in school**—asking children about school and what they learned could make them aware of education's importance. Parents who are supportive of appropriate homework also encourage their children to do well in school. Parents who talk with teachers about their children's progress also send the message that school is a positive force.

6. **Encourage reading, writing, and discussions among family members**—this can be accomplished around the dinner table, but another fun activity is to read books together as a family and discuss what is being read. Helping children reach a higher level of thinking is an amazing thing to witness.

## Involvement in Education

There are many opportunities for parents as their children move through the school system: volunteering in the classroom, participating on the Parent-Teacher Association, and collaboration with the community. One thing that school does for children is help them become aware of their community at large. Children start to see many different things that they can do around them and within their community. This can include after-school programs, sports, tutoring, lessons and programs, and culturally based opportunities. Parents who are aware of their community resources can help children and teachers connect classroom learning with opportunities around them. This can strengthen the learning in the classroom and help children apply the learning.

Research has found that when parents are involved with their children and the education process the outcomes are favorable. These include higher grades and test scores, better school attendance, better self-esteem, decreased use of drugs and alcohol, and fewer instances of violent behavior.[24]

## Staying Involved with a Career

It seems that all the research suggests that parents spend lots of time involved with their children and their school for success. This is not the case. There are many things that parents can do at home to ensure that children will succeed in school. Jim Trelease wrote *The Read Aloud Handbook*.[25] In this book, he writes about three crucial things families can do to help children become lifelong readers (which can lead to becoming lifelong learners). These three things are easy for any parent to incorporate. The first is giving children books of their own. These books should be for the child only, even if there are other siblings in the home. There can be shared books, but children also need their own books. When they have their own books, they need a place to put them. This can be a bookshelf or a basket; it doesn't have to be anything big or fancy. The last thing is a lamp near the bed so children can read before they go to sleep. When families establish these things at home for their children, they are more likely to read. Thinking about the children's room and including these items is a simple way working parents can send a simple message about the importance of reading.[26]

Parents often equate involvement in education to volunteering in the classroom. This is definitely not the case! Teachers succeed in the classroom when they have many resources. Going and helping once a week is not the only way parents can help. Maybe a parent has a special skill like computer graphics and can put together a newsletter for the classroom. This can help out the teacher by saving time, and can help out parents by their knowing what is going on in the classroom. Talking with a teacher is one of the best things that a parent can do. Then parent and teacher can work out together different ways a parent can help. It can include grading papers at home, calling parents for fieldtrips, gathering resources for a special project, etc. Teachers know what they need, and if they know they can call on a parent for help, they will find a way to use it.

It's important that working parents don't overlook the importance of helping their children attend school every day prepared for what needs to happen. Completed homework, nightly reading, well-fed and well-rested children can make a teacher's day! Parents can encourage these behaviors by setting a simple routine for children to follow. This can be a fun time of learning and growth for parent and child if parents understand their potential and make use of it.

## Extracurricular Activities

It really would be easier if your child arrived with a book of instructions, but not having one is part of the fun and excitement of parenting. You have to figure out the questions, and then find the answers. How can families figure out when enough is enough? Is there a worksheet that parents can fill out to determine if they have a balance? What is the best approach for families to make this decision? Is there anything proven in research to help our families maintain harmony? What about practical approaches to everyday tasks that can help us save time? Just thinking about it all can get overwhelming!

### The Martins (Rob)

*I have watched Maria run herself ragged so many different times in the past seventeen years. There have been times when the children have been involved in too many activities, and we have lost our sense of family. There have been other times that we have done too little for too long, and it has affected the stimulation and learning of the children. It has been hard to determine a balance and then stick with it. It seems like it should be easy, but there are so many external factors that can upset the balance. Each child is different and handles different amounts of stimulation. The distance we have to drive to get the children where they need to go is a huge factor. If other parents can help us share the burden by carpooling, and if a special project or holiday is upcoming are all things that affect the fragile balance we work so hard to establish. Sometimes I think Maria gets too emotionally tied to helping our children succeed and have different experiences. I feel like I have to bring her back to earth sometimes and say enough is enough! If we can't have a meal together a few times a week, we lose our connection!*

## How Children Spend Their Time

All children spend part of their days eating, sleeping, and involved in personal care. In a study conducted by Sandberg and Hofferth, they also found that most children spend part of each day watching television (2–3 hours each day on average) and playing.[27] How much time do children have, and how do they choose to spend that time? In this study, children averaged about 51 hours of unstructured time each week. Most children spent about fifteen hours watching television; five hours involved in sports, lessons, or other instruction outside of school; one hour in church; three hours visiting friends; one hour outside; and about 26 hours in unstructured play.[28]

Parental attitudes, perceptions, and values affect the way that children spend this discretionary time each week. Family structure and size affect the abilities of parents to monitor their children and transport them to various activities. There are a lot of variations that affect if, how, and when children are engaging in extracurricular activities.

Structured activities for children, ranging from sports practices to dancing to music lessons, are associated with higher cognitive and emotional development. Children have the opportunity to learn to solve problems, gain skills associated with the activity, and practice social skills. Parents often perceive extracurricular activities as a good thing and seek out informed guidance as to how to direct their children's activities. Parents need to be careful about planning structured activities for children. Children also benefit from time at home talking, interacting, and eating with their families. It's also important that children have enough sleep. Children who spend time with their families tend to have lower incidences of behavior problems. Families must seek out a balance between time at home and time away from home.

One way that I like to look at how my children spend their time is compare their time to a budget. Just like opportunity costs with our money (if we have a car payment, opportunity costs are the things we could have spent our money on or saved instead of the car payment), I think that my children have opportunity costs with their time. Watching 1 hour of television isn't necessarily a bad thing, but I weigh that hour against what my children are choosing NOT to do with their time. There are times that it's more important that my children are spending time with the family, completing homework, reading, or engaging in unstructured play instead of watching television for that hour. This type of thinking can help parents keep things in perspective, and it's an easy concept to teach children as they learn to make decisions.

## Parents Really Do Have the Answers: Supports for Families

There are many supports for families, some easier to recognize than others. Those supports create a safety net for children to obtain experience and understanding about life in a situation hopefully set up for their success. Many individuals serve as mentors and models for your children. Teachers and others with whom your child interacts in their school can provide encouragement to children, promote responsibility and competence in children, and provide an educational support net for parents.

Parenting programs and classes within neighborhoods can help parents in many ways. Obviously, they can teach specific skills to parents; they can also help parents reduce children's behavioral difficulties. Many times parents reach out to parenting classes during times of stress or times of transitions (childhood to adolescence). Classes, teachers, and other parents attending the class can help reduce the stress of parenting, and in turn increase parents' self-confidence.

Some government and community agencies can help parents as they adjust to difficulties ranging from temporary job loss, homelessness, or even disabilities of a family member. These agencies can also help educate parents about skills that can improve family life.

One last area parents can turn for support is to churches. Children who engage in religious activity with their families can develop a sense of security. This security and belonging can be similar to the feeling created by family rituals. Religion can offer guidelines for daily conduct so children and parents know how to behave. Some churches might also be able to provide services for children and families when they are needed.

All of these different support systems can help create anchors in children's lives so they feel a connection with their community, religion, school, and peers. These anchors create daily activities for children that can lead to better outcomes. Anchors help children know that they belong somewhere and that they are wanted. This is crucial if we want to develop resiliency in our children. Resiliency can help our children survive many life storms.

## Making the Best Decisions for Children

Regardless of what message society tries to send to families, parents really can be the best individuals to make decisions for their children. There are a few things parents need to develop an understanding of as they think about the future of their children.[29] The first is having a high level of personal self-awareness. Parents who understand their own strengths and weaknesses have a better working knowledge of their children and what is acceptable. Parents need to know what their children like and dislike so they can follow through with those expectations on behavior. Parents who don't like a lot of loud sounds probably shouldn't encourage young children to play with pots and spoons. The noise may lead a parent to their breaking point, where they may respond to the child in a manner that doesn't reflect their usual consistency. I can handle a lot of mess at my house, so we spend a lot of time playing with things like sand, rice, or shaving cream in the sensory table (explained in Chapter 12). We also like to paint and do lots of crafty types of things. I have also learned over time that it's important to me that my house be put back in order before bedtime. This means that we get out the mess and play hard, and then we all pick up so we can do it again another day.[30]

The next component is being in tune with your child. What are their strengths and weaknesses, and are they different from yours? Keeping in mind the desires a child might have can help parents make reasonable choices for their children. This step requires a lot of work for parents. One way that I like to keep up with my children and open the lines of communication is to take them on "dates." About once a month I take each child to go do something, just the two of us. I truly treasure these times because I have found that my children often open up and talk candidly to me. I then have better information to make more effective decisions.[31]

The last part of this is to take that information, as well as knowledge about culture, family goals, individual children, and make an effective decision. It's okay to change your mind at a later time, and it's okay to go away from societal norms. Keeping your eyes trained on the important factors of family, child, and connection will encourage good decision making.[32]

There isn't a template for parents to plug numbers into, but by establishing awareness about self, children, and family, parents can make effective decisions. Parents can see what is best for their children and can then plan accordingly. Parents also need to remember that families do need time to be together in order to create feelings of closeness and love. Some of that time together should include traditions, rituals, and celebrations. It can also include planned structured activities for children and vacations.

Families also need unstructured time to be together. This is probably the biggest struggle for working families—literally taking time and relaxing together. Sometimes the temptation to fill the time with household responsibilities or catching up on homework and work outside of the home can be overwhelming. Families need to fight the temptation and instead make time for each other. This time away from the grindstone will help families maintain balance as well. Reflection and appreciation will come more readily in moments of unstructured time than at any other time. Parents who foster, respect, and maintain unstructured family time set up the potential for children to feel accepted. These relaxing and fun times lend themselves to more spontaneity and encourage memories to form.

## Practical Implications

One way that a family can maintain balance is to start slow. Allow each child to pick one structured activity each week. After a few weeks, evaluate the situation. Is there added stress to the parent or child? Does the child enjoy the activity? Is it affordable? Make changes at that point. If everything is going okay, parents might want to consider adding another activity. This process needs to be very thoughtful and methodical. Some children can and want to be involved in more activities than other children. Yet others succeed with more unstructured free time. Follow your child's lead, and tune into yourself and your child. Success is sure to come.

## References

[1] Blades, J., & Rowe-Finkheiner, K. (2006). *Motherhood manifesto*. New York, NY: Nation Books.

[2] Clarke-Stewart, A., & Allhusen, V. (2005). *What we know about Childcare*. Harvard University Press.

[3] Clarke-Stewart, A., & Allhusen, V. (2005). *What we know about Childcare*. Harvard University Press.

[4] Clarke-Stewart, A., & Allhusen, V. (2005). *What we know about Childcare*. Harvard University Press.

[5] Clarke-Stewart, A., & Allhusen, V. (2005). *What we know about Childcare*. Harvard University Press.

[6] Clarke-Stewart, A., & Allhusen, V. (2005). *What we know about Childcare*. Harvard University Press.

[7] Clarke-Stewart, A., & Allhusen, V. (2005). *What we know about Childcare*. Harvard University Press.

[8] Clarke-Stewart, A., & Allhusen, V. (2005). *What we know about Childcare*. Harvard University Press.

[9] NICHD Early Child Care Research Network. (Ed.) (2005). Child care and child development: Results of the NICHD study of early child care and youth development. New York: Guildford Press.

[10] Ramey, S. L. (2005). Human developmental science serving children and families: Contributions of the NICHD study of early child care. In The NICHD Early Child Care Research Network Child Care and Child Development: Results of the NICHD study of early child care and youth Development. New York: Guilford Press.

[11] May, K. (2009). What is the difference between self-concept and self-esteem? Associated Content, Aug. 05. Retrieved February 24, 2010, from Associated Content.

[12] May, K. (2009). What is the difference between self-concept and self-esteem? Associated Content, Aug. 05. Retrieved February 24, 2010, from Associated Content.

[13] Dobson, J. (1999). *The new hide or seek*. Ada, MI: Revell.

Notes

[14] Davis, S., Eppler-Wolff, N. (2009). *Raising children who soar: A guide to healthy risk-taking in an uncertain world*. New York: Teachers College Press.

[15] Garbarino, J. (1995). *Raising children in a socially toxic environment*. San Francisco: CA: Jossey-Bass.

[16] Louv, R. (2005). *The last child in the woods: Saving our children from nature-deficit disorder*. (p. 178). Algonquin Books of Chapel Hill, Chapel Hill, NC.

[17] Davis, S., Eppler-Wolff, N. (2009). *Raising children who soar: A guide to healthy risk-taking in an uncertain world*. New York: Teachers College Press.

[18] Davis, S., Eppler-Wolff, N. (2009). *Raising children who soar: A guide to healthy risk-taking in an uncertain world*. New York: Teachers College Press.

[19] Davis, S., Eppler-Wolff, N. (2009). *Raising children who soar: A guide to healthy risk-taking in an uncertain world*. New York: Teachers College Press.

[20] U.S. Department of Education. (2005). Helping your child succeed in school. U.S. Department of Education, Office of Communications and Outreach. Washington, D.C.: Education Publication Center.

[21] U.S. Department of Education. (2005). Helping your child succeed in school. U.S. Department of Education, Office of Communications and Outreach. Washington, D.C.: Education Publication Center.

[22] Elkind, D. (2009). *The power of play: learning what comes naturally*. Philadelphia, PA: Da Capo Press Books.

[23] U.S. Department of Education. (2005). Helping your child succeed in school. U.S. Department of Education, Office of Communications and Outreach. Washington, D.C.: Education Publication Center.

[24] U.S. Department of Education. (2005). Helping your child succeed in school. U.S. Department of Education, Office of Communications and Outreach. Washington, D.C.: Education Publication Center.

[25] Trelease, J. (2006). *The Read Aloud Handbook*. 5th edition. New York, NY: Penguin Group.

[26] Trelease, J. (2006). *The Read Aloud Handbook*. 5th edition. New York, NY: Penguin Group.

[27] Sandberg, J. F. & Hofferth, S. L., (2001). Changes in children's time with parents: United States, 1981–1997. *Demography*, 38, 423–436.

[28] Sandberg, J. F. & Hofferth, S. L., (2001). Changes in children's time with parents: United States, 1981–1997. *Demography*, 38, 423–436.

[29] Lerner, C. & Dombro, A. L. (2005). Bringing up baby: Three steps to making good decisions in your child's first years. *Zero to Three.*

[30] Lerner, C. & Dombro, A. L. (2005). Bringing up baby: Three steps to making good decisions in your child's first years. *Zero to Three.*

[31] Lerner, C. & Dombro, A. L. (2005). Bringing up baby: Three steps to making good decisions in your child's first years. *Zero to Three.*

[32] Lerner, C. & Dombro, A. L. (2005). Bringing up baby: Three steps to making good decisions in your child's first years. *Zero to Three.*

Notes

# Chapter 14

## Play: Why It's Important for Both Parent and Child

# Play: Why It's Important for Both Parent and Child

I look back fondly on the times when I was younger and would play with my brothers and friends. We were always outside, and even though I am sure I am making it better than it really was, it seems there was always an adventure waiting for us. In life now, I feel like I don't have the time to just spontaneously play; however, from my children, I have learned the importance of taking time to play. I believe that play has a major role in a balanced life.

### The Martins (Maria)

*I always wanted to be the "fun" mom. I wanted to have the house that all the children on the block wanted to go to, and knew they were welcome. I thought it would be easy. I just had to have punch and cookies and great toys. It's not that easy! This is really hard for me. I love when my children invite their friends over, but I really struggle with my desire for a clean house. The children come over, and I can be playful and fun for a little while, and then I start thinking, "I hope they clean this up. I don't have time to clean this up." I have to fight my inner mom that wants everything perfectly clean and realize that everything is perfect because the children are playing and having fun.*

The following paragraph was taken from the introduction of the position statement put forth by the Association for Childhood Education International (ACEI), a professional organization for early childhood education. The position they have taken is that play is essential for all children at all ages and that adults need to provide materials, time, and support for children's play. The best way that you can support play is to allow and encourage your own children to play.

*Children are growing up in a rapidly changing world characterized by dramatic shifts in what all children are expected to know and be able to do. Higher and tougher standards of learning for all populations of students are focusing on a narrow view of learning. Consequently, students have less time and opportunity to play than did children of previous generations. Few would disagree that the primary goal of education is student learning and that all educators, families, and policymakers bear the responsibility of making learning accessible to all children. Decades of research has documented that play has a crucial role in the optimal growth, learning, and development of children from infancy through adolescence. Yet, this need is being challenged, and so children's right to play must be defended by all adults, especially educators and parents. The time has come to advocate strongly in support of play for all children.[1]*

Research has shown that children learn through play.[2] Some of the skills they learn through their play include problem-solving skills, increased creativity, enhanced language and social skills, and better and longer attention spans. Play is defined as something that is pleasurable and enjoyable to the individual. There are not any extrinsic goals associated with the play—it's spontaneous and voluntary, the participant is actively engaged, and there is an element of make-believe to the play. Play is ultimately children's way of controlling their environment. Have you ever noticed how often young children play house, for example? They are figuring out their place in the family. When children feel like they are in control, they are more likely to have a strong sense of self, which in turn will affect their self-esteem. Exploration and play are connected for children. They don't think of them as disconnected activities, but those that go hand in hand. Children need time to explore and play, and they also need time to process the information they have gained through their explorations.[3]

Play is such an important element of life for young children, and something that parents can utilize to connect and relax with their children. I would like to look at different kinds of play and how they can help children develop. Morrison defined 6 types of play.[4] They are explained in the following paragraphs.

Social play involves play with peers. Children work out turn taking, and in so doing they learn how to resolve conflicts and continue play. Language skills can increase in social play as well because children are talking and sharing ideas. Children engage in social play in different ways. It might look like playing trains, working playdough, or stacking blocks.

Cognitive play requires active participation from children. As they practice skills over and over, like walking or cartwheels, children develop muscle control and strength. Pretending a block is a phone or that they are "mommy" helps them learn about social interactions. In constructive play, children build and create things with different materials. They might build a tower or a house for their doll. They learn how things fit together. As children get older their play becomes more defined by rules. These rules establish limits and expectations. Children work with their peers to determine the rules, and they learn about social interactions.

In sociodramatic play children experiment with roles. They might try on realistic identities like playing house or grocery store, or they might embrace a more fantasy type of play imitating superheroes or fairytale characters. With sociodramatic play, children have the opportunity to participate in a wide variety of roles, and interact with their friends. I also learn a lot about the ways my children interpret what I say and do. When my daughters play house, I like to listen in and see what rules they set up in their house and how they maintain them. It's a reflection on actual happenings in the house I have set up.

Outdoor play is crucial because it allows children to release tension that may build up as they sit still. When children move their arms and legs and run, their muscles develop. Pretend play can take on different elements outside as well. During the summer, we like to create a fairy garden with flowers and rocks for our children to play in.

In one way or another all children engage in rough and tumble play. Children learn the subtle differences in facial expressions in rough and tumble play. They learn to recognize what a "game face" is compared to when someone is hurt or seeking revenge. The emotional learning can transfer to body language as well.

Play is a natural way for children to learn.[5] They are intrinsically drawn to exploration and play, and this can build their curiosities. Recognizing the importance of play is one way that parents can build parenting skills. Supporting and encouraging play by providing time, props (because cardboard boxes can be more fun than toys!), and friends can make your house the most popular one on the block!

### The Martins (Rob)

*One of my favorite times of the day is coming home from work. I love to walk in the door and yell, "Daddy's going to get you!" Maria has got after me several times about getting the children riled up, but it's so much fun! I can chase after Luke, sneering that I am going to get him, while laughing an evil and sinister laugh, and he knows this is in fun. It really helps me unwind to run around and wrestle for a minute. I know it bothers Maria, but I can't seem to explain what this means to me.*

## Playful Parenting

Adults who are trying to slow down the pace of life recognize the importance of play in the lives of their children.[6] They value the time they get to spend with their children on the floor engaged in active play, or outside exploring new environments. Years ago when I was starting my family, my older brother, who I love and adore, told me, "You'll be a great mom." I told him, "Thank you," and moved on to the next thought in our conversation, but he stopped me and said again, "You'll be a great mom." Hearing this a second time, I stopped and looked him in the eye and asked, "Why do you say that?" My brother responded, "You'll let your boys play in the dirt and get messy, and you won't yell. That is important." This thought has always stuck with me. My brother, a parent himself, was reaching out and complimenting me on something he recognized as part of my personality, something that would be valuable for young children. I don't think he understands the impact this had on my early parenting philosophies. I made choices not to yell or get upset with messes because those words were in my head. I do let my children get messy, and because of his statement sometimes I encourage them to get messy.

David Elkind, in his book titled *The Power of Play*, coined the term "lighthearted parenting." "Parents make an ongoing effort to integrate play, love, and work into their child-rearing practices."[7] Lighthearted or playful interactions can make childrearing easier, more fun, and more effective. I like these thoughts because while I did decide to have children to fit my adult developmental tasks, I also had children because I wanted fun in my life. It's easy to forget that children are fun, and parenting is too! Parents can get so caught up in meeting the next deadline, planning the next meeting, paying the bills, or even cooking dinner. If parents can instead integrate playful interactions, including humor, with what we must accomplish anyway, it can make it easier, more fun, and more effective.

I have tried to incorporate these principles of fun, play, and humor into my parenting over the years. Through my many failures, I have learned some great tricks that help me succeed at bringing play and humor into our family. For example, our family cooks together. I cook big meals on the weekends so we have leftovers throughout the week. My favorite times are when my children are in the kitchen with me, and I have my five-year-old cracking eggs, my thirteen-year-old chopping vegetables, my eight-year-old mixing batter, and my one-year-old emptying the cupboards. It sounds chaotic, doesn't it! Well, it is, but I love the noise, the questions, the laughter, and everything! When I look around and see all of us working together and having fun, I know that life is good, and I know that my children understand that they belong. They feel, see, and know that I love them.

Parents all have different parenting styles. Not all parents enjoy messy play. For some, having everyone in the kitchen is frustrating. I think that variety is delightful. It adds to the challenge of parenting. It's more crucial that parents ask themselves, "How can I enjoy parenting more?" or "Can I be more playful with my children?" When parents ask those questions and truthfully answer them, they find their strengths. It might be something as simple as telling jokes on the way to school, or as complex as playing restaurant at dinner. The key is doing what parents are happy doing and want to do and stopping there.

My children have always loved to put on "shows" for the family. My husband and I have encouraged these interactions by providing simple props and dress-up. A few years back, I was noticing some talent with my children, and I really wanted to give them a stage area in our house. I talked about pulling up carpet and having wood floors installed in my house. My husband quickly brought me back to earth by asking, "Is the outcome going to outweigh the effort?" This is a good way to maintain balance. A stage would've been nice, but my husband knows me well. I would've reached and gone beyond my breaking point with such a fun project.

This may seem like an ideal approach to parenting that if parents live, work, and play together that everything will be bright and beautiful and that it will never rain over your house. I don't believe that, but I do believe that the relationship parents form with children is a part of their foundational understanding about life. Peggy O'Mara, the publisher, editor, and owner of *Mothering Magazine* has been quoted, "Be careful how you speak to your children, one day it will become their inner voice." I really hope that my children know I love them and want to be around them. Deep down I want them to think that I believe the sun and moon rise and set because of them. I want that because I know there will be times that are hard. If parents have a secure attachment and common experiences from playful interactions, then learning about life lessons will be easier.

One thing that I have learned over the years is that my actions do speak louder than words. Playing with my children, looking them in the eyes when we talk, sharing hopes and dreams have shown my children I am an active part of their lives. Problems still occur, but I feel I can be a help to them because I have seen them in action and can understand how they feel. I know what questions to ask them, and I can talk with them before small problems become out of hand. Our connections really bring us together.

### The Martins

> Hopefully Rob will learn a little bit about play. His interactions with the children are important for building a strong foundation for learning and social interaction. It might be a good idea for him to work with Maria and figure out how he can engage in the rough and tumble play with the children and not upset the household. Working together, Maria and Rob can determine the best playful interactions for getting their work done and being together.

## Parenting Stages and Styles

While parents and individuals may travel different roads to parenting, Ellen Galinsky found that most parents experiences stages of transformation in their parenting ideals.[8] (Refer to the following table for her stages of parenting.) These are commonalities that link us as parents. I love talking with other parents and hearing their stories because I can generally think of something similar I've experienced with my children.

Galinsky's stages of parenting are nice to know because it helps explain how people think about parenting and why parents might do things during various stages of their children's development. This is one more tool that parents can use to learn about their own strengths and weaknesses as they make decisions about how they want to parent. Looking at the different stages, I can see why I interact in different ways with my five-year-old and my thirteen-year-old. They have different needs and perspectives on life and it's my responsibility to accommodate those changes. This flexibility is another way that parents can find success in families. Having more information about child development and parenting allows parents to make more effective decisions.

| | |
|---|---|
| Image-Making Stage (Through Pregnancy) | The timing for this stage is usually pregnancy, and parents are preparing for the changes that are going to occur in their lives. Parents often think about what they want for themselves and their child. |
| Nurturing Stage (Birth–18 months) | Parents realign their "imagined child" with their actual child. Parents become attached to their child and become caregivers. They work to balance the responsibilities in their lives with their child. |
| Authority Stage (18 months–5 years) | Parents learn importance of structure and boundaries for their child's success. They establish patterns of interacting. |
| Interpretive Stage (5 years–12 years) | These are the teaching years where parents help children interpret the social world around them and help them establish a way of life. |
| Interdependent Stage (Adolescence) | The formation of a new relationship between parent and child occurs during this stage. While parents are still the authority, their power is shared. Parents must balance monitoring, responsibility, and personal freedom in the relationship with their child. |
| Departure Stage (Young Adulthood) | Parents evaluate themselves as their children leave the house. Parents must also again reestablish a relationship with their adult child that fosters both independence and close personal ties. |

## Strategies Parents Use to Meet Needs

Couples and parents must consciously make decisions about how, when they are away from home working, to meet the needs of their children. Most working parents do this by focusing their energies on the children while at home. They may decide to, instead of vacuuming the hallway, help children with their homework. Multitasking may be an important part of this. For example, as parents drive children to a music lesson, they may ask questions about their day at school, discuss upcoming homework projects, and plan out a time for a birthday party in two weeks.

The struggle for parents is making sure they get the important things done. Most parents plan and create a schedule to make sure this happens. Some parents have weekly planning meetings. One strategy we have used in our family is to sit down every Sunday evening and discuss the week with a calendar. Each family member lists appointments, lessons, and projects in a different color of ink on the calendar, and we plan out who is in charge of each item and how and when it will get done. This may seem complicated, but families may want to try a variation of this technique.

Monitoring children and their behaviors is another important struggle working couples face. Where the children are and what they are doing after school can be hard when parents are not home. The few hours after school until a parent returns home are times of great concern for parents. Some parents may find relief from this worry by having their children in after-school programs. Others may choose to have older teens come home. Most parents actively set up systems and plans to help monitor their children when they are not home. Some parents have the children call them upon arriving home from school. Other parents may have a neighbor check in on the child and call if there is a problem. Parents may leave lists of things children must accomplish by the time they return home. However parents choose to monitor their children doesn't particularly matter, as long as there is something in place and parents have a knowledge about who, what, where, and how, as well as safety.

To help meet the needs of the family, parents may also encourage family cooperation in household work. Working parents can often find effective and efficient ways to accomplish jobs with the whole family. That way the household responsibilities are getting done, and there is also family togetherness. Working families may decide to have everyone go together to the grocery store so they can spend time together. They may divide out the house chores, but have everyone work on them at the same time. Working together to accomplish household tasks may allow for parent and child to talk while they work and parents can use this time to talk about life experiences with their child.

Another strategy some working parents use is to have their younger children maintain a unique routine. Maybe a parent might keep a child up late into the evening because they work a swing shift and want to tuck their child in. Then the child sleeps late in the morning. Working parents and their children tend to maintain similar sleep-wake cycles and activities. Some working parents may make sure that their children are in bed at a certain time most days, but if they don't have school or other activities the next day, they may keep their children up late to spend a few extra minutes with them.

The key to successful strategies in balancing work and family is to mindfully decide what the family needs and goals parents have for their children and then come up with a plan to see what works. I have an example of this. I love to have the beds made in our house. It is important to me. One goal I have is that I want my children to know how to make their beds. I didn't care so much about how they got made as long as they were made by the time we left each morning. I realized that it was important to me to have the beds made, and I didn't want to negatively impact my relationship with my child or upset the morning by yelling. It ended up being better to make beds with my children each morning. I learned over time that both my children and myself had needs met. I had beds that were made, and my children each got time with me in the morning. I also had time to visit about the things the children were looking forward to during the day. It was a great way to start the day!

## Parenting Styles and Resiliency

Parenting is obviously critical to the development of resiliency.[9] Whereas dysfunctional or neglectful parenting can be one of the major risk factors for children, a close relationship with a parent who provides unconditional love and support (behavioral guidance and supervision) is generally agreed to be the most significant protection a child can have against psychopathology and other problems later in life. Parents provide children with their basic roadmap for navigating life. Their capacity to cope with and overcome adversity is directly related to the skills and attitudes with which their parents have equipped them.

Resiliency research has demonstrated that the three key factors of the foundations for developing resiliency are caring relationships, high expectations, and opportunities for involvement. Warmth, responsiveness and emotional closeness provide children with the sense of security, trust, and self-esteem that are fundamental to resiliency. High expectations and clear boundaries provide the structure, discipline, and sense of self-efficacy which children need in order to master important academic and life skills.[10]

This is a brief summary of some of the ways that parents can promote resiliency. Involved parents are parents who take a close interest in their children, are responsive to their needs, and are intimately involved in their children's lives. Uninvolved parents, on the other hand, are relatively remote and unresponsive, and take relatively less interest in the "ins and outs" of their children's lives. Demanding parents have high expectations of their children in terms of behavior and responsibility, are firm, and set clear boundaries. Undemanding parents have relatively lower behavioral standards, allow their children more freedom to do as they please, and impose fewer boundaries, if any.

Diana Baumrind[5] identified authoritative, authoritarian, and permissive parenting styles.[11] A parenting style is a set of attitudes toward the child that a parent transmits to the child to create an emotional climate surrounding parent–child exchanges. Parenting style is different from parenting behaviors, which are characterized by specific actions and socialization goals. The combination of parental warmth and demandingness is central to conceptualization of parenting style.

| Authoritarian | Authoritative |
|---|---|
| Low Responsiveness High Demandingness | High Responsiveness High Demandingness |
| Neglectful | Permissive |
| Low Responsiveness Low Demandingness | High Responsiveness Low Demandingness |

Authoritative parents display a warm, accepting attitude toward their children while maintaining firm, consistent, and clear expectations of and restrictions on children's behavior. Open communication between parent and child is facilitated within this emotional climate. These parents allow and accept their children's independence and freedom of expression. These parents focus on giving choices. Long-term outcomes for children and adolescents of authoritative parents are more favorable compared to outcomes for children of authoritarian or permissive parents. For instance, Baumrind found that adolescent sons of authoritative parents were more competent in comparison to children reared with other parenting styles.[12]

The authoritarian parenting style is characterized by a harsh, rigid emotional climate combined with high demands and little communication. These highly controlling parents value obedience, and rely on punishment for discipline. They are parents that give orders. Baumrind found in her longitudinal study that boys with authoritarian parents were particularly vulnerable in terms of both cognitive and social competence.[13]

Permissive parents display some warmth and acceptance toward their children but do not place demands or restrictions on children's behavior. Some of these parents could be viewed as non-traditional, and they are lenient. They do not have expectations about a child's behavior, and they are very warm and accepting toward their children. They tend to be the parents giving in to their children. Uninvolved parents are not demanding or responsive toward their children. They do not have expectations for their children and they are extremely lenient. These characteristics put their children at risk for many social, cognitive, and behavioral problems with an "I don't care about you or what you do" attitude toward their children.[14]

Behavioral scientists have continued to conduct research based on Baumrind's parenting styles. Findings have confirmed positive outcomes for offspring of authoritative parents, in particular, better academic achievement.[15]

## Quiet Availability

Trying to provide the best for growing children can feel like an immense undertaking at times. It's easy to get caught up in taking your child here, teaching them there, and trying to motivate them to look toward the future. When parents are child-centered in their approach to parenting as opposed to adult-centered, children have better outcomes. Children need to have opportunities to explore and learn on their own. They need parents who provide for safety, but are not helicopters, hovering over them constantly.

Child-centeredness is not a specific set of techniques that parents adopt and check off on the road of raising children. It's more an attitude. Children are curious, and they can work on things by themselves. Child-centeredness is the art of "being constantly present and yet not being present."[16] In other words, parents are nearby to provide for safety without imposing a sense of fears, anxieties, or instructions about how to accomplish the task. Quiet availability can give children courage to explore on their own and accomplish the things that are important to them.

Let me explain this with an example from an interview with a mother. Her grown daughter was a student at George Washington University majoring in international affairs with a specialty in security and defense. She was choosing a career of uncertainty and fear:

*When Julia was very little, when we went outdoors, rather than telling her to "be careful," I encouraged her to "pay attention"—which doesn't instill fear, but works against fear. Of all the times we were together outdoors, we never encountered any creatures that made either of us fearful. I hope that I taught her to use good judgment. For instance, when climbing around on rocks, it isn't prudent to put your fingers into a crevice that you haven't first examined. [17]*

Parents' unobtrusive presence usually requires a good deal of patience. It takes patience to just stand by while an infant perfects the skills of walking or investigates a bug crawling on a blade of grass. It requires patience for someone to hold still while a baby explores their face by touching their cheeks, eyes, and lips. However, it soon pays off when parents find themselves taking silent pleasure in the intensity of our child's actions. Patience and unobtrusiveness can be just the thing that leads to a child's security and freedom to explore and feel confident about their world.

Quiet availability is really about the little things in life. I danced all my life, and was on the high school drill team. I can't remember a time that my parents didn't make it to a performance, even if it meant traveling for hours. My parents didn't make a big deal about it; I just knew they would be there. One thing they did, probably without much thought, was to sit in the same place in every gymnasium. They always sat about three quarters of the way up the bleachers and just left of center court. I knew I could look up at them, and they would be there. The morning of my state dance competition my mom left a good luck card on my dresser. She never said anything about the card, but the message came through. I knew she loved me and was proud of me. As an adolescent, I would've been horrified if she would've yelled and screamed at the competition, but her simple card meant so much. Her quiet availability in my life strengthened our relationship.

### The Martins

*Maria and Rob have so much going for them. They are good parents, and if they can continue to seek out playful interactions with their children, their relationships will grow. By being sensitive and responsive to his children, Rob has established a fun way to reconnect at the end of the workday. Finding ways to build in the daily work of life and family so it's done together and in fun ways will encourage the children to help Rob and Maria. Taking time to talk and share ideas helps to maintain the secure attachment through life. It may seem simple, but the back and forth interactions with parents build the strongest foundations for young children.*

# Parenting Is Not a Test

The ideas presented in this chapter may sound great. Parents should want to be with their children and find playful ways to get things done. It is easy to get caught up in wanting to do the right thing for our children, wanting only the best. I follow several blogs and there are times when I click on a post about the best playdate, or the most exciting birthday party, and I feel I fall short in my parenting. It is easy for me to compare what I have done with the bigger and better things I perceive others doing. Parenting is not a test. I have to remember that the best person to make decisions for my children is me. I know my children best, I know their dreams and hopes, I know their history, and I can use this information and make decisions about their care.

Parents want their children to be happy. Barry Schwartz, a professor of social theory at Swarthmore College, said in an interview, "Happiness as a byproduct of living your life is a great thing, but happiness as a goal is a recipe for disaster."[18] In trying to do the right thing parents may feel they should do anything to avoid having their children experience discomfort, anxiety, or disappointment. Dan Kindlon warns parents against a "discomfort with discomfort," saying that children need to experience hardship and less-than-perfect situations to learn coping skills. He explains that this is like our body's immune system: "You have to be exposed to pathogens, or your body won't know how to respond to an attack. Kids also need exposure to discomfort, failure and struggle."[19] Children need to take risks and struggle to be resilient. Skills in perseverance and resiliency may be better predictors of life fulfillment.

Jean Twenge, a co-author of *The Narcissism Epidemic* and professor of psychology at San Diego State University, says that indicators of self-esteem have risen consistently since the 1980s among middle-school, high-school, and college students. This healthy start can quickly change into a sense of self-absorption. Twenge gives the example of parents constantly telling their children how special and talented they are and how it can lead to an inflated view of oneself—a self-absorption and sense of entitlement. Interestingly, rates of anxiety and depression have risen in tandem with self-esteem. This may be evidence that instead of children feeling good about themselves, they feel better than everyone else.[20]

Parenting is not a test; it is enjoying time together, seeing the relationship as bidirectional and reciprocal. Parents do need to dedicate a large amount of time, energy, and resources to raising their children, but they must keep in mind it is for their child's benefit. Finding balance between what you want to do (perfect) and what you can do (reality) will help families find happiness. It is often the simple things that build the strongest connections with our children. Putting together puzzles, making playdough monsters, and cooking dinner together are great playful experiences we can have with our children.

# Summary

There are so many different ways parents can be effective. Keeping in mind ways to be playful and fun can help parents find the daily joys in parenting. Children need both quality and quantity time with their parents. Connecting the ages of children with parenting ideals can help parents understand how parenting changes over time. Finally, it's important to recognize that certain parenting styles can help build resiliency for children to bounce back from the struggles they may face in life.

### References

[1] Association for Childhood Education International/Isenberg, J., & Quisenberry, N. (1988). *Play: A necessity for all children*. A position paper. Olney, MD: Association for Childhood Education International.

[2] Elkind, D. (2009). *The power of play: Learning what comes naturally*. Philadelphia, PA: Da Capo Press Books.

[3] Morrison, G. S. (2009). *Early childhood education today*. 11th Ed. Columbus, OH: Pearson Education.

[4] Morrison, G. S. (2009). *Early childhood education today*. 11th Ed. Columbus, OH: Pearson Education.

[5] Elkind, D. (2009). *The power of play: Learning what comes naturally*. Philadelphia, PA: Da Capo Press Books.

[6] Honore, C. (2004). *In praise of slowness: Challenging the cult of speed*. New York, NY: HarperCollins Publishers.

[7] Elkind, D. (2009). *The power of play: Learning what comes naturally*. (p. 171). Philadelphia, PA: Da Capo Press Books.

[8] Galinsky, E. (1987). *The six stages of parenthood*. Reading, MA: Addison-Wesley.

[9] Garbarino, J. (1995). *Raising children in a socially toxic environment*. San Francisco, CA: Jossey-Bass.

[10] Garbarino, J. (1995). *Raising children in a socially toxic environment*. San Francisco, CA: Jossey-Bass.

[11] Baumrind, D. (1973). The development of instrument competence through socialization. In A. D. Pick (Ed.), *Minnesota symposia on child psychology* (Vol. 7., pp. 3–46). Minneapolis: University of Minnesota Press.

[12] Baumrind, D. (1991). Parenting styles and adolescent development. In R. M. Lerner, A. C. Petersen, & J. Brooks-Gunn (Eds.), *Encyclopedia of adolescence*. Vol. 11 (pp. 746–758). New York: Garland.

[13] Baumrind, D. (1991). Parenting styles and adolescent development. In R. M. Lerner, A. C. Petersen, & J. Brooks-Gunn (Eds.), *Encyclopedia of adolescence*. Vol. 11 (pp. 746–758). New York: Garland.

[14] Baumrind, D. (1991). Parenting styles and adolescent development. In R. M. Lerner, A. C. Petersen, & J. Brooks-Gunn (Eds.), *Encyclopedia of adolescence*. Vol. 11 (pp. 746–758). New York: Garland.

[15] Baumrind, D. (1991). Parenting styles and adolescent development. In R. M. Lerner, A. C. Petersen, & J. Brooks-Gunn (Eds.), *Encyclopedia of adolescence*. Vol. 11 (pp. 746–758). New York: Garland.

[16] Crain, W. (2003). *Reclaiming childhood; Letting children be children in our achievement-oriented society*. New York, NY: Holt Paperbacks.

[17] Louv, R. (2005). *The last child in the woods: Saving our children from nature-deficit disorder*. (p. 178). Algonquin Books of Chapel Hill, Chapel Hill, NC.

[18] Gottlieb, L. (2011). *How to land your kids in therapy*. The Atlantic Monthly Group. http://www.theatlantic.com/magazine/archive/2011/07/how-to-land-your-kid-in-therapy/308555/

[19] Gottlieb, L. (2011). *How to land your kids in therapy*. The Atlantic Monthly Group. http://www.theatlantic.com/magazine/archive/2011/07/how-to-land-your-kid-in-therapy/308555/

[20] Gottlieb, L. (2011). *How to land your kids in therapy*. The Atlantic Monthly Group. http://www.theatlantic.com/magazine/archive/2011/07/how-to-land-your-kid-in-therapy/308555/

Chapter

**15**

# Finding the Balance

# Finding the Balance

Wouldn't it be fun to go into a McFamilies and order up items that will guarantee success? What would that menu look like? What would be the most ordered item? While the idea may be fun to entertain, unfortunately it wouldn't work. The reason is because people are all different, and people all have different needs. What works for your parents may not work for you. That is why people have to approach parenting like a recipe book instead of a restaurant. People have to work from scratch, carefully consider the ingredients, and figure out how to cook it in ways that bring out the flavors and avoid weighing down the food.

I have presented an idyllic parenting model throughout the last chapters. Successful parenting, regardless of what parenting philosophies you adhere to, will only work when beliefs and values align with our actual practices. You can follow something simple, or more elaborate, but it comes down to "to thine own self be true"!

### The Martins (Maria)

*I have enjoyed being busy, both at home and volunteering. Some days it's really hard to get everything in, but most of the time things are fine. One thing that I have learned over the years is that I really like to start the evening with a family dinner. I used to think that this meant I had to cook something homemade and wonderful every evening. Then the family would join me around the table dressed in nice, clean clothes. Smiling at one another, we would share our experiences from the day and bond. It paints a pretty picture, but reality forced me to realize the most important part of that "pretty picture" is being together and talking. I have quickly learned that we can share our day while we eat peanut butter sandwiches!*

## Creating Special Times

Setting aside time each day, week, or month as special, dedicated time with children establishes an atmosphere in which they feel loved and appreciated. When parents designate these moments as special, they convey the message to their children that they are important and that they enjoy having uninterrupted time to spend with them. Parents should make every effort to adhere to these schedules. Obviously, this should not preclude having other, spontaneous moments, and there may be circumstances in which special times have to be moved. However, when the time is arranged and set aside each week for the children together, as well as each child alone, it sends the message they are important and that they are loved.

Although many families set aside times each week when all family members are present, often during dinner or a family outing, setting aside times for each child individually is the most powerful way of communicating appreciation. My husband and I have tried on a regular basis to take each child individually out to dinner. These times with our children are great for communication and sharing. I really look at these times for building a strong foundation of trust in my relationship with each child. I do have to add a caution here though. If a trusting relationship hasn't been established with a child that allows for talking and sharing, just taking your child to dinner will not create that automatically. A strong relationship is built over time step by step.

I love to take my children to a nice restaurant, let them order whatever they want, and practice making choices. I also love being a sounding board for them. I think that children need time to talk about and process life. I enjoy listening to them talk and learning their opinions. Then the next time we go out, I sometimes find that their opinions have changed. Their level of awareness grows as they express their emotions and knowledge.

When children are young, special times often consist of outings to the playground or reading before bed. Regrettably, while parents may see this time as special, many children do not. To change that impression, you can highlight the importance of the time spent with children by actually telling them, "When I read to you, it's such an important time that even if the phone rings, I won't answer it." Parents can also convey their feelings by their actions. Make sure that you don't answer the phone, and instead ask questions about your children's day or how they feel, and then most importantly listen to them. Show them that you love them for whom they are.

Sherry Turkle, director of the Massachusetts Institute of Technology Initiative on Technology and Self, has been studying how parental use of technology affects children. Dr. Turkle said, "Over and over, kids raised the same three examples of feelings hurt and not wanting to show it when their mom or dad would be on their devices instead of paying attention to them: at meals, during pickup after either school or an extracurricular activity, and during sports events."[1] It is hard not to recognize that it is tough to unplug, and even more challenging to give our children undivided attention. On the other hand, the study might be dismissed as another parental guilt trip.[2] Regardless, this study seems to affirm that children want our attention at certain sensitive times. It is advantageous to be mindful of these times and try to limit distractions.

All of these things take time. This is the commodity that busy parents are usually short on. I know that some days I don't have a lot of time to spend with my children, but I really try to be with them as often as I can. I also look forward to the days when I have more time to spend with them, and I talk to them about those upcoming times. Other times I have caught myself not spending as much time with my children as I should. When I do, I start to make changes. One thing that has worked for me is to literally put my children on my schedule until better habits are formed. I know that sounds like if my children don't have an appointment I can't help them, but rest assured, that is far from the case. I put playtime with my children on my schedule because that is something I value. Homework, helping with lessons, or clean-up time always finds their way into my day, but the fun interactions I want with my children don't always make it. Sometimes I have to find ways to ensure that they do.

I know I have just touched on planning fun and playful times with your children, but I don't want that to overshadow how much spontaneous enjoyment can add to a relationship. Several years ago my husband and I ran into a book called *Dad's Dinosaur Day*.[3] In this story, the Dad changes into a dinosaur, and so he must take the day off work. He walks his son to school, and stays and plays. They eat pizza for dinner and spend time reading books. The message of this simple children's book is that it's really crucial to spend time with children when it isn't planned. Every once in a while my children and I have a dinosaur day!

## Family Traditions

When you think of the four seasons, are there different things you remember or do with your family? Do you snowshoe in the winter, or visit the beach in the summer? Is there a park in the neighborhood where family reunions are held? Traditions are the glue that holds families together. Activities and rituals help us create memories and tell others around us that this is where I belong because I know what to do.

When I was a little girl, my parents lived in a small town. My father enjoyed helping others around us. We had several older widows in the neighborhood that needed help maintaining their homes. My parents were glad to provide assistance. On Saturdays they would pack up the lawn mower or snow shovel, depending upon the time of the year, and drive around the neighborhood. When we found a house that needed some work, my parents would get us out of the car. My father and brothers would work in the yard, while I would go with my mother to visit for a minute and share some cookies we had baked. I always felt like I was getting the raw end of the deal because my brothers could stay outside; I came to learn that they felt just the opposite.

It doesn't take long, now that we are adults, for our memories to surface at family get-togethers. I love hearing my brothers' recollections of mowing the neighbors' lawns before they could see over the handle. My parents are teased, but I can also see the values my parents taught me of hard work, talking with neighbors, looking out for others around us, and so many other life lessons. They never had to say a word; their example and weekly ritual taught it better than any words could ever express.

Traditions can range from something that happens on a yearly basis to our daily routines. Sometimes parents put a lot of planning and thought into what traditions they want in their family. Other times it's not planned, but is established through repetition and daily responsibility.

Established traditions can make us long for home, especially those associated with special occasions and holidays. At one point in her life, my grandmother worked in a candy store. She excelled at candy making and loved to share her talent with her grandchildren. She took hours to create a fist-size sugar and chocolate egg for every grandchild each year at the Easter holiday. I still expect to see my name on a candy egg each year. It was always an amazing sight to see all 21 eggs decorated and carefully placed on the table as we went to visit. It was so exciting to get to bring them home at the end of the day. Children need these experiences to help them understand that they are important times for the family, and have something to look forward to.

## Definition of Rituals

John D. Friesen defined the differences between celebrations, traditions, and routines.[4] Knowing these differences can help families establish habits that can help them succeed and connect on a regular basis. The familiarity of repeated activities and schedules can also help empower children because they know what to expect. Here are his definitions.

### Family Celebrations

**Family celebrations** are rituals in which the family observes holidays or occasions that are widely practiced by the culture and that are special within the family, or what many people think of as holiday traditions. Occasions such as funerals, weddings, baptisms, bar mitzvahs; religious holidays such as Christmas, Easter, and the Passover Seder; and secular holidays such as New Year's, the Fourth of July, and Thanksgiving are family celebrations. These rituals are observed broadly by the cultural groups and provide an opportunity for larger group identification for the family.

### Family Traditions

**Family traditions** are activities, which are less culture-specific and more unique to each family. They are not necessarily celebrated annually, although they occur regularly in families. They are more moderately organized than celebrations. The events included in this category are summer vacations, visits to and from extended family members, anniversary and birthday customs, parties with special food and music, participation in community events, and activities with kin.

## Family Routines

**Family routines** are rituals that are most frequently enacted but least consciously planned by the participants. They are the least deliberate and yet the most evident in the family. They include activities such as regular meals, bedtime routines for children, leisure activities, and discipline of children, everyday greetings, and goodbyes. These rituals organize everyday life and define family roles and responsibilities.

> **Family Rituals**—the umbrella term for family traditions, celebrations, and daily routines.

> **Family Celebrations**—for example, caroling with neighbors at Christmas (key = you celebrate something similar to neighbors)

> **Family Traditions**—for example, eating dinner on a red plate when it's your birthday (key = these activities are family unique)

> **Family Routines**—for example, nightly cleanup done to songs on the radio (key = maintain daily roles)

## Family Celebrations and Traditions

Celebrations are fun, and often create special meaning for holidays or other cultural events in our lives. Busy parents are wise when they find a few celebrations that they maintain over the years, but not so many that it's overwhelming or time consuming to put them together and carry them out. My favorite celebrations are the easy ones that my children can help me with. That way we enjoy the celebration and the time preparing for it. In the month of December, our family has a celebration where we read a book every evening about one of the many holidays celebrated in the month of December. These books are special to our family, and we bring them out only during the month of December. My children help get the books out of storage boxes and place them around our couch for easy access. They spend many hours throughout the month looking through and reading the books on their own, but the special part is reading them together.

Family traditions are important for family connectedness. Traditions are also important for individual children and their parents. Time parents set aside to spend with their children can develop into family traditions. Whatever you decide to implement, from date night to a dinosaur day, can become part of the family fabric over time. Children expect them to happen, and their security and importance in the family are conveyed. The traditions that become part of your life can also create special memories that your children will remember for a lifetime.

## Daily Connection Rituals

Celebrations and traditions play an important part in the family, but for busy families the routines of life can be a redeeming factor. One thing I have learned over the years is that I can plan a routine and make sure everything gets done, or we can haphazardly go through our day. Either way, what we do becomes a habit. I know that for my family, having a routine helps us get things accomplished more efficiently. It has also helped my children to know what they need to do to get ready for the day. This takes some of the burden off my husband and me.

My first child was 7 weeks old when I started a new job. I was both excited for the job and devastated to leave him. I was so torn. I wanted him to know that I wasn't going to abandon him, and that the time we were apart was short. One thing I did was to massage him. We had a little routine, and I would take fifteen minutes before work to massage him and let him know we were going to be apart, and then fifteen minutes when I returned home to reconnect. This was so wonderful. We had a preparation, a routine, and a reconnection. I felt lucky to have found a way to build my attachment with my son, while also finding personal fulfillment with my employment.

Those times together created a framework for daily connection rituals. As my son outgrew the massage, I replaced this time with songs, talking about the day, and preparing the evening meal. As we had more children, it became harder for me to feel successful at these daily connection rituals. I wanted desperately to have time each day with all my children alone to talk. It was overwhelming to find the time to communicate with each child and still complete the daily tasks of living. More recently the thing that has worked the best for me is to stagger the bedtimes at our house. This allows for snuggle and connection time every evening as the children go to sleep. Another fun thing that came from staggered bedtimes is that we have staggered awakenings too! This presents another opportunity for connections. I love starting and ending the day with these personal, important, and quiet ways with my children.

I slowly learned over time, and by watching my children, that they need time with parents alone and with all the family together. They learn different things in those situations. I quickly learned the importance of fixing the evening meal together and talking all together. This was something that helped my children learn how to work with others (even when I might feel grumpy or tired), find common interests, and share common experiences. We have also learned how to be happy for each other, and empathize together in moments of joy and sadness. These have been crucial lessons for my children and have developed into a connection ritual for our family.

Daily connection rituals do not always have to be centered on communication. One of my favorite times of the day is when we turn on some music really loudly, and yell that we are all going to clean the house for two songs. Then we are done for the night. These few minutes are so helpful in maintaining the house, but I also have memories of my children singing and yelling at the tops of their voices to music as they pick up toys, or shaking their hips as they hang up clothes. These mental pictures always make me smile, and remind me that I love my children and that we have fun together.

Daily connection rituals have also saved me on many evenings! We have a family calendar on which we organize our schedules. With my children at young ages, we usually have a few nights a week without a planned activity. We like to plan out family fun (as we call it). This is one example of how I have scheduled my children into my day. In this instance having our activity on the family calendar also helped my children recognize the importance of what we are doing. We take the phone off the hook for a few hours and play together. We have puzzle night, Lego night, book night, cookie night, playdough night, movie night, and so on. When I come home exhausted from a busy day of work, I am so glad that something is planned and I can unwind with my family. It makes all the difference for me to actually get to interact with my family because something was on the calendar, instead of asking, "What should we do tonight?" and doing nothing because we were all too tired to think.

We are not glued to these plans either. Occasionally someone likes to change the plans. We might decide to go get ice cream at the last minute, or maybe one of our children learned about a great activity at school that day. We do change our plans! The wonderful thing about this is that family time and togetherness is planned, so we have flexibility in what we do. It's also fun to see what activities are favorites for our children. This gives me as a parent a lot of information about the development of my child and how I can help them continue in their development.

## Benefits of Working Traditions into Daily Habits

Some individuals might feel that traditions are not helpful because they might be able to take away the spontaneity of the moment, day, or holiday celebration. This is a big concern that families need to acknowledge, as they think about what types of traditions to include in family activities. Some things to keep in mind are that more successful traditions and rituals are those that are easy and simple. Convenience in putting together a ritual over and over again increases the likelihood that parents will take the time to make sure that it happens.

Traditions need to be simple, but they also need to bring families together. Whether it's the cake that is a secret family recipe, or a book to read aloud, or the football game on a Friday night, it's about being together. It's easy to get so involved in preparations, taking pictures, dressing just right that the importance of being with the people you love is overlooked. This time needs to be about taking time to enjoy each other's company, share thoughts and memories, and help children build the story of their lives. The sharing will lead to creating memories, sharing love, and strengthening the bonds between family members.

The predictability and dependability of the ritual will help children gain a sense of security and a sense of belonging to something they love and understand. One tradition shared in our home is talking about extended family members. It's fun to say, "You like to run? Did you know that Grandpa liked to run too?" Then we might tell the story of how Grandpa ran to school every day. This helps children find similarities and differences between family members. Telling family stories to children helps them align themselves with what they see going on around them and connecting to it. It builds self-esteem, and children have an easier time under-standing themselves. This is best when parents are also supportive of children's individual interests and have avoided pushing them to do things in which they are not interested just to be like Uncle Johnnie.

## Household Organization

I am sure you have noticed that I use a lot of daily rituals to maintain the house and complete household tasks. Does it really matter if the house gets a little messy? I know that there are times when I am finishing up a big project or juggling a lot of different assignments, and maintaining the house is the thing I drop from my list. Does it make a difference? In the last decade, a study conducted by UCLA's Center on Everyday Lives of Families, followed 32 middle-class families to look at the interplay between house and family.[5]

Social archaeologists, anthropologists, consumer experts, sociologists, and econo-mists videotaped and recorded the ways the families communicated, how and where they interacted, and the organization of the house, literally making blue-prints of the house and where different objects were stored. Several of the findings are insightful. Researchers found a correlation between how many items were on a refrigerator and how much clutter was found throughout the rest of the house.

Notes

Another finding is that most homes had multiple television sets. If television sets were located in a living room or family room, all the furniture was oriented toward the television. This also impacted interactions between family members. Kitchens were found to be the central hub of the family as well. Kitchens are used to cook food of course, but they are also the place where children complete their homework (even if they had a desk in their room), parents teach and socialize with their children, and for coordination of schedules. Researchers also found that having a baby increased possessions in the household by 30%.[6]

Eliminating clutter from the house and being a mindful consumer helps me feel that my house is more calm and organized. Other studies have found that living in a predictable household can help family function and child development.[7] High levels of household chaos (noise, clutter, disarray, and lack of routines) and the stress associated in the home can have a negative impact on parenting behaviors and lead to poorer cognitive and social-emotional outcomes for children and adolescents.[8] Reducing stress by being discriminate consumers and donating or recycling items not being used may be a simple solution to making housekeeping a little easier. Combining those habits with routines may optimize healthy development for all family members.

## But What about Dinner?

Several researchers have identified that daily rituals and routines can help families survive the negative spillover effects between work and home.[9] Family dinners are one routine that has been considered a positive buffer against stress associated with work overload.[10] More recent research has specifically looked at work interference with family dinner.[11] This research found that families had higher levels of work–family conflict when a parent worked longer hours and missed the dinner hour about thirty times in a six-month period of time.[12] Additional hypotheses showed evidence that longer work hours can result in a negative perspective of success in personal life, relationships with a spouse or partner, relationships with children, and a lower perception of the workplace being emotionally healthy. This is particularly true for women who miss the family dinnertime on a frequent basis because of long work hours.

Families that identify dinner as a time that is valued and set aside for reconnecting may be more resilient to the stresses associated with spillover from work. It's not clearly understood what part of a frequent family dinner ritual helps reduce the work—family conflict, but eating dinner together as a family seems to provide some sort of buffer against stress. It could be that the dinnertime itself provides a time for connection between family members. Parents also could feel they are actively meeting the needs of their children by cooking for them and communicating about the day. For whatever reason, dinner is a ritual that provides meaning for a lot of families.

Dinnertime is an important time in our family. When I first thought about dinnertime and what I wanted it to look like, I envisioned a nice, healthy, home-cooked from scratch meal, my children clean and shiny with proper manners eating and talking around the dinner table. I have learned through experience that really the main thing for me is that we sit down together and talk about the day. All the meals are not home-cooked from scratch, but I work hard to make sure they are healthy. My children may not always have the best manners at the table, but they have clean hands. And we talk. We love to share the best thing that has happened to each of us throughout the day. We love to celebrate these little moments with each other. It's something that we look forward to. I consider it the best way to end my day!

### The Martins

*Maria has learned that finding time to connect every day helps their children understand that they belong. Sitting down at the dinner table and sharing a meal is more than just eating for a lot of families. The communication and sharing that occurs around the table can help the children feel that they belong and are loved. Families that think about what they can do to encourage connection are families that generally do well. The establishment of connection rituals and taking time for each other creates a strong foundation for family interaction.*

## Summary

Rituals are tools that families can use to help children with transitions (seasons, childbirth, starting school). Rituals give children something constant in their life when other things are changing. This helps them continue to maintain secure attachments with their parents. Rituals can also be used to transmit values and beliefs to children. Rituals help children know how they should act in certain situations, like visiting neighbors. It also helps them construct their cognitive maps of society that are rooted to their personal family history, but experienced in the future. Lastly, rituals help children provide support for others and create a sense of safety and security within their homes. Children learn how to appropriately show their feelings through rituals (think over-excitement with Christmas or a birthday!), and as they interact with other family members they feel less lonely or isolated from others.

Balancing work and family in the real world may seem like a daunting task, and at times even impossible. However, families can find balance and harmony in their interactions, activities, and relationships. Taking time to think about what is valued in everyday life and then aligning that with what you actually do can bring a sense of fulfillment. Enjoying playful interactions and sharing through communication

Notes

can build stronger relationships between family members. Common goals and interests can provide opportunities to spend time together, and everyday household tasks can be divided to create ease and fun. Balancing work and family is a process and each family will find a different path to that balance.

---

### References

[1] Scelfo, J. (2010). *The Risks of Parenting While Plugged In*. Retrieved January 15, 2013, from http://www.nytimes.com/2010/06/10/garden/10childtech.html?pagewanted=1&_r=0

[2] Lansbury, J. (2013). *Do wired parents need time out...or less guilt*. Retrieved February 1, 2013, from http://www.janetlansbury.com/2010/06/do-wired-parents-need-time-out-or-less-guilt/

[3] Hearn, D. D. (1999). *Dad's Dinosaur Day*. New York, NY: Aladdin Paperbacks.

[4] Friesen, J. D. (1990). Rituals and family strengths. *Direction*, 19(1), 39–48. Retrieved May 18, 2008, from http://www.direction-journal.org/article/?654.

[5] Arnold, Graesch, Ragazzini, Ochs. (2012). *Life at Home in the Twenty-first Century: 32 Families Open their Doors*. Cotsen Institute of Archaeology.

[6] Arnold, Graesch, Ragazzini, Ochs. (2012). *Life at Home in the Twenty-first Century: 32 Families Open their Doors*. Cotsen Institute of Archaeology.

[7] Matheny, A. P., Wachs, T. D., Ludwig, J. L., & Phillips, K. (1995). Bringing Order Out of Chaos: Psychometric Characteristics of the Confusion, Hubbub, and Order Scale. *Journal of Applied Developmental Psychology*.

[8] Deater-Deckard, K., Chen, N., Wang, Z., Bell, M. (2012). Socioeconomic risk moderates the link between household chaos and maternal executive function. *Journal of Family Psychology* 26.3 (June 2012): 391–399.

[9] Anderson, E. A., & Leslie, L. A. (1991). Coping with employment and family stress: Employment arrangements and gender differences. *Sex Roles*, 24, 223–237.

[10] Eisenberg, M. E., Olson, R. E., Neumark-Sztainer, D., Story, M., & Bearinger, L. H. (2004). Correlations between family meals and psychosocial well-being among adolescents. *Archives of Pediatrics and Adolescent Medicine*, 158, 792–296.

[11] Jacob, J. I., Allen, S., Hill, E. J., Mead, N. L., & Ferris M. (2008). Work interference with dinnertime as a mediator and moderator between work hours and work and family outcomes. *Family and Consumer Sciences Research Journal*, 36(4), 310–327.

[12] Jacob, J. I., Allen, S., Hill, E. J., Mead, N. L., & Ferris M. (2008). Work interference with dinnertime as a mediator and moderator between work hours and work and family outcomes. *Family and Consumer Sciences Research Journal*, 36(4), 310–327.